The Graywolf Short Fiction Series

1 9 9 0

Name and Tears

& OTHER STORIES

FORTY YEARS OF
ITALIAN FICTION

Edited and Translated

by Kathrine Jason

Graywolf Press / *Saint Paul*

The editor gratefully acknowledges the generous support from the National
Endowment of the Arts which made this work possible.

Publication of this anthology is made possible by the generous donations Graywolf
Press receives from corporations, foundations, and individuals, including the
Minnesota State Arts Board and the National Endowment for the Arts.
Graywolf Press is a member organization of United Arts, Saint Paul.

The editor would like to thank the following individuals for their help with this
project: Elena Andrenelli, for her hospitality in the Marche and generosity in
helping the editor hash out difficult questions. Rosanna de Longis-Zuppi,
who helped launch the project by providing an enlightened view of books and
writers to consider and whose hospitality made several stays in Rome possible.
Gloria Dori, who discussed shades of meaning for hours. Lucille Jason,
for her meticulous editing of parts of the manuscript. And the editor's
husband, Peter Rondinone, for support both literary and spiritual.

Published by GRAYWOLF PRESS
2402 University Avenue, Suite 203
Saint Paul, Minnesota 55114
All rights reserved.
9   8   7   6   5   4   3   2
First Paperback Printing, 1991

Library of Congress Cataloging-in-Publication Data
Name and tears and other stories : forty years of Italian fiction /
edited and translated by Kathrine Jason.
p.   cm. – (The Graywolf short fiction series)
Translated from Italian.
ISBN 1-55597-126-1 : $10.00 (pbk.)
ISBN 1-55597-132-6 : $17.95
1. Italian fiction – 20th century – Translations into English.
2. Short stories, Italian – Translations into English. 3. Short
stories, English – Translations from Italian.   I. Series.
PQ4257.E5N36   1990
853'.0108'09045 – dc20   89-77990

This book is for Micole

future reader

ACKNOWLEDGMENTS

GIOVANNI ARPINO. "The Peacock" from *Un gran mare di gente*. Copyright © 1981 by Rizzóli Editore. Reprinted by permission of Caterina Arpino.

GIUSEPPE BONAVIRI. "The Missed Marriage" from *Il sarto della stradalunga*. Copyright © 1954 by Giulio Einaudi Editore. "The Tailor's Son" from *Novelle Saracene*. Copyright © 1980 by Rizzoli Editore. Both stories reprinted by permission of the author.

VITALIANO BRANCATI. "Arrival in the City" from *Sogno di un valzer*. Copyright © 1982 by Bompiani. Reprinted by permission of Bompiani.

GESUALDO BUFALINO. "The Invaded Man" from *L'uomo invaso e altre invenzioni*. Copyright © 1986 by Bompiani. Reprinted by permission of Bompiani.

DINO BUZZATI. "Something That Begins with L" from *60 racconti*. Copyright © 1958 by Arnoldo Mondadori Editore. Reprinted by permission of Arnoldo Mondadori Editore.

ITALO CALVINO. "Adam, One Afternoon" from *Difficult Loves*, translated by William Weaver, copyright © 1949 by Giulio Einaudi Editore, Torino, copyright © 1958 by Giulio Einaudi Editore S.p.A. Torino, English translation copyright © 1984 by Harcourt Brace Jovanovich, Inc., reprinted by permission of Harcourt Brace Jovanovich, Inc.

CARLO CASSOLA. "At the Station" from *La Visita*. Copyright © 1942 by Giulio Einaudi Editore. Graywolf Press has made every effort to contact the holder of rights to this story.

UMBERTO ECO. "The Discovery of America" from *Diario minimo*. Copyright © 1963 by Bompiani. Reprinted by permission of Harcourt Brace Jovanovich.

BEPPE FENOGLIO. "The Boss Doesn't Pay" from *Un giorno di fuoco*. Copyright © 1973 by Giulio Einaudi Editore. Reprinted by permission of Agenzia Letteraria Internazionale.

CARLO EMILIO GADDA. "The Thieving Magpie" from *I racconti*. Copyright © 1963 by Garzanti Editore. Reprinted by permission of Garzanti Editore.

NATALIA GINZBURG. "House at the Sea" from *Cinque romanzi brevi*, Copyright © 1964 by Giulio Einaudi Editore. Reprinted by permission of Guilio Einaudi Editore.

RAFFAELE LA CAPRIA. "This Has Nothing to Do with Me" from *Nuovi Argomenti* (nuova serie) 9. Copyright © 1968 by Raffaela La Capria. Reprinted by permission of the author.

TOMMASO LANDOLFI. "Words in Commotion" from *Words in Commotion* by Tommaso Landolfi. Copyright © 1982 by Rizzoli Editore, English translation copyright © 1986 by Viking Penguin Inc. Used by permission of Viking Penguin, a division of Penguin Books USA. "Gogol's Wife" from *Gogol's Wife and Other Stories*. Copyright © 1961, 1963 by New Directions Publishing Corporation.

TABLE OF CONTENTS

Introduction

Historically, Italy is a place that has fired the imagination. In his study, *The Italians*, Luigi Barzini traces what he calls the "Eternal Pilgrimage," analyzing the elements in the natural and cultural landscape that have drawn foreigners, particularly artists and writers, over the centuries. These have ranged from diplomacy to religion, from spiritual and aesthetic edification to sensual excess. There is a whole body of literature set on Italian soil which celebrates the "fatal spell" of the land, a whole tradition of praise from which Barzini quotes. Henry Adams, for instance, remarked: "Italy was mostly an emotion and the emotion mostly centered in Rome. . . . The shadows breathed and glowed full of soft forms felt by lost senses." Gogol said: "Who has been in Italy can forget all other regions. Who has been in Heaven does not desire the Earth." And Henry James, after his first day in Rome, recorded these words in his diary: "At last – for the first time – I live!"

The geography we call Italy is mythopoeic, an amalgam of images and symbols which reach back to antiquity. And although many have celebrated elements of the "spell" – the landscape, the clime, the spectacle of history, the regional cultures, the artistic patrimony and living artistic and artisan traditions – the spell itself seems to elude definition. Whatever the essence of Italy may be, it originates in what the Romans called the genius, or spirit, of the place: that is, not only in the landscape but also in its history, in its art and artifact. "It is as if Italy were not only the home of Art, but an immense *objet d'art* herself," writes Barzini.

In fact, history imposes so compellingly, so powerfully on the present in Italy – consider the unflawed medieval aspect of Florence or Tuscan hilltowns like Gubbio – that the casual visitor, knowing no better, may be tempted to focus on the past, whether he or she actually knows or merely construes it in his imagination, rather than seeking out the realities of the present. In my mind, the dynamic, sophisticated capital that Rome is today merges with the imagined ancient city that suggests itself from every crumbling column and expanse of wall around the city, fusing a single image, complex and seductive. In any case, the Italy beloved of foreigners, Barzini believes, "is mainly an imaginary country, not entirely corresponding to the Italy of the Italians."

"The Italy of the Italians" is, in fact, rather difficult to define as a simple geographical entity, not to mention a political and social one: to begin with, the Italy of today has only existed since the Unification in 1861. It is made up of regions which historically have been autonomous – some politically, most culturally and linguistically – up until very recently.

In their essay, "The Transformation of Post-War Italy," Michael Ceasar and Peter Hainsworth explore the radical changes which have taken place in Italian society and culture over the past forty years, providing a context in which to view modern literary movements. In the 1950s, for instance, the Italian language was still spoken by only 18 percent of the population, though not exclusively; 20 percent spoke only dialect. Thus, it is not surprising that the forging of a dynamic national language that could serve as a vehicle for a literature written for the people and not merely for the few literati, as had been the case for centuries, has been central to Italian literature since Manzoni and the *veristi* of the late nineteenth century.

If there are continuities both in Italian life and literature, recent Italian history – by which I mean the period since World War II – is singular precisely for its discontinuity. In the mid-1950s, Italy was still "a relatively poor, traditionalist, largely agrarian country," write Ceasar and Hainsworth. The subsequent rapid industrialization and economic expansion of the 1960s, particularly the period between 1959 and 1965 known as the "boom" or "economic miracle," transformed the country into one of the ten leading industrial powers in the world. Perhaps Barzini had these changes in mind

when he wrote that contemporary Italy is "too disturbing and difficult" for the foreigner "to understand." And if the composer Gioac-
chino Rossini could have remarked in the mid-1800s, "Thank God
for the Spaniards. . . . If there were no Spaniards, Italy would be the
last country in Europe," it couldn't be further from the truth in 1989.

The effects of these economic changes were sweeping. Ceasar and
Hainsworth point out that whereas 78 percent of Italians had been illiterate in 1861, by 1951 the figure had fallen to 12.9 percent (24
percent in the south). Secondary education became compulsory in
1964, and the numbers of students attending universities rose
dramatically, from 168,000 in 1948–49 to 360,000 in 1964 and just
over 800,000 in 1972–73. The advent of a consumer culture and
mass media also helped to replace dialect with Italian. Nevertheless,
even "in 1974 it was calculated that 28.9 percent of people used
dialect as their normal spoken language. . . and only 25 percent
used Italian exclusively," write Ceasar and Hainsworth. Naturally,
the domain of writing and publishing has also been transformed by
literacy and higher education: the number of books published in a
year rose from 9,182 in 1966 to just about 17,000 in 1978.

The sixties and seventies were not only a time of economic expansion, of cultural ferment and opening to ideas from the outside, but
also of social and political change. There have been forty-eight gov-
ernments in Italy since World War II. The student and union upris-
ings of 1968 and 1969 were followed by a decade of terrorism, both
from the left and the right, which, according to Ceasar and Hainsworth, claimed more than 400 lives. These were the aftershocks of
the war and subsequent economic expansion, the fissures created in
the social fabric.

This anthology, then, reflects this particularly cataclysmic period
of history. I hope it will cast the light – however partial and fleeting
– that statistics cannot. For who can better suggest the textures of
everyday life as it was lived in Italy for the past forty years than its
writers?

*   *   *   *   *   *   *

In 1978, I went to Italy on a Fulbright, as a student of literature
and a translator, and as a casual visitor. I had every intention, come

the end of that year, of leaving. In some sense, I have never left. The language and the writing I discovered that year, but above all the place itself, took hold in my imagination. *Name and Tears & Other Stories: Forty Years of Italian Fiction* is the culmination of twelve years of exploration, of reading and translating contemporary Italian writers.

With any anthology, the first step is to define purpose and scope, to draw boundaries. As my aim was to present a broad picture of contemporary short fiction, I first had to define "contemporary." For example, should one go back as far as Luigi Pirandello and Italo Svevo, both of whom mark the turning point in Italian literature and culture reached during the first decade of this century? Although both those writers are precursors for much that came later, I decided that a selection of that magnitude would be too difficult to publish commercially.

Instead, I chose 1945 as a point of departure for the contemporary period: in the years following the Second World War as the country was attempting to rebuild, writers too were debating the purposes and means of literature. During these years of ideological and literary ferment, the predominant movement, neorealism, reached its zenith. A number of the elder neorealists, such as Alberto Moravia, had been publishing throughout the thirties and forties; but they continued to publish work of considerable importance and to exert a major influence in the decades that followed – unlike, say, Cesare Pavese. Central as he was to Italian literary culture as poet and fiction writer, and as translator and editor, his death in 1950 places him on the margins of the period covered by this anthology.

Most critics view neorealism as a literary movement rooted in leftist ideology, specifically in the experience of the Italian resistance; not surprisingly, the war and the resistance loom large in the fiction of this period. Emerging from the war with the task of re-inventing a culture stifled by years of fascism, many intellectuals and writers believed the mission of literature was to portray the heroes of the resistance; to reflect the struggle of the proletariat and of the common man and woman of the various rural Italys; and to give those previously unknown Italys a natural, spoken language rather than a literary one. Hence, the use or abuse of regional dialect, along with prescribed subject matter, was thought by some to be the order of the day. Nevertheless, in the preface to the 1964 edition of his first novel, *The Path to the Nest of Spiders*, speaking of the generation of writers who came to the fore after the war, Calvino states, "With our renewed freedom of speech, all at first felt a rage to narrate. . . , we moved in a varicolored universe of stories. . . . But the secret of how one wrote them did not lie only in this elementary universality of content; that was not its mainspring. . . . On the contrary, it had never been so clear that the stories were raw material. . . . Though we were supposed to be concerned with content, there were never more dogged formalists than we. . . . Language, style, pace had so much importance for us, for this realism of ours." Vittorini, Pavese, and Gadda had also argued that language and not subject matter were at the heart of neorealism. In Pavese's view, "Behind the warning all too often addressed to writers lies the crude presumption that writing stories of left-wing cities, the heroism of war, hunger and prison, in other words, everything which is labeled as a heart-pounding news item, will make our literature richer, truer, or, as they say, more human. . . while the truly authentic, the pure in art, has its roots not in the arduousness or the enormity of events suffered but only in the mind and in the heart. . . . "

If, in the decade 1945–1955, neorealism began to lose vitality, by the early 1960s the new, industrialized, affluent Italy was spurring writers to approach writing differently. In general, Italian culture was wide open to the influences of other cultures and took novel directions. As Michael Ceasar and Peter Hainsworth observe, "partly from a widespread sense that a new culture was developing which needed to be articulated, partly from a feeling that in many ways Italy needed to catch up with other countries, new foreign writing has been rapidly translated and made readily available. Semiotics, structuralism, modern Marxist thought, new theories of psychoanalysis all penetrated Italian literary culture before they were known in Britain." With this flood of new ideas, the trend, especially in poetry, was toward the avant-garde and experimental.

The historic anthology of poets, *I novissimi (The Newest)*, was published in 1961 by the poet Alfredo Giuliani; and then on October 3, 1963, the avant-garde took visible shape and identity when at a meeting in Palermo a group of writers named itself "Il Gruppo '63." The group's theoretical basis was largely articulated in Umberto Eco's *Opera aperta* (1961), and especially in the essay, "Del modo di formare come impegno sulla realtà." In an informative overview of the avant-garde, Christopher Wagstaff points out that Eco's major contribution to the ideology of the Gruppo '63 was the belief that the modern artist must reflect the disorder of the world rather than conventionally reflecting a (false) sense of order and perpetuating a false system. In order for art to be an instrument of change, it must be ambiguous enough to allow the reader or viewer to interpret or find a meaning rather than finding it dictated. To achieve this openness, the writer has to work against the conventions of language and form. The work of the Gruppo '63, much of it theoretical, was published by Feltrinelli in a series called "Materiali," effectively introducing these ideas into mainstream culture, until the group disbanded in 1968.

How much did this spirit of engagement and experimentation influence the writers included in this anthology? There's no doubt that poetry was the primary focus of experimentation while fiction, which lent itself to a wider mass audience, retained certain conventions, at least on the surface. In fact, most of the stories here are conventional. Interestingly enough, the most "open" piece in this selection is Vittorini's now famous "Name and Tears," which was written in the thirties, under the constraints of fascist censorship. Paradoxically, the ambiguity and "openness" which arose out of the need to be textually apolitical later came to be seen as an instrument of political action. Still, some of the pieces here innovate by subtly modifying traditional story form.

The tale, or "novella," a genre that is native to Italian literary tradition, has its roots in the fourteenth century. Its earliest and best-known masters are Boccaccio and Sacchetti. The "novella" continued to be a popular narrative form up until the first "racconti" – what we call short stories – developed into the more popular form of short prose fiction in the late nineteenth century. In the introduction to his *Racconti italiani del Novecento (Italian Short Stories of the Twentieth Century)* Enzo Siciliano writes that ". . . the story, as we understand it in modern terms, in twentieth-century terms, is something separated, almost completely, from the form of the classic novella" which is "still anchored, according to the Tuscan and Italian tradition, to the narration of an anecdote or of a parable. . . . "

There are some examples of "novella" in this collection – Giuseppe Bonaviri's "The Tailor's Son," for example. "Blocked," by Moravia, also displays the clean lines of the tale, as does Sgorlon's "The Grey Stain."

There are also pieces that deliberately play with our expectations of what happens in a short story, sometimes a stripping down of fictional elements. Characters, for instance, may merely be labeled as "a man," "a young woman," or "the man who lived in the upstairs apartment"; we may not be provided with details that would make "believable" or "motivated" or "rounded" characters. In fact, these characters are often purposefully "flat," defined only by their movement through the fictional situation. Parise's lyrical pieces, which resemble prose poems, exemplify this tendency to portray a moment or situation taking shape. The narrators in Malerba's pieces seem more like disembodied voices than full-bodied characters. Setting, too, may be minimal; time is often atemporal; place is non-specific, or only generically specified. Other stories play with structure. Eco's "The Discovery of America" is written as a play, or teleplay, would be; in Bonaviri's "The Missed Marriage," narration alternates with playlike dialogue, although the effect is of various voices addressing the reader rather than each other. In Pontiggia's "Publisher's Reader," stories within the story constitute the plot and the conflict.

Interestingly enough, in the past five years, there has not only been a return to the more conventional short story, but also evidence of greater diversity of sensibility and approach to fiction. Also, for the first time in decades, "the young" and "the new" writer has been sought out and marketed. Antonio Tabucchi and Gesualdo Bufalino, both of whom have made their reputations in the past five years, represent this trend toward idiosyncratic style and subject matter.

*　*　*　*　*　*　*

Twelve years ago when I went to Rome to participate in a workshop with American and Italian writers and translators, our hope was to promote literary translations from both languages, especially of young and lesser-known writers. At that time, most contemporary Italian writing was virtually unknown here. Only the handful of writers who had earned international reputations after the war with the sudden and short-lived interest in Italian culture – Giorgio Bassani, Elsa Morante, Alberto Moravia, Mario Soldati and Italo Calvino – were available to English readers.

We arrived in Rome feeling a bit like explorers of territory that was for us uncharted. We quickly discovered a thriving literary scene, which was particularly remarkable in its diversity. The fact was that several generations of Italian writers were unknown here, except perhaps to scholars and Italophiles.

On my return to the United States, I undertook a systematic search for translations of contemporary Italian fiction. The results confirmed what I already knew: the books that had been translated in the fifties and sixties were generally out of print. The three once-existing Penguin anthologies – *Italian Short Stories/Penguin Parallel Text*, Vol. I, 1965, and Vol. II, 1967, and *Italian Writing Today*, 1967 – were likewise long out of print.

The situation has improved over the past ten years. At present, eighteen (of the twenty-seven) writers in the anthology are available in English translation, as are a number of those not included here. And although it would be an exaggeration to equate this to the Latin American "boom" of the 1970s, the comparison may be instructive; for, like the great success of García Márquez's *One Hundred Years of Solitude*, which generated so much interest in Latin American literature, the resounding success of Umberto Eco's *The Name of The Rose*, in 1980, performed, I think, a similar function for Italian fiction. In addition, the consistent popularity of the work of Italo Calvino, and more recently, of Primo Levi, has motivated publishers to look toward Italy for new voices. Nevertheless, it must be said that a handful of publishers with a commitment to literary translation, and to Italian literature in particular, have been responsible for this small renaissance: the British publisher Carcanet, the Marlboro Press, Richard Seaver Books, and Eridanos Press have published "literary" Italian titles that larger houses would not take on. And while many of the major houses have published one or two translations from Italian, these are the exception to the rule. Not surprisingly, this anthology did not, indeed could not, have taken shape as a commercial enterprise. Its existence is due to a translation grant which I received from the National Endowment for the Arts in 1985.

Because *Name and Tears* is the first anthology of Italian fiction to appear in twenty years, I wanted to present an overview of the period between 1945–1985. My basic premises for inclusion of stories were these: first, to include those writers whose contributions have been considered of major importance; secondly, to choose stories that have not appeared previously in English translation; and finally, to favor recent work, especially in the case of older writers, like Moravia, whose careers may span more than five decades.

The basic source and guide for my own selection was *Racconti italiani del Novecento*, edited by Enzo Siciliano (Mondadori, 1983), which was, in 1985, the only authoritative Italian anthology of contemporary short stories. In his foreword Siciliano writes, "An anthology is always a thing of will, and there is no criteria of presumed objectivity that can justify it. An anthology is a manual for reading — but also for reading that which falls outside of it."

Looking at the table of contents as it stands, I am struck by its divergence from the one I originally envisioned: by the degree to which my initial definitions have been blurred and my intentions thwarted. "That which falls outside" seems to be particularly at issue here. Because if the "reading manual," shaped by that odd coupling of subjective and critical judgment, is an ideal product, the finished book is a real product of the literary marketplace, with all its caprices.

It would be impossible to enumerate the myriad reasons for the omissions and substitutions I finally made. In any case, many lie not in aesthetics, but in the complex business of acquiring rights (complex because translation rights may lie with the author himself, with his publisher, his literary agent or lawyer, and if the story has been published in English or is contracted to be, with the English-language publisher).

Thus, to some extent, the literary marketplace dictated the table of contents. Several stories I had chosen, and in some cases even translated and previously published, for example, could not be reprinted here. Some writers are absent altogether, although their inclusion was intended – Primo Levi, Elsa Morante, and Giorgio Bassani. The Calvino story originally chosen ("Signora Palutim"), being previously unpublished in an English volume, could not be used, so another was chosen in its place and retranslated.

One more point about the selection. This is an anthology of short fiction, rather than excerpts from longer fictional works. Most Italian novelists write short fiction as well, publishing it in the literary page of newspapers, in literary magazines, and eventually in collections. But some novelists have written few stories or only long ones. That is why a major writer like Pier Paolo Pasolini who produced relatively few short stories in a vast opus (and these were published by the Marlboro Press in a translation by John Shepley, in 1986) is not represented here. Other novelists I'd hoped to include – Alberto Arbasino, Anna Banti, and Francesca Ramondino – write stories, but again, they were too long for my purposes. And similarly, several of the young novelists I'd planned to include – Andrea Del Carlo, Daniele Del Giudice, Roberto Pazzi – did not have stories to offer. On the other hand, in the end I did include two excerpts: "The Arhant," a chapter from Antonio Tabucchi's expressionistic novella *Notturno indiano*, and a chapter from Giuseppe Bonaviri's novel *Il sarto della stradalunga*.

This selection reflects, as all selections must, my own sensibilities and sense of Italy, its language, and its writers. I hope other anthologies will follow to broaden the perspective.

KATHRINE JASON
December, 1989

WORKS CITED

BARZINI, LUIGI. *The Italians*. New York: Atheneum, 1980.

CALVINO, ITALO. Preface. *The Path to the Nest of Spiders*. William Weaver, trans. New York: Harcourt Brace Jovanovich, 1967.

CEASAR, MICHAEL AND PETER HAINSWORTH. "The Transformation of Post-War Italy." *Writers & Society in Contemporary Italy: A Collec-*

tion Of Essays. Ceasar and Hainsworth, eds. Warwickshire: Berg Publishers Ltd., 1984. 1–34.

GIOANOLA, ELIO. "La situazione della letterature dopo il '50." *Storia letteraria del Novecento in Italia*. Torino: Societa Editrice Internazionale, 1983. 298–319.

SICILIANO, ENZO. Introduction. *Racconti italiani del Novecento*. Milano: Arnoldo Mondadori Editore, 1983. xi–xxviii.

WAGSTAFF, CHRISTOPHER. "The Neo-avantgarde." *Writers & Society in Contemporary Italy: A Collection Of Essays*. Michael Ceasar and Peter Hainsworth, eds. Warwickshire: Berg Publishers, Ltd., 1984. 35–61.

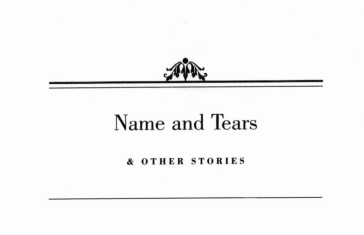

Name and Tears

& OTHER STORIES

GIOVANNI ARPINO

The Peacock

GIOVANNI ARPINO (1927–1987) A fiction writer, journalist and poet, Arpino is best known for his early neorealist work and his later so-called neonaturalist novels, among them *L'ombra delle colline*, which won the Strega Prize in 1964. Arpino has been called a "spiritual existentialist," a term which can be understood by the story included here, which portrays the restless but seemingly doomed search for meaning in a disaffected physician's daily routine. This story exemplifies too the tendency of Arpino's later work towards the fantastic: here the simple image of a peacock spurs a moment of transcendence in the protagonist's otherwise bleak life. "The Peacock" is from the collection *Un gran mare di gente*, 1981.

He looked out the window at the hospital courtyard petrified in the sun. At the end, beyond the pitiful border of grass turned bronze in the city heat, several frumpy women appeared to be melting into boiling spots of varnish. Their dresses flared and their aching legs sought new points of equilibrium with each tottering step they took in their impossible heels. It was torture just to watch them, but not for him. After decades he was used to their anxious, suspicious faces as they came and went through the garden and hallways of the dermatology and venereal medicine department which he directed.

He yawned, pushing his fists deeper into his jacket pockets. The summer weighed on him. As much as he loved it, every year only made him feel older and more breathless as he sought a moment's rest along the contours of the days which seemed to stretch on endlessly between examinations, words, and more words, mouthfuls of blood, microscope slides, and again words – of reproach, consolation, or whatever. . . And as much as he looked forward to it, the summer was always just that: arid and violent, the fan going round and round on the desk, and the women going round and round the corridors and the examining rooms in their dresses that were too red or too yellow; and then the empty, withered evenings in the city's open-air trattorias where the food lay heavily in the plates and each glass of chilled wine brought a sense of urgency and humiliation, especially for someone like him who envied the youth all around him.

He turned on his heels, leaving the window, and huddled behind the desk, craning his neck towards the fan. His mail lay unopened among unwrapped magazines, square and rectangular packages sealed with lead or wax, heaps of opened yellow envelopes, the usual infinitude of invitations, queries, new products, all of it a bore.

He shifted slightly to favor the hot side of his neck. Swallowing hot saliva, he studied the verdigris box filled with cigars but managed to find the will to deny himself.

Summer's a bitch, he thought suddenly; but that statement, which in mixed company, say a beautiful woman's, he would've insisted was meant ironically and defended, only left him feeling more alone and overheated now.

"Professor. . ." a voice called hesitantly from the door.

Surely he didn't have to answer, the usual glance over his glasses would suffice.

"Two people are here to see you. . . that man who called this morning, the accountant. . ." his nurse murmured quickly.

"Hmmm, what, who. . . ?" he gurgled, more to take hold of himself and connect. Pushing back into his memory, he saw the accountant from the fifth floor, his decorous and irreproachable tenant, appear in all his corpulence and courtesy.

He gurgled again, in assent, and the nurse disappeared. Then in the black space of the threshold, he saw the woman appear, shoved forward by the accountant; tall, fresh in her delicate colors, she had an immaculate white, white face around large eyes.

"Oh yes, yes," was all the professor said as he stood to greet them, to show them in.

He sat down again, suddenly feeling wide awake before the woman, whose light flowered dress covered her from neck to knees, shoulders to wrists. She was smiling at him, calmly, politely.

"We've come to thank you," said the accountant, already exploding out of his chair, "we just got the test results, and they're perfect, perfect..."

He giggled, momentarily ill at ease.

"Perfect," he continued quickly, "but we didn't want to leave without paying our thanks."

"Ah yes, yes, the tests, right," the professor mumbled. "Good. The results are no surprise..., of course."

All three smiled, the accountant more composed now, the woman briefly lowering her dark eyelids.

"Purely a formality, of course, I know," the accountant said, venting his formidable propriety. "But for any couple that wants to marry and have children nowadays, it's only right to take the tests and be sure... They should pass a law to make the premarital examination obligatory... Public health, as you know better than anyone..."

"Yes, right," the professor agreed passively.

Meanwhile she sat there, letting all the words rush by her. Her head slightly bent, she clutched the straw bag on her knees. She was smiling inwardly, her eyes lowered, as if she were unaware, untouchable.

"And anyway, since you're my landlord, it would have been foolish not to take advantage..." the accountant said cheerfully.

"Certainly, certainly," the professor blurted.

He fingered the cigars in the box, which made little squeaking noises, then decided again to resist.

"And what about the wedding?" he forced himself to ask.

"In about two weeks, the proper two weeks." The accountant laughed openly, reaching inside his summer jacket.

"All my best," the professor grunted.

"Ah, I don't regret bringing my Gina here," the accountant was already adding: "It's a horrible place, if you don't mind my saying so, but there are things to be learned. .... Isn't that so? Gina here has actually travelled around the world, but as we know, there are things that a woman knows only after she marries. As they say, a woman is born three times: when she's born, when. . ."

Raising his eyes, the professor saw the woman looking at him, palely and a bit anxiously. The heat had brought out the slightest, delicate hint of perspiration around her nostrils. But already a tiny handkerchief was produced, directed by swift fingers in white perforated gloves to tidy up.

"Fine, fine," the professor finally grunted.

He forced himself to look at the accountant and saw that he was suddenly embarrassed, struggling, no doubt, with the question of the fee, the "bother."

Wishing to avoid any further conflict of politesse between landlord and tenant, he gestured.

"No, no," he said, stopping the accountant from launching into details; "the nurse will tell you how much you owe the clinic. Nothing else, no, really, please. Anyway, I didn't do a thing myself, it was Doctor what's-his-name, Doctor M., wasn't it? You pay only what you owe the clinic in these cases. . . the nurse will tell you. . ."

"I'll go right now." The accountant leapt up.

She was still sitting still, leaning over slightly to scrutinize the words of an English magazine.

"Do you know English?" the professor mumbled cautiously.

"English? Why, she knows six languages and one hundred dialects, even some Indian dialects," the accountant shouted from the door.

"Ah," the professor grunted, sitting down.

She was looking at him, twisting her gloved fingers around the hand of her purse.

"Please, please," she whispered breathlessly, but clearly, "tell me when I can come back to see you alone, maybe later or tomorrow, but alone. . ."

"What?" The professor leaned forward.

"When. Please. I must speak to you. It's about something very serious," the woman enunciated, her eyelids fluttering; she went pale then suddenly flushed.

She had leaned slightly towards the desk with that splendid, immaculate face of hers which shone in the shadows of the room like a piece of frozen fruit.

"Let's see," the professor said, searching his mind quickly. "Yes, tomorrow morning, no, tomorrow afternoon would be better, at the same time... Is that right: at this same time?

In silent agreement, she looked down gravely at the upside-down title of a magazine.

"Here I am," the accountant announced boldly as he entered the room.

The salutations were brief; the professor stood to make a false bow.

Falling back in the chair, he watched her disappear into the shadows, the current of the fan following her and then lifting her light dress in a flutter.

Alone, he reached his hand out willfully and savored the familiar crunching of the cigars before choosing one and lighting up.

"I've turned on the red light, so we can relax. Nobody will bother us. Now what can I do for you?" he had urged.

The woman sat calmly with the hint of a smile, the slightest shadow of embarrassment. She nodded silently.

"Go on," he said, amused. "Come on, let's have a smoke. Do you have a cigarette? I'm just an old snuffer, but one cigarette..."

He pulled one out of the pack she held out and continued studying her through the smoke, relishing the moment. Her back, her dizzying white back; moved, he wanted to proceed slowly.

"You're not sick, that's obvious," he said jokingly. "What then?"

She shook her head, a shoulder, in mild denial.

"Can you understand?" she said to him then, her eyes lowered.

"What?"

"Can you understand," the woman repeated softly, without changing her tone. "You're a doctor, professor, I know... but men are so slow to understand. They don't seem to want to understand. . . . That I have learned. No, this has nothing to do with illness, thank goodness..."

"What then," the professor encouraged awkwardly, cursing the inadequacy of his vocabulary.

Putting her glasses down, she slid her elbows forward on the table. She looked at him, smiling, returning into her untouchable silence.

"Let's see if I understand," the professor tried. "Go on, go on, tell me."

She shook her head docilely.

"Even if it's not an illness, it's still some sort of trouble. Isn't that so?" the man continued slowly, content to have found a tone at least, and a precise definition. "Otherwise, why me? Right?"

"Exactly," the woman sighed.

"And you haven't mentioned anything to him, to the . . . ?" the professor asked.

"Oh no, that's impossible," the woman breathed, suddenly overcome. "That's exactly why I need your help. . . . Good grief! My fiancé, you know him, he's your tenant, is a person who's overly . . . overly, what's the word? . . . proper."

"Yes" the professor said becoming irritated. "So let's talk about it. Speak to me."

"It's a tattoo," the woman exhaled in a tone that was more calm than confessional. "A tattoo. I want to have it removed, but I don't know if that's possible."

"Oh," the professor said, disappointed, letting himself go slack against the back of the armchair. "Oh, of course, now I understand . . ."

"Look," she began quietly, more freely, "my life has been so unusual . . . I don't know why . . . but anyway, that's how it went. Years ago, five years ago, I worked on several ships, as a hostess, you know? On a line between Calcutta and Madagascar too. That's where they gave me the tattoo . . ."

"*Gave?*" He looked at her wearily over the rims of his glasses.

She smiled, shaking her head.

"I mean, I was forced to," she went on. "They tattooed me and I had to let them. At sea, you know . . ."

"What?" blurted the professor.

The woman sat perfectly still, her eyes resting on the handle of her purse, as if concentrating to remember. Then she looked up, gazed about here and there as though lost in thought, and finally smiled again calmly.

"Yes, there were two of us girls on the boat," she told him. "As you can guess, I wasn't about to accept the propositions of the entire crew. They were Dutch, all but one Scandinavian. So to punish me, since I wasn't as nice as the other girl, they tattooed me. Oh, it was all a game, a joke: And I even liked it afterwards, but now..."

"Yes?" the man assented mildly.

"Now," and she became a bit muddled, "my fiancé... you know how he is. He wouldn't understand, he couldn't understand. Tattooed like this! In the two years we've been engaged, he's never even seen me in a bathing suit. On some of our holidays at the beach, I've stayed shut up in the room, faking terrible headaches so I wouldn't have to get undressed. You know him. I wouldn't want to make him unhappy. And I've never had the courage to tell him the truth."

Pulling the cigar box to him, the professor stared inside sleepily. And he nodded to every word of the story, somehow distant now, professionally courteous and dominant.

"Did you say something?" the woman ventured softly.

"Huh? No, no, go on. Then we'll see..." the professor urged again. "You know, some tattoos are easy to erase and others are impossible.... It depends..."

The woman let out a little breath.

"This one is impossible," she sighed. "Impossible. I know. they've already told me. It's... it's per-fect."

"What do you mean?"

"An entire design, colors..." the woman said confused, trailing off in a gesture. "I was so happy! When I got engaged, I mean. Because women are like that, inferior, weak. I always thought I could manage on my own.... But at a certain age, you discover that you can only put your life in order by marrying.... Am I being clear? Oh, I know I'm boring you, I'm sorry."

"No, please, go on," the professor muttered.

Though he knew he wouldn't light it, he chose a cigar and rolled it between the tips of his fingers until the veins of the dark fiber showed through.

For a moment, only the hum of the fan animated the room. The sunlight filtered through the opaque windows, staining objects and angles, wood and paper, with a uniform coat of hot, thick varnish.

"Yes," the professor took a breath, "let's have a look."

But the woman remained seated. She was shaking her head, no longer smiling but pressing her lips together in a subtle expression of apprehension.

"Don't worry," the man said, raising his hand. "Please, go behind that screen."

Suddenly, the woman stood meekly, and leaving her bag on the armchair, disappeared behind the screen.

"Don't turn the light on, please," she said plaintively.

"Of course I won't, I can see perfectly well like this, don't worry," he assured her curtly.

He sat looking remorsefully at his cigar once again, feeling the spiralling lazy gloom of those summer hours, and the long, slow waves of drowsiness inside him.

"Yes?" he said, simply not to let her fuss.

"I'll be right out," she called amidst the sound of rustling.

He laid the cigar in its box, his hands motionless on the desk top, not even spurring himself on to imagine what base markings a sailor's imagination had carved on that appealing flesh.

"There," the woman breathed, from far off.

And then, raising his eyes, the professor almost saw nothing; for several seconds he foundered like a drunk man before that unexpected spectacle.

She stood there, her stupendous colors trailing off, bright yellows, blues, greens, violets, and a blue that was black but hot as honey; and dozens of eyes, immobile in the thicket, were lined up in rows from the nape of her neck down to the top of her buttocks. There were feathers, wings, a glorious web of frightening shrew-eyes and tiger-eyes.

"You see?" The woman's voice arrived as if from afar.

Stunned, he couldn't even answer, and now the woman was walking backwards towards him gracefully, elbows drawn tight against her sides, bringing her tapestry of nightingales closer and closer.

Beneath it, under the clean edge of the design, her buttocks and legs seemed to belong to another person, someone belittled by that supreme treasure, transformed into a miserable phantom by such intensity.

"You see?" the woman explained feebly, without turning, "this way, it's one thing... but if I move, it's something else. If I move it's... it's. ... That's why they tattooed the peacock. So that when I moved...

She raised her elbows slightly.

And then shifting upwards in a geometric shudder, all those eyes moved, winking then reeling briefly in wide or cleverly truncated curves.

"You see the peacock?" the woman whispered, overwhelmed.

She stood right across the desk from him now; the sumptuous movement came to life and then stopped and came to life again.

The professor gazed at it.

"May I get dressed now?" she said.

And as if she'd heard a "yes," she headed for the screen; then she returned to the desk where the professor sat humbled, pinned to his seat.

"What can be done? Please tell me. . ." She sat down, attentive.

The professor shook his head negatively.

"Nothing, right? I know. They've all said that. I keep hoping, but obviously, I'm just a fool," the woman murmured, as she slipped the perforated gloves back on.

"There's no skin transplant that could. . ." the professor began.

"Yes, yes," she said, already resigned, downcast.

"But who did it, how. . . ," he couldn't keep himself from saying.

"A Scandinavian. He was wonderful. It hardly hurt. Everyone said he was a master," the woman replied softly.

She was smiling again, a smile of resignation. She said nothing, waiting.

"Somehow I must find the courage to tell him," she said finally to break the silence into which the professor had fallen at his desk.

"Right" was all he could manage to add.

The woman shifted.

"Look, I said to you before that men don't understand," she confided patiently. "I know that there was nothing wrong with it. But he. . . who knows what he'll think? The truth is, it was the other girl on the ship who they demanded things from, without a stop, they reduced her to a state. . . . All they asked me to do after the peacock was finished. . . was to parade around. . . .

"And how long did it take to finish it?"

The woman smiled, her eyes half-closed.

"Oh, fifteen days, I remember perfectly," she answered. "But you know? Nobody bothered me. When they had decided on the peacock — because somebody suggested a tiger, if you can believe it! — when they decided, nobody wanted to see it until it was finished. Everybody waited, even the officers. But afterwards, they wouldn't let me stop parading around, you know what I mean?"

The professor nodded slowly.

"How am I going to tell him?" The woman stood up.

Using the desk for leverage, the man pulled himself up too.

"We'll have to see it again," he blurted, looking for words, desperate. "Reconsider. . . You know, it's a unique case, I. . . . Perhaps it wouldn't be impossible to reduce, to bleach the colors. . . ."

"Oh, no," the woman smiled knowingly, "I understand right away when a specialist says no. To tell you the truth, it wasn't that I really expected you. . . . Anyway, they told me the same thing at the Y clinic, in London."

"Then it is impossible," he exclaimed, as if resigned. "You'll have to tell him."

They crossed the room slowly, without another hopeful word.

"You see?" the woman stopped.

Standing erect, she lifted one elbow up to her shoulder.

"You see?" she explained, "If I do that with both arms, even without turning my back, two eyes appear on the sides of my breast, excuse me. . . . And even if I'm perfect from the front, I would have to stay perfectly still, from my arms up, not to show what I'm hiding in back."

"Ah, yes." The professor drew a breath.

They stood looking at one another, the woman's slight smile now breaking across her lips.

"Perhaps you would like me, since I'm a doctor, to bring it up with him myself," he suggested. "I've known the accountant for years. Perhaps I could. . . "

"Yes?" The woman pressed him on expectantly.

"I could, for example," he managed to say, biting his lip,

"because, well. . . because it's a marvelous thing, and he should accept it, he has to accept it. That's all there is to it."

"Yes," she said, looking down. "I know. Very well. But look, the man. . ."

"I know," the professor said curtly, trying to control his voice, to sound hopeful, "I know."

"Would you really try to talk to him? You're a professor, an expert, and then you're also the landlord," the woman said.

The professor interrupted, nodding pensively in agreement.

Perspiring, he leaned against a corner of the wall, furious, broken-hearted that his great hope was vanishing in silence and absurd prattle.

"But," he finally managed to say, swallowing hard, "but I want to see it again. You understand that, right? Again, just like before. Those eyes too, the way they move forward, all right?"

The woman gave him a serious smile, blinked.

"You won't think badly of me, professor?" she answered softly.

"Why no, no Signora. . . why?" he protested quickly, raising his arms.

She let out a light sigh.

"You'll do it then?" the professor attempted again, addressing her with greater confidence, "whenever you want, wherever you want, even here."

The woman consented with several quick nods.

"If you don't think badly of me," she repeated quietly.

"But no, no," the other stammered.

They stood close together at the door, sheltered by the still, opaque light of the room.

She still smiled as she whispered her telephone number and address.

"My dear friend," she said, extending her hand.

He watched her disappear, straight as a sword, into the bright, high sun in the corridor. Her dress blazed in a play of colors that seemed so banal to him now, so unworthy of those other gardens.

The Missed Marriage

GIUSEPPE BONAVIRI (1924–) A physician and writer, Giuseppe Bonaviri was launched in Vittorini's Gettoni series of young writers when his *Il sarto della stradalunga* (from which the first selection here is taken) appeared in 1954. Bonaviri is a master teller of tales from and about his native Sicily, in which the texture of the real is often transformed into the fantastic and in the words of Italo Calvino, "the countryside explodes into a biological poem." His writing is often highly stylized and naive in tone. Bonaviri was nominated for the Nobel Prize in 1985. "The Missed Marriage" is from *Il sarto della stradalunga*, 1954; "The Tailor's Son" is from *Novelle Saracene*, 1980.

My sister Pina is much older than me. When I was a kid she loved to sew clothes for me and whenever the hen laid an egg, she wrote my name on it so that the hen would hatch a pretty little chick just for me. I remember her smiling as she stood beside the rustling coops, the stray bits of straw poking through the mesh cover.

My sister Pina with her crown of curly hair: She'll hatch you a chick with a furry neck. Then she'll lay eggs for her little master and be the envy of the whole neighborhood.

They used to say my sister was a beautiful girl who would make a wonderful marriage if only fate would help my mother and father to put together a good trousseau. Another sister had died long before I was born, so she remained alone. But all kinds of adversity came our way and botched it every time a young peasant or a well-off young man proposed. I'll never forget Ciccio Incarbone who raved outside our house day and night; whenever he saw me, he'd touch my face with his large hands and whisper in my ear: "Oh, my angel, if only you could make my wish come true." But the next year, he had to leave to find work in America after a misfortune had impoverished his family. When he'd come, clutching his beret in his hands, his face haggard, my father had responded definitively.

My father, raising his voice: I don't give any daughter of mine to a starving man. A stew with two pieces of wood in it doesn't boil. Go to America instead. God willing, you'll make yourself a home over there.

The years passed and things went badly in our house too. My sister Pina was no longer considered a girl fit for a husband, and she no longer wanted to waste time sewing new dresses and endlessly brushing out her long hair, which she watched growing brittle in the mirror.

By now she had decided to follow me into my own adversity and to make herself as useful as she could in my house. Then one day, five years ago when my sister was forty, Turi the cripple, the local matchmaker who worked like a dog to put food on his table, came to find me in the workshop on the long road. I was sewing a pair of socks for a worker. It was February. Luigi was not there and the wind was swirling around on the streets, raising little dark cones of dirt and garbage into the air.

Turi the cripple: Master, this time we'll make the wedding. I want to be among the witnesses and carry the burning candle.

I had a vague sense of what he was referring to, but I didn't say a word and continued to work the needle into that dark, tough fabric, waiting for the matchmaker to make himself clear.

Turi the cripple: No offense meant, sir, but the husband is good. If we can do this thing cautiously, everything should go well.

Me, tersely: Who is he?

Turi the cripple: I'm telling you we're on the right road this time. Even if Don Napoleone was a bit disorganized once, now he's forty-nine and has many pots on the fire.

Uneasy, and flushed with shame for my sister, who said nothing but sat gazing at her yellowed, rough hands, I talked it over with him; I went to see Don Napoleone who lived with a sister in Sant'Aggripina in a little cobblestoned alley where wind descended in gusts raising wet mud and withered leaves from the blackberry bushes. As soon as I'd climbed the polished marble steps that led to the little red door and placed my hand on the knocker, I saw that everything was bound to fail. Donna Peppina, the sister, received me in her room.

Donna Peppina: Come in, come in. Welcome to our house and may God bless you.

Her bed, which stood next to the window and received the grey afternoon light, was made of wrought iron that had been polished with oil and vinegar and had a sculpted half-naked Christ on the headrest. A little altar with the image of an afflicted saint I didn't recognize, numerous candles arranged in tin cups and a bunch of artificial flowers stood facing the door. I remembered that the woman was a fanatical bigot who spent day and night in church and the sacristy; it was said she'd had dubious relations with Father Cianci.

Donna Peppina: My brother has a little cold today. Wait while I tell him you're here.

Don Napoleone was lying in a matrimonial bed. He had a bullish neck and his stomach was so high and round that it made a huge arc which lifted the blankets.

Don Napoleone with his lustful smile: Come forward, Tailor.

Ropes of sausage turning dry and brown hung on a wire strung between the bar of his bed and a wicker chair, giving off the acrid scent of sweat and rotten meat. They had me sit in a green armchair with a flowered rug at its feet, and I couldn't but notice that it clashed with all the other dusty old furniture and the common clay tiles on the floor.

Don Napoleone in an arrogant tone: Peppina, bring us some pastries. One should eat something sweet before making a deal.

The tray on which the little, hard, tasteless pastries arrived, covered by an embroidered napkin, had filaments of rust in the corners and strands of dust here and there. Don Napoleone had arranged a pile of cushions so that he could sit up in bed, and he pulled his shirt closed over his chest and his pink, pendulous breasts. Meanwhile, I nibbled patiently at one of the pastries, gazing beyond the balcony at the arid, cracked stones of the Salemi Wall and the garbage heap that rose into the air, furrowed and stirred up by a cold, whistling north wind.

Donna Peppina, all serious: Don't be polite, eat up. We'll all be family anyway soon, if the Madonna of Carmine approves.

But the whole thing failed, just as I expected: Don Napoleone's terms were dishonest, to say the least, and too difficult for my sister and me to meet.

But it's better that I stop writing the part of the story that concerns me. Going on would only make me bitter again, I know, and maybe even more muddled than I was in the past. I'm thirty-two years old and there's no way out anymore. The years to come will bring poverty and hunger. I should give this a happy ending like a real story, but thinking of the fate that awaits me and my sister Pina, I can't.

The Tailor's Son

Once upon a time there was a tailor who had it very bad. Carnival time was approaching, and the old heart of the people was coming to life again. The wind hummed in the silent forest, the river was dry, the cold mist darkened the olive trees. In their houses people made sweets, ruffled their dresses, they joked, they made macaroni and meats. But the tailor, who had three children, a mannequin, a needle, and yarn didn't even have a loaf of bread. The oldest child said to his father:

"Father, we should enjoy the carnival this year. Everybody but us eats and laughs."

The tailor answered, a knot of tears in his throat: "And how can we manage, son, if we have no money, no silver, or gold?"

"I'll take care of it, you'll see."

"Be careful son, don't steal because you'll go to jail, and life is futile there. Your mother is dead, and we're alone on this sorrowful earth."

"Don't worry, father."

The boy left for the countryside, which is dead and has no sparkling sun, only rocks and scrub. He came to a lovely, large half-green pasture where the oxen of Don Antonio Fragala, the principal priest of our village, were grazing. Seeing so many oxen, the boy sighed and listened to the mournful harmony the little oxen were making. He saw a small one, grabbed it by the horns, and fled into a cave where he cut the ox's neck and emptied out the entrails, saving only the legs and the shoulders. These he took with him; the shepherd was not to be seen, having gone to the spring. The tailor's son, who we can call Salvatore, after the glory of our Lord, arrived in the village at night. Three lamps were lit, the church bell was ringing out, the village was plunged in a well of darkness. He knocked at the door. The father: "Who's there at this hour?"

"It's me, father."

The father got out of bed, lit the oil lamp and went to open up. He was frightened.

"All this meat, my son? I told you that it would end badly. Where did you get this little oxen?"

"In Don Fragala's field."

"Now you'll end up in jail. I can already hear the trotting of the police horse and the birds' crying."

"Don't worry. Let's eat while we can. Thank God!"

God was thanked and adored, as they sat down on the floor to eat roasted oxen, delicious onions, hard bread. The house shone, for outside Sirius was shining clear and beautiful on the roof. And that's all.

Leaving them to the delights of the palate, we meet the farmhand of Antonio Fragala, parish priest of our village. This farmhand came back from the fountain with a gallon of water on his back and saw that the ox named Colombo was missing.

"Colombo! Colombo!" he cried.

The mother moaned a moan of bitter grief. The boy ran, leaped over pits, blackberry bushes, saw the village above him, arrived. Tup, tup—he knocked.

"Who is it?" asked Don Antonio, the priest.

"It's me, Father."

"At this hour? What is it?"

"It's that Colombo the little ox is missing. They stole him."

"And where were you? Who did it? How on earth did it happen?"

"I don't know anything. I was gone getting water."

He said no more. Don Antonio made the sign of the cross and said, "I'll find the devil of a thief."

Lent came, the sky was in ashes, the faithful Catholic folk heard the bells ringing like a river.

"Let's go to church and confess," they said.

The father, who was a fervent Catholic, an enemy of Macone Dio, said to his son: "Salvatore, you must go and confess."

"Yes, father."

"But how will you do it? What will you say to Don Antonio, the parish priest?"

"Don't worry."

He left on the road where it was hardly raining, raindrops fine as ashes. The priest said to him, "Get down on your knees and tell me everything, even if you robbed, otherwise I can't give you the holy consecrated wafer."

In the church of Santa Maria, the villagers were kneeling on the cold marble, and some on this side and some on that were crying for their sins and for the penitence which would undo them, beat by beat and in the slow Lord's prayer.

When Father Antonio Fragala learned what the tailor's son had done, he said to him: "Salvatore, let's do this: there are two pulpits in the church. I'll go up in one, you go up into the other one. You must tell the people from up there that you robbed my calf. That way, everybody will hear it."

Salvatore answered, his head bent: "Yes sir, parish priest."

When the young man got up on the pulpit, he said nothing. Then he asked Don Antonio loudly, "Do I have to say it? Do I really have to?" The echo of his voice was magnified above the lit candelabra, above the jasper of the columns, above the heads of the villagers and the women.

"Say it, say it; what are you waiting for, son?" the priest thundered.

"So I'll say it."

"Yes, yes, yes, that way the people will hear it."

"Good, Catholic friends, as you see, he, Don Fragala, our parish priest, is making me say this."

"We're listening, Salvatore," said the women.

"He's making me say that all you women here are Don Fragala's whores!"

Oh, dark horror! The villagers ran to get hoes, pickaxes, pitchforks, the wives clambered up on the pulpit. The priest was impaled on a fork, his cries mute in his throat.

"Go on, get him, go on!" cried the others dragging themselves towards him. And there were Saracens among them, there were French and Spaniards and Normans.

"Go on, go on!"

The men and women of the village hurled forks into all the bodily orifices of Don Antonio Fragala, whose hands and head went up in sulfurous flames. The fable ends here, at long last. Amen. And what else could we ask?

VITALIANO BRANCATI

Arrival in the City

VITALIANO BRANCATI (1907–1954) A scathing social satirist who exposed the manners and mores of his native Sicily in the years of fascist rule, Brancati's central theme is Gallismo, or the obsession with virility and power at the heart of fascist ideology. His most successful works are the novels *Il Bell' Antonio*, the unfinished novel *Paolo Il Caldo*, and many of the stories, particularly "Il vecchio con gli stivali," which is considered a masterpiece. Brancati was also an essayist, journalist and dramatist. "Arrival in the City" is from *Sogno di un valzer*, 1982.

Dozing off in the second-class compartment, Luigi Arlini knew exactly what he was going to feel when he set foot in the big city: nostalgia, embarrassment and sea sickness.

At the pensione which his friend Artusi had already described in detail, he would sleep in a pentagonal room, next to the enormous one where a baroness lived with her husband. The tenant who had slept in the bed in the pentagonal room before him was a young lawyer, "thin, five feet ten, with a slightly hoarse voice, but healthy just the same." The baroness was a beautiful woman, a gypsy of sorts who played the piano at the most inappropriate hours of the day and dined in her own room with her husband. Occasionally, however, a barbaric mania compelled her to eat alone, huddled in her armchair like a hyena; and whenever that happened, her husband was seen leaving the pensione smiling, a gardenia in his buttonhole, repeating the phrase "Je mangerai dehors, Je mangerai dehors" like a refrain.

The little lawyer — according to his friend Artusi's letter — fell in love with the baroness; but being timid and small, he had sat on his little bed for days on end, listening to his neighbor's voice, her music, her footsteps, and breathing those subtle moods, now violent, now sweet, which reached him from the adjoining room across the wall that divided them.

No, he, Artusi, would've behaved differently. The baroness was some kind of gypsy, and as such, was also romantic. Two days after he arrived, Artusi would have sent the baroness a letter (and so he advised his friend to do) expressing his gratitude and his admiration for the music he was hearing; then a bunch of roses; and then a second letter, this, a romantic one ("Imagine, romantic") about his dreams of becoming a painter and feminine charms.

Thus, given his friend's advice and information, and given certain duties which he considered necessary to his private life, Luigi Arlini knew precisely how he would spend his first day in the pensione, in the big city. He could already see the details: the bed in which a stranger had slept, repellent and sibylline; the yellow walls of the room on which the light traced faces he'd never seen, faces of men who had lived a hundred years ago; the great, futile noise that rose from the street; waiters with their fleeting, indifferent gazes; the voices, sounds and manners of his native city rediscovered in certain voices, sounds and manners, but somehow exaggerated by a comic spirit; the footsteps of a pensione guest mistaken, momentarily for his mother's; nostalgia; fear; the baroness' music filling these voids like icy water; and the delicate letters, the first dreams of his easy and hard life.

But instead, as soon as he lay down on the bed in the pentagonal room, his shoulders sinking into the pillows, he felt a sense of love pervading him and giving him strength. Sleeping on the still warm impression left by another man, he had the same feeling he'd had at three when he'd been lost and his father lifted him up off the street and hugged him to his chest.

The ceiling vault above the yellow walls was suffused by a mysterious and motionless delight. The furniture, well-used by people he didn't know rather than by strangers, seemed full of spirit and chatter, amusing, like an album where everybody scrawls a thought, a little comment. . . . On the right, a old woman was coughing. In the baroness' room, somebody was walking back and forth slowly. The sound of a violin came softly from the end of the corridor. His friend Artusi was running water in the bathroom. Passing close to the door, a young girl said: "Tomorrow, okay!" The telephone rang and somebody laughed; a comical "Reeeeady!" was heard. Something blurred and poetic beckoned lightly at the window: lights, noises, the sound of a radio, unfamiliar views.

A feeling of unanticipated well-being flowed through him and unsettled him. He began to feel troubled: what kind of man was he, what was he made of, if his impressions were hardly normal, common? Why did he feel good when he should've been feeling awful?

He wanted to think of gloomy things: what if he fell ill and died all alone in that pensione!. . . . He made a great effort to find evidence for the thought. And in fact, it was painful to think of falling ill and dying alone, in that pensione! But it was the *alone* he couldn't get a sense of. All around him voices, footsteps, the banging of doors and ringing of bells breathed the light, warm breath of human life on his skin. And even if those people were unknown to him, they were present just the same. Wasn't this the best way, he thought, to overcome solitude? We love our fathers, mothers, brothers and sisters too much because they're companions, they give us that pure courage that compels us to take action without a second thought. And because we adore them so, they're frightful beings, subject to the perils of mystery. . . .

He put on his slippers, opened the door and crossed the corridor. The violin fell silent like the sound of woodworms which seems to be coming from some piece of furniture until we approach and no longer hear it, perhaps because it wasn't coming from that piece of furniture after all. An old woman emerged from a doorway and slipped quickly into another one. A half-naked young man was doing gymnastics in a square room.

The telephone was in the most dimly lit corner of the room.

"Where is the damn light?" Luigi muttered as he searched for the switch. "Where is this damn light?" he repeated with a kind of delight, as if that crude question gave him more power. But he found the switch and turned it on.

"I'll call that beast Arno."

He dialed the number, listened to the bleating sound (like a lost sheep) that the new telephones made; then the full voice of a woman came across the cable in the vast, unknown city like a voice from the center of a labyrinth. "Hello, who is it?"

Luigi paused for a second to savor the inflections of that voice once again.

"Hello? Who is it?"

"Luigi Arlini. Is Commander Arno there?"

"I'll go see. Hold on please."

He could hear the inside of the Arno house through the receiver; a dog howling, the sound of a piano, several hard little knocks which he couldn't make out.

"Hello?"

"The commander went out a minute ago."

"Goodbye."

And he hung up: "That animal went out!" He crossed the corridor again and entered his room. Opening a window which gave onto the courtyard, he stretched out on the bed.

Two women were talking in the courtyard below.

"He came this morning, my good lady."

"So, the room is rented"

"No, he didn't want it."

"Why?"

"Why, he's a crude... ! He inspected everything minutely, then he said to me: 'I don't want to be alone, at night.' 'Are you afraid?' I asked, to make light of it. 'No,' he said, 'I get bored,' and then after thinking a moment: 'But naturally, you'll sleep with me three times a week.... '"

"Oh, what a rogue!"

"And you should've seen his face – totally serious and calm!"

"And what did you do, Signora?"

"But what could I do? I told him it was impossible... and goodbye."

"And you lost a guest!"

"Sure, I lost him... but that's life.... What would you have done?"

"Nothing. I would've pretended not to understand, and then I would've seen what happened. Was he attractive?"

"A handsome man."

"Ha, we even have to rent our bodies out these days."

Both women laughed.

"Great!" thought Luigi, dropping, at the sound of those crude words, into a blissful sleep.

One day as Luigi was typing a letter, the door opened and a porter came timidly into the room. He seemed amused.

"What is it?" Luigi asked.

"Pardon, Signore, don't take it the wrong way. But the baroness has asked me to tell you that the sound of the typewriter is disturbing her."

"It's shattering my eardrums," corrected the baroness, who must've been standing at the door.

"Fine. Tell the baroness that it's generous of me to pay her back for the horrible piano playing of hers with a typewriter."

"Bastard!" the woman yelled, and the door slammed violently.

Embarrassed, the porter withdrew, and Luigi went on typing the letter, throughout which insults slowly began to appear.

Their relationship grew more and more tense after that incident. The baroness spoke loudly of "certain bastards who she'd like to whip!" As soon as she sat down at the piano, Luigi would leave his room quickly and noisily, as if a fire had broken out.

One night he came back later than usual. He didn't even turn on the light. The glimmer of a glass door faintly lit the corridor.

Numerous shoes were lined up near the doorways, giving the fabulous impression of slippers that having danced away, now in the presence of a stranger, had hurried fearfully back to their rows against the wall. He heard the old woman coughing quietly. He heard the false silence of sleeping people that seemed so audible in pensiones.

Luigi walked down the corridor. But in the corner between his doorway and the adjoining one, he found the baroness standing in her pajamas, mute. With that precise, cold sensation of touching, not an object, but something important and unknown, rich with fine detail and a history – a being – he reached out to that corner; and he felt the slightly damp hands of the woman. Then he wrapped his arm around her and slowly pulled her into his room.

As he shut his door, he saw his enormous hand, as though projected from a distance in the light of universal judgment, turning the doorknob, turning the key, and then finding the woman's shoulders again. And with a sense of disgust, he felt the reality of his life – a life condemned to luck and brutality.

The Invaded Man

GESUALDO BUFALINO (1920–) A self-defined "secret" writer for decades, the septuagenarian Bufalino made a clamorous debut in 1981 with his novel *Diceria dell' untore* (published in translation under the title *The Plague Sower*). Bufalino is a highly idiosyncratic stylist who tends toward the baroque and archaic and a whimsical fantasy. His broad frame of reference embraces the arcane, the historical, and the classical. "The Invaded Man," exemplifies Bufalino's idiosyncrasy. "The Invaded Man" is from *L'uomo invaso e altre invenzioni*, 1986.

Although I suspected it for some time, I was never brave enough to talk about it. But now the evidence is undeniable: I, Vincenzino La Grua, am no longer a man, but an angel, probably a seraphim.

I haven't the vaguest idea how it happened. But the fact is that the proof of my metamorphosis would convince a blind man. Still, God knows how fond I've become of the mediocre flesh (sweaty hands, strong breath) that has protected my days until now. The human condition—with all its thorns, its steppes of yellow ennui—has this much good: it guarantees each man, with the mayor's signature to boot, a self-evident identity; and while we call ourselves lifelong masters of the square meter or so that we occupy on this earth, that doesn't take away the comfort that we get from feeling equal to millions upon millions of distant creatures. . . .

I wake in the morning, and as I wake, I become one with everyone else in the world opening his eyes, each an owner, like me, of an odor, a face, a memory. And yet, at the same time, if I lean out the window and shout, "Vincenzo, Vincenzo, La Grua!" there's nobody out there who will lift his head and recognize himself in my voice; the syllables of the name I shout belong only to me, to this humble, solitary, exclusive, unique god.

And yet, now that a stranger has invaded me, I'll have to do without that terribly flawed certainty; from now on, who knows exactly who "I" am?

Let's start at the beginning. The first sign came in the bathroom, six months ago. I was standing in the shower, all white skin, teeth chattering. Then the hot water ran out, for no apparent reason, and a thousand cold spurts assailed me treacherously, all at once. So I maneuvered the faucet with inept fingers, all the while perilously poised on the edge of the rubber mat. And then suddenly I could no longer feel the mat beneath the soles of my feet, a lightness took over my bones, and I rose gracefully towards the ceiling. The first movement was timid, fearful: I was drawn up, naked and white, to the small opening that lets light into the room, flashing the sparse black bush of my pubis as I rose – the danger being that the lawyer's wife on the facing balcony might glimpse me and tremble indignantly for her little daughters.

It was fortunate that the episode only lasted a moment or so. I found myself sitting, somewhat unconsciously, on the floor, unable to figure out at first whether I'd been hovering in blessed flight or had only sustained one of those bourgeois household accidents that every slippery Sunday ablution threatens. . . .

Several weeks later the first bleeding began. Slyly at first, in the form of little pink drops, which I noticed along the seam of my sleeves whenever I changed my shirt. But one late night, returning in the tram from an opening at the opera, (in my free time I'm a *claqueur*; everyone in my family has always been either a musician or singer or a buff) I felt an odd warmth, a dampness all up and down both backbones, as if two veins of tepid mineral water had been opened up in my back. I got off at the next stop, unbuttoned my shirt under the street light, trying to reach around to the double spring, and saw my hands were red like the hands of an apprentice butcher. At home, craning my neck in the mirror, I could see two fresh wounds where it hurt, the blood hardened into a burning, livid crust, like the embers of an amputation. I was struck by the hilarious thought that my wings had been clipped at some point during my infancy and now the stumps were shooting up again, like the teeth that replace baby teeth. Perhaps these fresh wounds heralded a birth of sorts; perhaps a thick birdlike plumage would soon sprout from the top layer of skin. . . .

More reasonably, while I undressed for bed, I raged at Amalia as I had the night before, pointing to the evidence under my armpits. She protested and shouted, and I had to admit that these were not stigmatas or injuries of love, but something else. Since then the allusions are multiplying all around me; somebody seems to be trying to tell me something. For example, the hilt that I found in the attic inside my Uncle Ettore's theatrical trunk where he abandoned it after his unfortunate rendition of Manrico in Parma, in '49; sure, it could have well been the separated appendix of a prop man's sword. But, really, it was so powerful and strange; such a phosphorescent darkness emanated from the rags wrapped around it that it seemed a barber trophy or diadem, strewn with rubies. And finally, one day, I happened upon my copy of the Doré Bible that I haven't looked at for years, opened, on the top of my dresser, to the very page that tells the story of Tobias and one of his mysterious travelling companions.

I began to worry. I couldn't hold back the waves of disequilibrium I felt throughout my body. One morning my hair fell out in handfuls as if it had been mown by the unerring blade of a scythe; another day, it grew back in, but blond and soft, fine and supple to the touch, unlike my own. "Angel hair," Amalia called it, the name of a certain Sicilian spaghetti, as she caressed it. A useless seduction at that point – because the most incredible indifference towards women has come over me. On the other hand, I am becoming ever more aware of the attentions others pay me: women and young girls wink at me, they graze by me, whispering "Oh, blondie!" But so do hairy men who accost me in elevators or in the men's rooms of railway stations. One even insisted; he fell to his knees, kissing my hands, begging me. I had to force him to stand up and console him by pinching his cheek.

There is an amusing benefit to all these strange signs – a sense of fun. But it's not without its horrors, like the time I found a pile of white feathers on the floor at the foot of the sink, and leaning against the wall right beside it, a hatchet.

Now I can't stop thinking about it; but neither have I let myself lose sight of my first impression. As you can surely see, I'm a homebody, a calm fellow with little propensity for the metaphysics of the sublime. But if for a week I dream of dawn as an immense, frozen black space from which a bolt of incandescent lightning suddenly issues; if the sound of magisterial rowing on either side of my bed reaches me in my sleep, like the sound of wind in a great forest; if I feel as if I'm being lifted in this wind, higher and higher, until I cross a dizzying threshold, to be set down in God's eye like a drop in the thick of a perpetual flood; if, in more prosaic terms, I go up on the terrace to get a tan, now that June has arrived, and notice that my bare feet are leaving footprints in the floor that smoke and fume, as if they were oozing spoonfuls of melted iron... tell me, what am I to make of all that, what should I say?

Cautiously I went around asking questions. I went to the library to do research. The Pseudo Diogenes writes (according to the photocopy I'm looking at): "The scriptures not only speak of flaming wheels, but also of animals of fire and of so-called radiant men, and posit celestial clouds of flaming carbons and rivers which throw off fires with incredible force around these same substances, and shows that the sublime seraphim themselves, as their name indicates, are also fiery. . . . "

So, what should we make of it? If I rest my finger on Amalia's arm I burn her; if I put a thermometer in my mouth, I melt it. . . .

Amalia is incredulous, she reduces everything to her own terms. She says; "You're exaggerating, you see miracles everywhere you look. . . you're also slightly obsessed, to tell the truth. You're creating an incredible uproar, and all over a fall in the bathroom, two skin irritations, a little goose feather you happened to step on in the kitchen. Why don't you go to the doctor, really, go. . . you'll see, the fire you feel boiling in your body is only a flush from hypertension. . . .

Then I get angry and I hit her with a newspaper and accuse her of not listening. She isn't moved. "If you're really an angel," she challenges, "then give me the winning numbers for Lotto." So I give up, laughing. But I get my revenge now and then with a good joke, sometimes I scrawl some salacious curse on the mirror with her lipstick, sometimes I appear at the bedside at night in a white nightshirt and a tuba and blast a terrifying "Dies irae" in her ears.

Sophomoric pranks. They help me to put off the thoughts and doubts that still nag at me. So be it, I'm an angel, there's not a shadow of a doubt. But am I an angel who's being born or reborn? Am I undergoing a metamorphosis or being invaded? Is the being who is dwelling in my body a foreign guest or is my body host to an ancient, forgotten baptism?

When I brood over these questions as I lay awake with insomnia beside my snoring wife, or I ruminate aloud, filling both of us with shame, between courses at lunch, a feeling of anxiety grips my chest and I have to smoke a cigarette or take a drink to distract myself. The situation is so far gone by now that the woman is beginning to see the light, though in an oblique and spiteful way; she can't bear the idea that I could be possessed, if anything, it infuriates her. Although since she saw *The Exorcist* again on TV, she tends to believe mine is a possession of a different order – a more serious one. Indeed, on two or three occasions, I've caught her scrutinizing me from close up with the excuse of wanting to cut my toe nails, for instance: I suppose she suspects a cloven hoof. And when she sniffs the air and asks me if I've just lit a safety match, she must smell an odor of sulfur in the room, or pretend to. Nor do I believe that she's happened to invite the priest to dinner two days in a row.

On the other hand, I do believe that the thing that entered my body is good in nature. Even if I wonder, why me? I'm a simple man who doesn't deserve these visitations; my body is a poor house, my senses and intellect can't offer much illumination. . . . I don't understand. Unless the invader is simply a spirit who, being curious about the ways of the world, came to any old workshop to get experience, like the heirs to the throne who are sent out on hard duty or to join garrisons. Or else it is a displaced angel, who escaped from the sacred college as some kids here on earth do, catching the first passing train and returning a month later gripping a sullen policeman by the hand.

Sure, I feel violated, inhabited, forced to pit some feeble remainder of myself against an aggressive power. . . . And what if Amalia was right all along, damn her! What if the being inside me is a filthy little Satan in transit, fatuous and cruel enough to pass the time mistreating a poor fellow like me. . . .

In any case, one thing is undeniable: I'm suffering.

The final incident, which happened the day before yesterday, is definitive.

I was expecting it, but not so soon. The fact is the latest threat is affecting my speech. I normally use respectable, educated words, accompanied by mild gestures, but now, at first between long, then more frequent intervals, and finally every hour or half-hour, I am gripped by a sort of coprolingual fit: a vulgarity, or even worse an indecency, slips out as if it were nothing. If it happens when I'm in mixed company, I excuse myself like someone who feels the urgency to pass wind, and run to the bathroom, press my colored handkerchief to my lips and spit out the indecent word. This has made my dealings with the world difficult and infrequent and has led to a life of solitude. Still, if there was anywhere I felt more sure of myself, it was in the theatre where I had free admittance and could choose to stand behind a curtain far from all danger. Regardless of what happened, I always assumed I would be able to contain myself or to hide it if a fit came over me.

That time it didn't happen that way. I had come in on the sly, they were rehearsing one of those silly, obscure things that appeal to me, the oratory that the *carissimi* dedicate to the passion of Job. I went, inspired on two counts: to see the Ticinese contralto Gertrude, the passionate love of my youth, for her tenderness and melancholy (you must have heard of this contralto and her hoarse, dark, unforgettable Messalinas?); and since it's an angel who sings in the piece, to watch and see whether he was carrying a message from the superiors for me, from one colleague to another. I not only know Latin rather well, but also quavers and demisemiquavers. Therefore, I was taking in the words and music with a sense of warm pleasure, indeed, I confess, with tears in my eyes. But after the "Audi, Job," when I heard the melody repeat its sweet, resigned, impassive, "Sit nomen Domini benedictum" three or four times, I don't know why, but, overwhelmed by a fit of laughter and fury, I exploded into an incredible curse that drowned out voices and instruments alike and abruptly silenced them.

I was kicked, thrown out, it was the least they could have done. Then they had to call the madhouse.

Now I'm here and fine. Amalia brings me the newspaper, fresh linens, special food. Not that the meals are bad, but I have particular tastes, and I don't intend to change. As for the rest, there's fresh air, middle-aged but attractive nurses, a calming sweetness that dissolves in water, flowers in a vase on the window-sill.

I am coming to life again. I don't say ugly words anymore, I only think them. I address the spirit within me regularly, but in civil terms. An idea about this came to me: it must be an aborted creature who is doing everything it can to save itself from dying, and is sucking my human juices, usurping my memories to that end, to save itself from dying. I'll have to get used to us living together. As foe and friend. Reining him in and goading him on, as the case may be. Domesticating him. I will grow with him, he will become me, and I him, we'll exchange vices and virtues. I can already see myself driving with his hand, both of us paralytic and blind amidst the dizzying traffic; going from door to door announcing blessed motherhood, a lily in hand; standing vigil, a finger on my lip, before the rooms of the dying; and finally one dawn, vanquishing the dragon with a flaming sword.

Something That Begins with "L"

DINO BUZZATI (1906–1972) Buzzati's predilection for the fantastic, the allegorical and the Gothic, makes him a literary descendant of Poe and Kafka. But even in the most fantastic of the stories, there is the measured, documenting voice of the journalist – which, in fact, he was – exposing the tension, just below the surface of things, between the banal and the inexplicable or irrational in everyday life. The attitude described in "Something That Begins with *L*" is not so unlike attitudes we have witnessed recently in our own culture.

"Something That Begins with *L*" is from *60 racconti*, 1942.

When Cristoforo Schroder, a wood merchant, arrived in the village of Sisto and made his way to the usual inn – which he usually did two or three times a year – he went straight to bed, feeling unwell. Then he summoned Doctor Lugosi, whom he had known for years. The doctor came but seemed perplexed. Ruling out anything serious, he had the patient produce a urine specimen for analysis and promised to return that same day.

The next morning Schroder felt much better, so much so that he jumped up without even waiting for the doctor. He was in his shirt sleeves, shaving, when there was a knock at the door. It was the doctor. Schroder told him to come in.

"I'm feeling fine this morning," the merchant said without even turning from the mirror, and he continued shaving. "Thank you for coming, but you can go."

"What's the big rush?" the doctor asked, coughing slightly as if to express a certain embarrassment. "I've brought a friend along with me this morning."

Schroder turned and saw a man of about forty standing beside the doctor in the doorway, a sturdy, rather crude looking fellow with a flushed face and an insinuating smile. The merchant, a man who was always sure of himself and in the habit of taking charge, gave the doctor an irritated and questioning glance.

"A friend of mine," Lugosi repeated, "Don Valerio Melito. He must accompany me on a house call later, so I told him to come along."

"*Servitor suo,*" said Schroder icily. "Sit down, sit down."

"Anyway," the doctor went on to justify himself further, "you don't seem to need an examination today. The urine is fine. I only wanted to bleed you a little."

"Bleed me? What for?"

"It will do you good," the doctor said by way of explanation. "Afterwards you'll feel like a new man. It's always good for the composition of the blood. And it only takes two minutes, anyway."

Saying that, he took from his cloak a small glass bottle containing three leeches. Setting them down on a table, he added, "Put one on each wrist. Just hold them there for a moment and they'll cling to you. And please, do it yourself. I may have been a doctor for twenty years, but I've never been able to pick up a leech."

"Give it to me," said Schroder with that irritating, superior air of his. He took the small glass bottle, sat on the bed and put the two leeches on his wrists as if he'd been doing it his whole life.

In the meantime, the unfamiliar visitor, though not removing his heavy cloak, placed his hat on the table along with an oblong package, which gave off a metallic sound. Schroder noticed, with a vague feeling of unease, that the man was sitting almost on the threshold as if he were anxious to stay far away from him.

"You may not know this, but Don Valerio already knows you," the doctor said to Schroder, as he too, for some strange reason, sat down near the door.

"I don't recall having the honor," replied Schroder, who sat on the bed, his arms resting limply on the mattress, palms upturned, while the leeches sucked at his wrists. Then he added, "But tell me, Lugosi, was it raining this morning? I haven't looked outside yet. I have to make stops all day long; it'll be a nuisance if it rains."

"No, it's not raining," said the doctor, without giving much weight to this answer. "But Don Valerio really does know you and was anxious to see you again."

"You know," said Melito with a voice that was unpleasantly hollow. "You know, I've never had the honor of meeting you personally, but I know something about you that you'd never guess."

"I wouldn't have the slightest idea what it is," the merchant answered in a tone of complete indifference.

"Three months ago?" Melito asked. "Try to remember: three months ago, didn't you take the Old Border Road with your carriage?"

"That could be," Schroder said. "That could very well be, but I don't remember exactly."

"Fine. And don't you remember, in fact, that you skidded on a curve, skidded off the road?"

"Right, that's true," the merchant admitted, staring coldly at this new and unwelcome acquaintance.

"And a wheel went off the road and the horse couldn't pull it back up."

"That's right. But where were you?"

"Ah, I'll tell you that later," answered Melito, and letting out a laugh, he winked at the doctor. "And then you climbed down, but you couldn't pull the carriage back up, either. Tell us, isn't that what happened?"

"Exactly. And it was raining cats and dogs!"

"Good Lord, how it was raining!" Don Valerio continued, pleased with himself. "And while you were struggling, didn't a strange fellow appear, a tall man with a black face?"

"That part I don't remember," Schroder interrupted.

"Excuse me, doctor, but how much longer for these leeches? They've swelled up like toads. And I've had enough. I told you I have a lot to do today."

"Just one more minute," the doctor exhorted. "Have a little patience, dear Schroder! Afterwards you'll feel like a new man, you'll see. It's not even ten o'clock yet, for Heaven's sake, you'll have all the time you want."

"Wasn't there a tall man whose face was all black, with a strange cylindrical hat?" insisted Don Valerio. "And didn't he have some sort of bell? Don't you remember he kept on ringing it?

"Fine, yes, I remember," Schroder replied discourteously. "I'm sorry, but where is all this leading?"

"Nowhere!" said Melito. "I just wanted to tell you how I already knew you. And that I have a good memory. Unfortunately, that day I was far away, across a ravine, I was at least five hundred yards away. I was standing under a tree to stay dry, but I could see clearly."

"And who was that man, then?" asked Schroder harshly, as if to suggest that if Melito had something to say he'd better say it quickly.

"Ah, I don't know exactly who he was, I only saw him from a distance. But who do you think he was?"

"Some poor soul, that's all," said the merchant. "He seemed to be a deaf mute. When I asked him to help me, he began to moan. I didn't understand a word he said."

"And then you walked towards him, and he backed off, so then you took him by the arm and forced him to help you push the carriage. Isn't that how it happened? Tell us the truth."

"What does this have to do with anything?" Schroder retorted, growing suspicious. "I didn't do anything to him. In fact, afterwards I gave him two lire."

"Did you hear that?" Melito whispered to the doctor. Then, turning back to the merchant, he said in a louder voice: "Nothing's wrong with it, who says otherwise? But you admit that I saw the whole thing."

"There's no reason to get upset, dear Schroder," said the doctor, noticing that the merchant looked angry now. "This fine fellow here, Don Valerio, is a bit of a joker. He only wanted to make an impression on you."

Melito turned to the doctor, nodding his head in agreement. As he did, his cloak parted a bit and Schroder, who was staring at him, turned pale in the face.

"Excuse me, Don Valerio," he said in a rather less casual tone. "You're carrying a pistol. Certainly you could've left it downstairs.

They do that as a matter of course in these parts, if I'm not mistaken."

"Good God, forgive me!" Melito exclaimed, hitting his forehead to express remorse. "I don't know how to apologize. I usually never carry it with me, which is why I forgot. But today, since I have to go out into the countryside on horseback. . . ."

Though he seemed sincere, he was still holding the pistol at his waist. "But tell me," he went on still addressing Schroder. "What did you make of that poor devil?"

"What should I have made of him? A poor devil, a wretch."

"And what about that bell, that thing he kept ringing, did you wonder what it was?"

"Well," responded Schroder, weighing his words now that he sensed something insidious. "He could've been a gypsy, I suppose; I've often seen them ring a bell like that to attract attention."

"A gypsy!" Melito shouted, beginning to laugh as if the idea were the funniest thing in the world. "So you took him for a gypsy!"

Irritated, Schroder turned towards the doctor.

"What is this?" he asked firmly. "What is this interrogation all about? Listen, my dear Lugosi, I don't like this one bit! If you want something from me, you'll have to explain what's going on."

"Don't get excited, I beg you. . . ." answered the doctor, taken aback.

"If you're trying to say that this vagabond had some sort of accident and it's my fault, speak up," the merchant went on, his voice becoming more and more strident, "speak up, gentlemen. Are you trying to say that I killed him?"

"Killed him? Of course not!" said Melito, fully in control of the situation. "What are you thinking? I'm quite sorry if we've upset you. The doctor here said to me: 'Don Valerio, Cavalier Schroder is here, why don't you come up too?' 'Ah, I know him,' I said. 'Fine,' he said, 'come up with me, he'll be glad to see you.' I'm sorry if I've upset you. . . ."

The merchant realized he had gotten carried away.

"No, forgive me for being so impatient. It's just that you seemed to be interrogating me. If something's wrong, tell me straight out."

"All right," said the doctor with great caution. "All right: in fact, there is something."

"Have I been accused of something?" asked Schroder, becoming more and more sure of himself as he tried to put the leeches, which had come off during his outburst, back on his wrists. "Am I suspected of something?"

"Don Valerio," said the doctor. "Perhaps it would be better if you told him."

"Fine," Melito began. "Just let me ask if you can imagine who he was?"

"I don't know, a gypsy I thought, a vagabond."

"No, he wasn't a gypsy. Or if he once was, he wasn't one anymore. That man, to put it plainly, was something that begins with *L*."

"Something that begins with *L*," Schroder echoed mechanically, searching his memory. A shadow of apprehension covered his face.

"That's right. It begins with *L*," Melito repeated with a malicious smile.

"You mean a lout?" said the merchant, his face lightening with the confidence that he'd guessed correctly.

Don Valerio burst out laughing, "Ah, a lout! That's a good one! You were right, doctor: Schroder here is quite a comical character!" At that moment, rain started to fall audibly outside the window.

"Goodbye," said the merchant resolutely, removing the two leeches and placing them back in the bottle. "It's raining now. I have to go or I'll be late."

"Something that begins with *L*," insisted Melito, as he too stood up and arranged something under his ample cloak.

"I told you, I don't know. I don't like guessing games. Make up your minds if you have something to tell me. . . . Something that begins with *L*?. . . Ah, maybe a lansquenet?. . ." he added jokingly.

Melito and the doctor got up and leaned, side by side, against the door. Neither was smiling now.

"Not a lout and not a lansquenet. What he was was a leper," Melito said slowly.

The merchant looked at the two men, going pale as a dead man.

"And so? So what if he was a leper?"

"Unfortunately, that's just what he was," said the doctor, while he fearfully tried to position himself behind Don Valerio. "And now you are too!"

"That's enough!" shouted the merchant, trembling with rage. "Get out of here! I don't like these jokes. Out of here, both of you!"

Then Melito slipped the pistol out from under his cloak.

"I'm the mayor, my dear sir, you'd better calm down."

"I'll show you who I am!" shouted Schroder. "What do you plan to do to me now?"

Melito scrutinized Schroder, preparing to stave off a possible attack. "Your bell is in that package. Leave immediately and keep ringing it until you're out of the village, and then keep going until you're out of the county."

"I'll show you the bell!" Schroder came back, attempting to shout though his voice was dying in his throat and his heart turning cold at the horror of the revelation. Now he finally understood: when the doctor visited the day before, he was suspicious and went to warn the mayor, who three months ago, by pure chance, had seen him grab a leper by the arm – and now Schroder was condemned, too. They'd only used the leeches to gain time. He said again, "I'll go without your orders, scoundrels, I'll show you, I'll show you. . . "

"Put on the jacket," Melito ordered, his face illuminated by diabolical pleasure. "Take the jacket and move as fast as you can."

"Let me get my things," Schroder said, so much more feebly than before. "As soon as I've packed my things I'll go, I promise you."

"Your things have to be burned," sneered the mayor. "Take the bell, that's all."

"Let me take my things, at least!" exclaimed Schroder, who had been self-satisfied and intrepid until then; now he begged the mayor like a child. "My clothes, my money, at least let me keep those!"

"The jacket, the cloak, and that's it! The rest must be burned. We have already seen to the horse and carriage."

"What? What do you mean?" blurted the merchant.

"Horse and carriage have both been burned, as the law requires," answered the mayor, enjoying Schroder's desperation. "You don't think that a leper goes around in a horse and carriage, do you?"

And he let out a trivial, little laugh. Then he yelled violently, "Get out, out of here! Don't think that I'm going to stand here for hours discussing this with you. Get out immediately you dog!"

Large and sturdy as he was, Schroder was trembling all over; he left the room at gunpoint, with a slack jaw and a stupefied look.

"The bell!" Melito shouted again, causing him to jump. Melito hurled the package on the ground before him so that it gave out a metallic echo. "Take it out and tie it around your neck."

Schroder leaned down and took up the package with the effort of a decrepit old man, untied the twine, and pulled from the wrapping a copper bell with a turned wooden neck, all shiny and new. "Around your neck!" Melito shouted at him. "And if you don't put a move on, I'll shoot you, by God."

Schroder's hands were overtaken by such tremors that he could barely do as the mayor ordered. Still, the merchant managed to wrap the strap with the bell attached around his neck; hanging down to his stomach, it rang with every move he made.

"Take it in your hands and ring it, for God's sake! You'll be good, won't you, little old merchant. What a handsome leper you'll make," taunted Don Valerio while the doctor withdrew to a corner, stunned by the repulsive scene.

Schroder started moving down the steps like a sick man. His head was rolling back and forth like the village idiots that wander county roads. After two steps, he looked back to find the doctor and stared at him long and hard.

"It's not my fault," blurted Doctor Lugosi. "It was just a stroke of bad luck, very bad luck."

"Move on, move on," the mayor insisted, prodding Schroder like a beast. "Ring the bell, I tell you, people must be warned that you're coming."

Schroder began down the stairs again. Soon after, he appeared at the door of the inn, then moved slowly across the piazza. Dozens and dozens of people lined up to watch him pass and slowly drew back as he approached. The piazza was large, and long to cross. Mechanically now, he rang the bell—ding, ding, ding—the sound it made clear and festive.

Adam, One Afternoon

ITALO CALVINO (1923–1986) Calvino's unflagging narrative inventiveness has earned him the international reputation as Italy's most popular writer of the last thirty years. Though he is mainly known for his original science fictions and metafictions, Calvino's first novel, *The Path to the Nest of Spiders,* came out of the neorealist tradition. Even so, Cesare Pavese wrote in his review of the book that Calvino brought the Partisan struggle to light "on the wings of an inventiveness thrust freely towards the baroque structures of the imagination." "Adam, One Afternoon," a whimsical version of the Genesis tale, is an early story, but already Calvino's melding of the real and the fanciful is evident. Also a leading critic and editor, Calvino promoted the work of young writers in literary magazines and for the publishing house Einaudi. "Adam, One Afternoon" is from *I racconti,* 1967.

The new gardener was a boy with long hair tied back with a cloth bow. Now as he came up the path with a full watering can, he held his other arm out to balance the load. Slowly, very slowly, he watered the nasturtiums as if he were pouring out coffee and milk: at the foot of the small plants, a dark stain spread through the soil; when the stain was large and soft, he picked up the can and moved on to another plant. Gardening must've been a nice job because you could do everything so calmly. Maria-Nunziata stood watching him from the kitchen window. He was a young man, but he still wore short pants. And he looked like a girl with that long hair of his. She stopped rinsing the dishes and rapped on the window pane.

"Boy," she called.

The gardener-boy raised his head, saw Maria-Nunziata and

smiled. Maria-Nunziata began laughing back, in response, and because she had never seen a boy with such long hair tied back with a bow like that. Then the gardener-boy waved at her to "come here." Maria-Nunziata kept on laughing at his funny gestures and began gesturing too that she had dishes to wash. But the gardener-boy kept on waving her out with one hand while pointing to the pots of dahlias with the other. Why was he pointing to the pots of dahlias? Maria-Nunziata opened the window and stuck her head out.

"What?" she said, and she began laughing.

"Hey, want to see something pretty?"

"What is it?"

"Something pretty. Come and see. Hurry up."

"Tell me what."

"I'll give it to you. I'll give you something pretty."

"I have dishes to wash. If the signora comes, she won't find me here."

"Do you want it or not? Come on, come here."

"Wait there," said Maria-Nunziata, and she shut the window.

When she came out of the back door, the gardener-boy was still in the same spot, watering the nasturtiums.

"Ciao," said Maria-Nunziata.

Maria-Nunziata seemed taller because she was wearing her pretty cork-sole shoes, though it was a shame to use them for work, as she liked to. But her face was that of a child, small, surrounded by black curls, and her legs were still thin and childlike too, while her body, under the puffs of her apron, was already full and mature. And she was always laughing: at whatever she or anyone else said, she would laugh.

"Ciao," said the gardener-boy. The skin on his face, his neck and his chest was dark: maybe because he was always half-naked, like now.

"What's your name?" said Maria-Nunziata.

"Libereso," said the gardener-boy.

Maria-Nunziata laughed and repeated, "Libereso... Libereso, what kind of name is Libereso... ?"

"It's a name in Esperanto," he said. "It means liberty, in Esperanto."

"Esperanto," said Maria-Nunziata. "Are you Esperanto?"

Esperanto is a language," explained Libereso. "My father speaks Esperanto."

"I'm Calabrese," said Maria-Nunziata.

"What's your name?"

"Maria-Nunziata," and she laughed.

"Why do you laugh so much?"

"But why is your name Esperanto?"

"Not Esperanto: Libereso."

"Why?"

"Why is your name Maria-Nunziata?"

"It's the Madonna's name. I'm named after the Madonna and my brother's named after Saint Joseph."

"Sainjosef?"

Maria-Nunziata burst out laughing. "Saint Joseph! Joseph, not Sainjosef! Libereso!"

"My brother's name is Germinal," said Libereso, "and my sister's name is Omnia."

"That thing," said Maria-Nunziata, "show it to me."

"Come here," said Libereso. He put down the watering can and took her hand.

Maria-Nunziata dug her heels in. "First tell me what it is."

"You'll see," he said, "but you have to promise me that you'll take care of it."

"Are you giving it to me?"

"Yes, I'll give it to you." He led her to a corner near the garden wall. The potted dahlias were as tall as the two of them.

"It's there."

"What is?"

"Wait."

Maria-Nunziata peered around his shoulders. Libereso bent down to move a pot, lifted another closer to the garden wall, and pointed to the ground.

"There," he said.

"What?" said Maria-Nunziata. "I don't see anything." The corner was shaded, with damp leaves and mould.

"Look, it's moving," the boy said. Just then she saw a leafy stone moving, a damp thing with eyes and feet: a toad.

"Mammamia!"

Maria-Nunziata took off, leaping between the dahlias in her pretty cork-soled shoes. Libereso crouched near the toad, laughing, all white teeth in a dark face.

"You're afraid? It's a toad. What are you afraid of?"

"It's a toad," moaned Maria-Nunziata.

"Right, it's a toad. Come here," said Libereso.

She pointed a finger at it: "Kill it."

The boy put out his hands, as if to protect it: "I don't want to. It's good."

"It's a good toad?"

"They're all good. They eat the worms."

"Oh," said Maria-Nunziata, but she didn't budge. She chewed the edge of her apron, trying to glimpse it out of the corner of her eye.

"Look how pretty it is," and he reached down with his hand to touch it.

Maria-Nunziata came closer: she wasn't laughing anymore but staring, open-mouthed. "No, don't touch it!"

With one finger, Libereso caressed the toad's green-grey back, which was covered with slimy warts.

"Are you crazy? Don't you know it will burn you if you touch it? Your hand will swell up."

The boy showed her his large brown hands, the palms covered with a layer of yellow callous.

"It doesn't do anything to me," he said. "It's so pretty."

He had picked up the toad by its nape like a kitten and placed it on the palm of his hand. Chewing the edge of her apron, Maria-Nunziata drew closer and crouched beside him.

"Mammamia, what a sight," she said.

Both of them were crouching behind the dahlias, and Maria-Nunziata's pink knees grazed Libereso's brown, peeling knees. Libereso ran his hand, first the palm then the back, along the toad's back, and caught it each time it tried to slip out.

"Pet it, Maria-Nunziata," he said.

The girl hid her hands in her apron.

"No," she said.

"What?" he said, "You don't want it?"

Maria-Nunziata lowered her eyes, then looked at the toad and quickly looked down again.

"No," she said.

"But it's yours. I'm giving it to you," Libereso said.

Maria-Nunziata's eyes clouded up: she felt sad refusing a present because she never got any, but the toad really did disgust her.

"I'll let you take it inside if you want. It will keep you company."

"No," she said. Libereso put the toad back on the ground where it made off quickly to squat amidst the leaves.

"Ciao, Libereso."

"Wait."

"I have to finish washing the dishes. The signora doesn't want me in the garden."

"Wait. I want to give you something. Something really pretty. Come here."

She began to follow him along the little pebble paths. This Libereso was a strange boy, with his long hair and his habit of picking up toads with his bare hands.

"How old are you, Libereso?"

"Fifteen. And you?"

"Fourteen."

"Now or on your birthday?"

"My birthday's on Annunciation Day."

"Has it passed yet?"

"What, you don't know when the Annunciation is?" She began to laugh again.

"No."

"Annunciation Day, when they have the procession. Don't you go to the procession?"

"No, not me."

"In my village there are some really beautiful processions. My village is not like this. There are big fields full of bergamots, nothing but bergamots. And everyone works to gather them from morning until night. There were fourteen of us kids – five died when they were little – and we all gathered bergamots, until my mother got tetanus. Then we spent a week on the train to come to Uncle Carmelo's and all eight of us slept in a shed. Say, why is your hair so long?" They had come to a stop at a bed of lilies.

"Because it is. Yours is long too."

"I'm a girl. If you have long hair you're like a girl."

"No I'm not. It's not hair that makes someone like a boy or a girl."

"What do you mean it's not hair?"

"It's not hair."

"Why not?"

"You want a nice present?"

"Yes."

Libereso began wandering around the lilies. They were all in blossom, their white trumpets turned up to the sky. Libereso looked in each one, felt inside with two fingers then hid something in his tightly closed fist. Maria-Nunziata didn't enter the flower bed, but she watched him, laughing silently. Now what was Libereso doing? When he had checked all the lilies, he came back, his hands extended, one inside the other.

"Open your hands," he said. Maria-Nunziata cupped her hands but she was afraid to hold them under his.

"What's in there?"

"Something nice. You'll see."

"Let me see first."

Libereso opened his hands so she could look in. His hands were full of beetles, beetles of every color. The prettiest ones were green, but there were also reddish and black ones, and even a turquoise one. And they were buzzing and sliding onto each other's shelled backs, rolling their little legs in the air. Maria-Nunziata hid her hands under her apron.

"Hold them," said Libereso. "Don't you like them?"

"Yes, said Maria-Nunziata, still holding her hands under her apron.

"If you shut your hand tight, they tickle."

Timidly, Maria-Nunziata put out her hand, and Libereso let that little cascade of many-colored insects walk down.

"Don't be afraid, they don't bite."

"Mammamia!" She hadn't even considered that they'd bite. She opened her hand and released it to the air; the beetles spread their wings, and their pretty colors disappeared, leaving nothing more than a swarm of beetles flying and settling on the lilies.

"It's a shame. I have a present for you, and you don't want it."

"I have to go and wash the dishes. The signora will yell if she doesn't find me."

"Don't you want a present?"

"What are you going to give me?"

"Come here."

He was still leading her around the flower bed by the hand.

"I have to go back to the kitchen soon, Libereso. And I have a chicken to clean."

"Ugh."

"Ugh?' Why?"

"We don't eat the meat of dead animals."

"Are you always in Lent?"

"What?"

"What do you eat?"

"Lots of things. Artichokes, lettuce, tomatoes. My father doesn't like us to eat the meat of dead animals. Or coffee and sugar either."

"What do you do with your sugar ration?"

"We sell it on the black market."

They had come to a cascade of fleshy plants, all starred with red flowers.

"Pretty flowers," said Maria-Nunziata. "Don't you ever pick them?"

"What for?"

"To bring them to the Madonna. Flowers are to bring to the Madonna."

"*Mesembrianthemum*."

"What?"

"This plant is called *Mesembrianthemum* in Latin. All plants have Latin names."

"The mass is in Latin too."

"I don't know."

Libereso was peering at the branches that snaked along the wall.

"There it is," he said.

"What is it?"

A lizard, green with black designs, stood motionless in the sun. "I'm going to catch it."

"No."

But slowly, very slowly, he approached it with open hands, then lunged, and it was caught. Happy now, he laughed his white laugh in a dark face. "Look, he's getting away from me!" From his closed hands it squeezed out, first its little bewildered head, then its tail. Maria-Nunziata was laughing too, but each time she saw the lizard she jumped backwards, holding her skirt tightly between her knees.

"So you really don't want me to give you anything?" said Libereso, a little embarrassed, and very, very slowly, he set the lizard back on the wall where it shot off. Maria-Nunziata looked down.

"Come with me," Libereso said, taking her hand again.

"What I'd like is a little tube of lipstick that I could wear on Sundays to go dancing. And then a black veil to cover my head afterwards when I go for benediction."

"On Sunday," said Libereso, "I go to the woods with my brother and we fill two sacks with pine cones. Then, at night, my father reads aloud from the books of Eliseo Reclus. My father has long hair down to his shoulders and a beard all the way to his chest. And he wears short pants in summer and winter. And then I make drawings for the Italian Anarchist Federation windows. The men wearing top hats are bankers, the ones with the kepis are generals, and the ones with round hats are priests. Then I fill them in with watercolors."

They came to a pool full of the round, floating leaves of water-lily.

"Quiet," Libereso said.

A frog could be seen coming up through the water, thrusting and releasing its green arms. On the surface, it leapt onto a water-lily leaf and settled in the middle.

"There," said Libereso and he reached down to catch it, but Maria-Nunziata went, "Ugh," and the frog leapt back into the water. At that Libereso put his nose to the surface to look for it again.

"Down there."

He stuck his hand in and pulled it out in his fist.

"Two at once," he said. "Look. There are two, one on top of the other."

"Why?" said Maria-Nunziata.

"A male and female stuck together," said Libereso. "See what they're doing?"

And he tried to put the frogs in Maria-Nunziata's hand. Maria-Nunziata didn't know if she was afraid because they were frogs or because the male and female were stuck together.

"Leave them alone," she said, "you shouldn't touch them."

"Male and female," Libereso repeated. "They're making tadpoles."

A cloud passed over the sun. Suddenly Maria-Nunziata felt anxious.

"It's late. The signora must be looking for me."

But she didn't leave. They went on wandering through the garden that the sun had left. This time it was a snake. The little snake, a slowworm, was behind a bamboo hedge. Libereso wound it around his arm and pet its head.

"I used to train snakes, I had at least ten of them, even a real, real long yellow one, a water snake. But then it shed its skin and escaped. Look at this one, opening its mouth, look at its tongue cut in two. Pet it, it won't bite."

But Maria-Nunziata was also afraid of snakes. So they went to a little rock pool. First he showed her the spouts and then he turned on all the spigots, and this pleased her to no end. And he showed her the goldfish. It was a solitary old fish whose scales had begun to turn white. Finally, Maria-Nunziata liked the goldfish. Libereso began moving his hands around in the water to catch it, which was hard to do, but afterwards Maria-Nunziata could keep it in a tank in the kitchen. Once he'd caught it, he left it in the water so it wouldn't suffocate.

"Put your hands in, pet him," said Libereso, "You can feel him breathing; his fins feel like paper and his scales prick, but only a little."

But Maria-Nunziata didn't want to pet the fish, either.

In the petunia bed the soil was soft, and Libereso scratched around with his fingers and pulled out some very long and very soft earthworms.

Maria-Nunziata fled, letting out little yelps.

Then Libereso said, "Rest your hand here," pointing to the trunk of an old peach tree. Maria-Nunziata didn't understand why but she put her hand there, then screamed and ran to plunge it in the tub of water. When she'd taken her hand away, it was covered with ants. The whole peach tree was a coming-and-going of little "Argentine" ants.

"Look," said Libereso, resting his hand on the trunk. The ants could be seen going up and down his hand but he didn't pull it away.

"Why?" said Maria-Nunziata. "Why are you letting the ants crawl on you?"

His hand was already black, already the ants were crossing his wrist.

"Take your hand away," Maria-Nunziata moaned. "You're letting the ants crawl all over you."

Now they climbed up his bare arm, up to his elbow. By now his whole arm was covered by a veil of tiny, moving black points; finally the ants reached his armpit, but still he didn't budge.

"Get them off, Libereso, put your arm in the water."

Libereso laughed, and one or two ants even advanced from his neck onto his face.

"Libereso! Whatever you want! I'll take all the presents you give me."

She threw her arms around his neck and began to brush the ants off.

Then Libereso took his hand from the tree, laughing his white laugh in a dark face, and casually dusted off his arm. But clearly he was moved.

"Good, I've decided to give you a really big present. The biggest thing I can."

"What is it?"

"A hedgehog."

"Mammamia. . . The signora, the signora's calling me!"

Maria-Nunziata had finished washing the dishes when she heard a pebble hit the window pane. Libereso stood below with a big basket.

"Maria-Nunziata, let me in. I have a surprise for you."

"You can't come in. What's inside there?"

But just then the signora rang for her, and Maria-Nunziata disappeared.

When she returned to the kitchen, Libereso was gone. He wasn't inside, or below the window. Then she saw the surprise.

On every dish she'd set out to dry there were frogs hopping, a snake was twining itself in the casserole, the soup tureen was full of lizards, and slimy snails left iridescent trails on the crystal. The solitary old goldfish was swimming in the water-filled basin.

Maria-Nunziata took a step backwards, but she caught sight of a toad, a huge toad, beneath her feet. Not only that, but it must've been a female: following behind, her brood, five baby toads in a row, advanced in little leaps across the black and white tiles.

At the Station

CARLO CASSOLA (1917–1987) A writer who had great success in and out of Italy, Cassola writes primarily about his native region – the Tuscan Maremma – and the ordinary lives that unfold there. For the most part, Cassola stands outside the prevailing movements of his time, especially in his near total omission of historic and ideological reference which was at the heart of neorealism. What he aims to capture, instead, is the flow of existence, in its purest and most banal form – what he calls *il sublimare* (sublimation). Thus the positing of political and social reality as the root of evil and despair is only a distraction from the truth of the human condition, which is ahistoric and atemporal. Cassola's vision led him to use an increasingly spare and simple language and syntax that has often been called grey and neutral. "At the Station," a story which records a simple but emotionally loaded conversation between a mother and daughter, leaving it unresolved, is a good example of Cassola's narrative technique.

"At the Station" is from *La Visita*, 1942.

T he train was already a half hour late, and the railway worker said it would be even longer.

"That's just great," said Adriana's mother. "Let's hope your father's not waiting."

"If he goes to the station, they'll tell him it's delayed, mama."

"Yes, but you know how your father is."

They walked up and down the platform, stopping at the end of the station. Before them, the network of tracks gradually narrowed in the distance. A grey, cold air that grew heavier and heavier hung over the countryside.

"I wonder why it's late," said Adriana.

Her mother looked at her without saying anything.

"It's usually on time," she added.

Finding nothing more to say, she looked down. Her mother's silent gaze embarrassed her.

"You aren't pregnant, are you, Adriana?"

Her daughter shook her head emphatically.

"It's just as well," said her mother. "At least you can have some fun. You have plenty of time. You're still so young."

Two men were talking a way off: one was standing, the other sitting on a pile of railway ties. Adriana stood watching them, their gestures hazy in the dusk. Her mother looked over, too. The man standing said goodbye to the other and came towards them, swinging a lantern. As he passed, he gave Adriana an insistent look. Adriana turned to her mother.

"Promise me you'll come back soon," she said to her.

"My dear, it won't be easy with that man. I can't leave him alone."

"That's in your head, mama."

"Maybe," answered her mother. And after a moment, "Still, young couples should be left to themselves. I'm not one of those women who's always at her daughter's side, even for the silliest little thing."

"But in our case . . . ," said the daughter, "Mario likes you to come once in a while."

"And as you can see, I manage to escape now and then. But those women who set themselves up in their daughters' houses, or their sons', like your poor grandmother – God rest her soul. Every time she left, I breathed a sigh of relief."

"Mama!" her daughter scolded.

"I tell you, Adriana, it was torture. And that's when I promised myself: when your daughter gets married, you'll stay in your house, and she in hers, each with her own husband. I learned the hard way, and don't you forget it," she added after a moment's pause.

Suddenly the lights went on in the station. The women glanced out towards the fields and saw it was dark.

"The days are starting to get shorter," said the mother.

They walked back. Laughter floated out of the station master's office, and the station master appeared in the doorway smiling, a cigar in his mouth and a beret cocked to one side. Adriana greeted him.

He answered without looking at her.

"Will it be much longer?"

The station master turned back to the room to ask a question.

"At least ten more minutes," he said.

A small crowd, mostly workers, had gathered in the middle of the station. Now they broke into so many little groups. They talked excitedly, they laughed: no one seemed concerned about the delay.

"Adriana," the mother said abruptly, "tell me truthfully, you aren't angry with Mario, are you?"

"Of course not, mama," Adriana answered, "what are you thinking?"

"Nothing, I just thought. . . "

She glanced at her watch and then at the station clock.

"It's just that Mario is so busy," Adriana added. "He never gets home until after seven-thirty or eight at night; and he always goes out again after dinner."

"Men are all the same," the mother said. "They're a big bunch of egotists. I remember when I was nursing. . ."

The bell began to ring. There was an audible sigh of relief.

"Finally," said Adriana.

". . . But I hoped that women were a little more fortunate these days," her mother said. "I lived like a slave."

Adriana burst out laughing.

"I'm not exaggerating," her mother continued. "Laugh if you want. But think about it, Adriana: what enjoyment do we women get out of life? Sometimes I think it would have been better if I'd never been born."

They stood in silence listening to the conversations around them. Then suddenly they were forced to move aside to avoid being knocked down.

"Move back, folks, move back."

The red eyes of the train loomed out of the dark countryside. For a moment it appeared to be still, then to be racing madly, crazily, and finally it rolled in, stopping with a great lurch as people slowly gathered up their things.

Mother and daughter embraced. The mother got on on the first class compartments and leaning out, called Adriana, who stood below the window.

"There's still time," Adriana said. "They always wait a few minutes."

"Anyway, go if you have to."

"I have dinner ready," answered Adriana.

"It's seven-thirty," her mother said. "I can imagine just how that man will carry on. I can already hear him. He's always done whatever he pleases, while I. . ."

Now that the train was about to pull out, their conversation broke off.

"Send my best to everyone," Adriana said.

"Don't worry," her mother answered.

The station was empty now. Only three or four people waited to see their relatives off.

"There you go," said Adriana.

She'd seen the conductor raise the signal.

"Say goodbye to Mario for me. Tell him that I'm sorry I couldn't do it myself."

"Give dad a big kiss," Adriana shouted.

And she stood waving her handkerchief as long as she could see, or thought she saw something in the distance.

The Discovery of America

UMBERTO ECO (1932–) Eco was one of the major theoreticians of the avant-garde *Il Gruppo '63*. In his *Opera aperta* and other works he formulated many of the fundamental ideas about experimentation and the writer's role in contemporary society that have left a mark on Italian writing since the 1960s. Primarily a cultural and literary critic and the first professor to hold a chair in semiotics in the Italian university system, Eco transformed the themes and interests of his scholarly work into fiction in *The Name of the Rose*, which became an international best seller. His new novel, *Foucault's Pendulum*, was published in 1989. "The Discovery of America," a satire of Italian television, and television in general, works on an understated humor, which is an important concept in Eco's theoretical work. "The Discovery of America" is from *Diario minimo*, 1963.

TELMON[1]: Good evening. It's seven o'clock, October 11, 1492 and we're about to make a direct link-up with the admiral ship of the Columbus expedition, which by tomorrow at seven, October 12, 1492, should be the first European sea-voyager to reach the new world, a new planet, if I may use that metaphor; the unknown land which so many astronomers, geographers, cartographers and travelers have dreamed of, that some claim is India, approached from the West rather than the East, and that others claim is actually a huge, unexplored, new continent. From this moment onward, radio and television will stay in continuous contact for twenty-five consecutive hours. We will be linked to the admiral ship, the Santa

---

1. Sergio Telmon, Tito Stagno, Ruggiero Orlando, Mike Bongiorno, Pippo Baudo and Elio Sparano were leading telecasters and television personalities in the 1960s.

Maria, to the Canary Islands station, as well as to our Sforzesco broadcasting centers in Milan, the University of Salamanca and the University of Wittenberg.

Beside me is Professor Leonardo da Vinci, an eminent scientist and futurologist who will be providing us with the necessary explanations as we go along so that we can understand the technical particulars of this extraordinary undertaking. Go ahead, Stagno.

STAGNO: As you know, we cannot get a video link-up until they actually disembark. The television cameras were set up on the figureheads of the carvel's prows, but the antennae, which are attached to the maintop, can only be activated once the lookout has made his sighting and the veils are drawn up. At what point are the three carvels in this epic voyage now? We are holding our breaths as we witness this, the greatest undertaking in human history, the beginning of a new age, which some have called the modern age. Man is stepping out of the middle ages and taking yet another step in his spiritual evolution. Evidently the technicians of Cape Canary are overcome by the same emotion. . . . But in that regard, let's hear from Ruggiero Orlando, who came from Montecitorio especially for this historic telecast. Come in, Orlando. Do you hear me?

ORLANDO: Yes, I hear you. Can you hear me?

STAGNO: Ruggiero?

ORLANDO: Yes, can you hear me?

STAGNO: Do you hear me, Ruggiero?

ORLANDO: I was saying, yes, I do hear you. These are tense moments here at Cape Canary. The position of Columbus' three galleons. . .

STAGNO: Excuse me Orlando, I don't think they're galleons.

ORLANDO: One moment. . . here they're saying. . . there's an infernal racket at central control, three hundred barefoot Carmelites are chanting three hundred solemn prayers all at once to bless the voyage. . . yes, yes, they're not galleons, you're right, but three-sailed vessels called xebecs! The xebec is a common type of vessel.

STAGNO: Excuse me, Ruggiero but I hear them saying "carvels" on the audio here.

ORLANDO: What? I can't hear you. . . there's tremendous chaos here. Ah, there, yes, as I was saying, in fact they're carvels, the Niña, the Pen..., no, the Pinta and the Santa Radegonda.

STAGNO: Excuse me, Ruggiero, the ANSA wire I have here says Santa María...

ORLANDO: Actually, there's somebody here too saying Santa María, there are two theories on that. ... In any case, the carvel is a typical vessel, which I've had them make a little model of for me... I'm wearing the uniform that the Spanish Navy's ship boys wear... carvels...

TELMON: Excuse me, Ruggiero, but we have Professor Vinci here who can tell us something about the carvels' propulsion system. ...

LEONARDO: Sa nwonk drib egral a si ereht...

TELMON: One moment, uh, via Teulada control room... Professor Vinci has a strange habit of reading from right to left, you'll have to invert the camera; don't you remember, that's why we arranged in advance for a nine-second pause between shooting and the actual broadcasting. Hello? Cameraman, do you hear me? Good. Go ahead.

LEONARDO: There is a large bird known as...

TELMON: Excuse me, Professor Vinci... There are some twenty million television spectators watching. ... Perhaps it would be a good idea if you spoke more plainly.

LEONARDO: Yes, I'm sorry. All right, the carvel exploits a propulsion system known as "wind and veil" and stays afloat according to Archimedes' principle that a body immersed in liquid is buoyed up by a force equal to the weight of the liquid displaced. The sail, a basic element of propulsion, is connected along three yards, the main, the mizzen, and foreyard. The bowsprit, which the jib and flying jib energize, has a special function, while the fore topgallant sail and the gaffsail serve for steering.

TELMON: But does the sea-voyager depart and arrive whole or are some stages disengaged on the way?

LEONARDO: I'll say this: this sea-voyager undergoes a process of impoverishment which we usually call "kill and draw." That is, when a sailor behaves improperly towards the admiral, he is hit over the head and thrown into the sea. That's precisely when the "mutiny show-down" occurs. In the case of the Santa María, there have been three examples of "kill and draw," which are precisely the three sailors who allowed Admiral Columbus to regain control of the sea-voyager with what we would have to call manual or manhandler's command. . . . In these cases, the admiral must remain vigilant and intervene at exactly the right moment.

TELMON: Otherwise, he loses control of the boat, I understand. And tell me, what is the ship boy's technical function?

LEONARDO: Yes, it's an essential one. It's called a "feeding back" function. For the layman, we could call it a "safety valve." This is a technical problem which I have been working on for some time. . . . If you'd like I'll show you some of my anatomical drawings.

TELMON: Thank you, professor. But I think it's time for us to contact the studio in Salamanca. Go ahead Bongiorno!

BONGIORNO: Cheers! We're here at Salamanca's Studio 1 to interview some big brains who are considered "the tops" in their fields today. Let's first address a question to the Magnificent Rector of the University of Salamanca. Please, go on about that point marked in chalk. Would you tell us, Mr. Rector of Salamanca, what do you think this America that everybody is talking about so much really is?

RECTOR: Hot air, nothing more than hot air!

BONGIORNO: Forgive me, Mr. Rector of Salamanca, but I see that the experts wrote the word. . . "con. . . continent" here.

RECTOR: No, no, look I'm sorry about these experts. I have chosen the *Almagest* by Ptolemy as my basic text. If you refer to that, you'll see that the possibility of finding anything is minimal. Admiral Columbus presumes that he can *"buscar el levante por el ponente,"* but the undertaking lacks any foundation whatsoever. In fact, as most people well know, the earth ends beyond the Pillars of Hercules, and if the three carvels survive beyond that point, it is merely a television illusion created by demonic intervention. The Columbus case clearly demonstrates what happens when the knowledgeable authorities are too weak to oppose a student challenge. In fact, I'm preparing a book on this very topic for the publishing house Rusconi. On the other hand, even if the voyage were possible, the sea-voyager would eventually fail from the lack of angelical fuel. You see, as the minutes of numerous bishops councils have established, the problem lies in establishing how many angels can remain on the point of a needle, but there isn't the slightest suggestion in those minutes that angels can remain on the tip of a foremast. That would be comparable to Saint Elmo's fire, and being a diabolical process, not adequate to push a carvel towards a promised or unknown land, or whatever you want to call it.

BONGIORNO: These things are certainly quite complicated, I really don't know how to respond. Let's see what our experts decide, and good luck with "Risk-it-all."[2] But now let's hear from a very important expert who is "tops in his field," the Dean of the Royal Portuguese Cartographer's Society. Tell us, Dean of the Royal Portuguese Cartographer's Society, do you believe that Columbus is really navigating towards the Indies?

DEAN: This is not an easy question. Columbus' error is in trying to answer it empirically rather than proceeding to the definition of the essential problem. Look, *non sunt multiplicana entia sine necessitate,* and this would prompt us to postulate the existence of one, and only one, India. In that case, Columbus should land in the Levant on the furthest tip of Asiatic land, precisely at the mouth of the Ussuri River. If that were the case, the expedition wouldn't have the slightest interest, given the total political and geographical irrelevance of that piece of land. Or else, he could land on the eastern tip of Gipango Island, in which case the Mediterranean economy could suffer a terrible negative backlash: in fact, since the indigenous population engages in the malicious business of making transistorized imitations of the mechanical inventions of others, the markets of our sea-faring republics would soon be flooded by thousands of perfect imitations of our carvels at cheaper prices. And that would certainly bring about the economic collapse of the Republic of Venice, unless the Doge's cabinet was to provide for the construction of new shipyards at Porto Marghera, which would, however, have disastrous consequences for the equilibrium of the lagoons. . . .

BONGIORNO: I understand. But the Dean of Granada's faculty of law is here to tell us something about the juridical consequences of his discovery. Many people are wondering whom this new earth will

---

2. "Risk-it-all" (*"Rischiatutto"*) is the name of a popular quiz game show of the period.

belong to. To whom does the part of the ocean that Columbus is crossing belong?

DEAN: The question of international law is a rather serious one. Above all, there is the problem of division between Spain and Portugal, and I don't think I'm jumping the gun by saying that we will have to call a meeting at Tordesillas, or wherever, to trace an ideal line of demarcation between the spheres of influence...

ELIO SPARANO: Excuse me, Bongiorno, we're at the Sforzesco studio in Milan, and the group of eminent Milanese jurists here don't agree. They maintain that the whole problem is absurd. At any rate, since we must also consider England, another powerful sea republic, one would have to assume that eventually the new world will be divided between the Anglo-Saxon, Spanish and Portuguese spheres of influence. . . . This is pure science fiction! Professor Trimarchi wanted to say something in this regard. Professor! Where is he? One moment. Hello? Ah, they're saying that. . . it seems that some silly incident at the university has held the professor up. . . . Fine, I'm transferring the line to the studio in Wittenberg. Go ahead Pippo Baudo.

BAUDO: This is the Wittenberg studio. We would like to put a question to one of the brightest hopes of our Holy Catholic Church, a young but well-trained Augustinian theologian from Wittenberg. Tell us, Doctor Luther, do you think that this sail constitutes a real and lasting revolution in the history of man?

LUTHER: You know, there are not only technological revolutions. There are also spiritual changes which can have much greater, and more dramatic, more exciting, outcomes...

BAUDO: Brilliant indeed. . . but you don't mean that in the future we may see spiritual reforms that could be even more sensational than this great scientific event. . . .

LUTHER: Who knows?

BAUDO: Ah, ah, yes. Very sibylline. But you know, all kidding aside, I'm really inclined to believe it. My motto is, "Be a firm believer and a terrible sinner!" Ha, ha!

LUTHER: That's a good one! Let me write it down.

STAGNO: One moment, excuse me, gentlemen. Voices are coming over the audio. . . . It seems that land has been sighted. . . .

There, you can hear it clearly: they're screaming, "Land, land!" Orlando, do you hear it too?

ORLANDO: To tell the truth, I don't hear anything here. One moment, I'm going to get information from the Azores station. . . .

STAGNO: Yes, land has indeed been spotted. . . the ship is mooring. . . they've disembarked!!! Today, on this twelfth of October 1492, man has set foot on the New World for the first time. What are they saying down there, Orlando?

ORLANDO: Let's see. . . . It seems from the last report that the landing has been postponed for a month and that the land they sighted was actually the Lipari Islands. . . .

STAGNO: Ah no, Orlando. I heard differently!

TELMON: Hello? Yes? There. Both Stagno and Orlando are right. The ship has indeed dropped anchor as Stagno said, not on mainland but on San Salvador, a little island in the so-called Caribbean archipelago, which some geographer decided to name the Sea of Tranquility. But the television cameras posted atop the admiral ship's figurehead are on. There's Christopher Columbus setting foot on the beach to plant His Catholic Majesty's flag. It's a grand spectacle. A crowd of feathered characters is advancing toward the sea-voyagers from between the palm trees. Now, we're about to hear the first words spoken by man in the New World. The sailor leading the group, our own Baciccin Parodi, is about to say them.

PARODI: *Belin*[3], admiral, but they're naked!

STAGNO: What was that, Orlando?

ORLANDO: It didn't come across clearly, but these are not the words we'd agreed on. Somebody here is suggesting that there must be some interference phenomenon. Apparently, it's a common occurrence in the New World. But wait!. . . Admiral Columbus is about to speak!

COLUMBUS: It's a small step for a sailor, but a great one for His Catholic Majesty. . . *Belin*, but what's that on their necks? *Belandi Figieu*[4]! It's gold! Gold!

ORLANDO: The spectacle being transmitted to us via the televi-

---

3. An obscenity in Genovese dialect expressing marvel.
4. A milder variation of the above obscenity.

sion camera is truly grand! The sailors are hurling themselves towards the natives, in great leaps, leaps and bounds, man's first leaps
in this New World. . . . They're taking the mineral specimens right
off the natives' necks and dropping them in huge plastic bags. . . .
Now the natives are leaping too, trying to escape; and given the lack
of gravity, they might hurtle into space too if the sailors weren't
securing them with heavy chains. . . . But now the natives are lined
up in a civilized and orderly fashion, and the sailors are making their
way back to the ships, their heavy sacks full of the local mineral. The
sacks are terribly heavy; it seems they're struggling as hard to trans-
port them as they did when they filled them.

STAGNO: The white man's burden! This is an unforgettable spectacle! Vice President De Feo has already sent a telegram of congratulations. Today marks a whole new era of civilization!

BEPPE FENOGLIO

The Boss Doesn't Pay

BEPPE FENOGLIO (1922–1963) In the preface to his own first novel about
the resistance, Calvino wrote: "And it was the most solitary of all who succeeded
in creating the novel we had all dreamed of. . . . Beppe Fenoglio succeeded in
writing it, in *Il partigiano Johnny*, but not in finishing it." Fenoglio, who died at
41, though virtually unknown outside of Italy, is considered the best of the resistance writers. Fenoglio's models were English and American (the Elizabethans,
Coleridge and Melville), and *Il partigiano Johnny* is an ambitious linguistic experiment – a melange of Italian, English and neologism. Fenoglio is also known
for his use of dialect to portray the rough peasant life in the Langhe, as in the
stories of *La malora*. "The Boss Doesn't Pay" examines the belief underlying all
violent struggle – regardless of ideology – that "the ends justify the means," no
matter how seemingly inhuman and irrational. "The Boss Doesn't Pay"
is from *Un giorno di fuoco*, 1973.

D idn't you transfer from the Stella Rosa[1] like Jack and Matè?"
Gilera asked Oscar.

They were finishing their guard duty near the Mango Cemetery.
The day had come up and the air was already stirring with sounds,
but peaceful ones.

"No, not me," said Oscar. "I came straight into the Badogliani.
Actually, I had already made up my mind for the Stella Rosa, but my
cousin Alfredo, who enlisted a week before I left, suggested I wait for

---

1. Stella Rosa and Badogliani – these terms refer to two different partisan groups, the second of which takes the name of General Badolgio, who was made premier by King Vittorio
Emanuele III and negotiated an armistice with the Allies.

word from him. So I did, and after ten days I received the following postcard: 'The boss doesn't pay, Alfredo.' It didn't take much to figure out things weren't going as he'd expected in the Stella Rosa, and since my cousin and I have similar temperaments and needs, I went to enlist that night in the Badogliani."

"Ah, so that's how it happened," said Gilera.

"Actually," Oscar went on, "for the first two days my cousin got along fairly well, but that was because the organizing officer was away. He'd gone down to the valley to campaign. But when he came back on the third day and asked what was new, nothing was new except my cousin. This officer came from Brescia, his name was Ferdi, and he must've been about thirty-five years old. My cousin went over to him, and Ferdi said, 'So you're a partisan?'

"'So you see, sir?' said my cousin, who was fully equipped with alpine gear—it was February then—and a musket and a munitions belt.

"'Don't address me formally,' the officer said.

"'So you see,' my cousin repeated.

"'So you think you're a partisan like this?' said the officer, looking him up and down from head to foot.

"'I'm sorry, if you want me to take my jacket off. . . ,' my cousin said at this point.

"'I wouldn't think of it,' said the officer. 'I can see perfectly well that you're a partisan. What's your intention?'

"'To kill fascists,' my cousin announced quickly.

"'That's fine,' said Officer Ferdi, 'that's just fine for starters. And how will you kill them?'

"'I'll do my best,' said my cousin, 'I'll try to make the most of every opportunity. I'll track them down to kill them and I'll wait for them when they come to ambush us.'

"'Fine,' said Ferdi. 'And you have no scruples about killing them?'

"'Absolutely not a one,' said my cousin. 'Why should I? The fascists aren't even men. It's a greater sin to crush an ant than to kill a fascist.'"

"I would have said the same," said Gilera.

"Ferdi seemed to be satisfied, but he still wouldn't leave my cousin in peace. In fact, he suddenly started over again.

"'So you think you're a partisan?'

"And my cousin came back, sort of annoyed by now, 'Yes I am unless I wake up and find myself in the middle of a dream.'

"'Well,' the officer said, 'let's see what kind of partisan you are.'

"'At your command,' my cousin answered. He answered quickly but he was getting slightly anxious inside because Officer Ferdi seemed the type to send him on his first assignment on the spot. . . to go down to D and take the bunker just outside of town single-handed. Or something like that.

"Ferdi must've read his thoughts because he said, 'We'll find out in theory for now,' and my cousin breathed a sigh of relief and began to listen to him with the utmost attention.

"So the officer begins, 'Answer this, partisan. You have a sister, or if you don't, imagine one. You have a sister who also happens to be very beautiful and tempting. Your town is occupied by fascists, solidly occupied. This sister of yours attracts, or could attract an officer in the fascist garrison in your town. Now to get rid of a fascist officer is an important thing. . . '

"'A very important thing,' said my cousin.

"'So far we agree,' Ferdi says. 'So you try to set up traps, pitfalls, for this damned officer, you stalk him, for hours, for days, you go everywhere, but he never falls for it, or else he's just damn lucky and keeps getting away. At this point, partisan, would it occur to you to send your sister to make love with this fascist official, naturally in a place that you've studied carefully, on a hill or on the banks of the river, I mean in some isolated spot where you can blow him away surely and calmly? Wait before you answer. Naturally you could be waylaid and when you arrive he could have already done everything imaginable to your sister. Now give me your answer.'

"'Me, no,' my cousin answered plainly, 'I certainly wouldn't think of using my sister like that, not in a million years.'

"'Fine,' said Ferdi, poker-faced. 'You're a partisan and you wouldn't do such a thing. You're a partisan, you said so yourself, and you're completely convinced of it, but this sort of thing you won't do.'

"'No, I certainly wouldn't,' repeated my cousin.

"'Then that point is clear,' said Ferdi, still calm. 'Let's take another example. Let's imagine that a nice little group of officers takes their meals in such and such a restaurant in your city. They always eat their lunch in the courtyard that gives onto a certain street. You know all the streets, all the piazzas, all the courtyards and alleyways, all the little nooks and crannies of your city like the palm of your hand because you spent countless summers playing hide-and-seek there.'

"'Like the palm of my hand,' my cousin says.

"'Fine,' says Ferdi, and he continues. 'One fine day, I'm not saying tomorrow, or day after tomorrow, but some fine day, you say to yourself: I want to do something special. I'm sick and tired of simply doing my duty and I want to do something special.'

"'Yes,' says my cousin firmly, though in reality he doesn't know where the commander is going to end up with this restaurant, those alleyways, etc., etc. And the commander continues, 'So you finally decide to throw a grenade into the room in that restaurant just when the fascist officials all are sitting around the table. Okay? And that's what you do. You wear civilian clothes, with your good bomb under your shirt and naturally you have wrapped some padding around your chest so that the hump of the bomb doesn't stick out too much. You go down to your city. You don't enter by the doors which are all blockaded, but through some little hole that you know perfectly because it's your city. You enter and since you know the streets blindfolded, slipping through doorways, taking cover behind columns, crossing connected courtyards and so on, you manage to approach the courtyard of that restaurant. It's afternoon. Finally you come out on that street which gives onto that famous courtyard which the officials' dining room looks out on. Now imagine you peek out, just missing one of their patrols by a split second.'

"'Right,' my cousin says in total seriousness, 'I have to keep their patrols in mind.'

"'Right,' Ferdi says and continues. 'You're facing the courtyard. Empty. There's a portico where you can take cover a few feet from the dining room window. You walk until you're under the portico. Now you can hear the silverware clanking, the chatter and laughing. You reach the pillar at the end of the portico. You can see the window easily from there. You're really lucky. Once that window had a grill on it, but they recently removed it. In fact, you're quite lucky: the inside panes are open because it's the first really warm day of the year, so to throw the bomb, you don't even have to break the glass.'

"'Yes,' says my cousin, beads of sweat beginning to form on his forehead at ten degrees. And Ferdi goes on: 'You leap all the way across the wall and back up to the window on tiptoes. Craning your neck a little, you manage to get a glimpse of them. They're all sitting close together, they all have their faces in the plates, you can massacre them. It's virtually impossible for you not to massacre them. They will all croak within a fraction of a second, pieces of them will be stuck to the chandelier. But. . . there's a but. Serving the table are two little waitresses, two slender, attractive serving girls, the older of whom can't be a day over twenty. You throw the bomb anyway. . . '

"'No I don't!' shouts my cousin, 'I wouldn't throw any bomb. I couldn't throw it with those poor girls hanging around. I'd go back the way I came.'

"'Ah, of course,' says Ferdi, rubbing a hand across his forehead, 'naturally. Because you're a partisan. I understand. But let's take another example.'

"'Officer,' says my cousin, 'to tell you the truth, I've had enough. If you don't mind, I've had enough now.'

"But Ferdi hasn't.

"'Hold on,' he says, 'this is the last thing. I'll be quick. Let's keep talking about your city. You love your city. You were born there, you feel comfortable there, you hope you'll never have to leave it, you plan to die there peacefully, after a reasonable number of years. But right now your city is occupied by fascists. You can't bear the thought that your city is occupied, infested, the thought keeps you up at night. You grind your teeth whenever you think about it, you see red, you're overwhelmed with hatred for them and shame for yourself.'

"'Yes,' says my cousin, who now felt his head had swelled to twice the size of Mussolini's.

"'Let's go on,' said the officer. 'The fascist garrison in your city is very strong. Not because your city is so important in its own right but because it has access to two or three valleys.'

"'I understand perfectly,' says my cousin.

"And Ferdi answers: 'So that's how things stand. Your city is impenetrable. Even if there were five hundred more of us and we were armed to the gills, we couldn't dream of taking it. We might only be able to take it if some unforeseen circumstances wiped out the garrison units and actually threw the enemy into a state of panic. Do you understand me?'

"'I can't say I do,' confesses my cousin.

"'I'm talking about an aerial bombardment,' explains the officer. 'A half-dozen English fighter-bombers which suddenly appear overhead and drop them from a low altitude. The English, as you well know, don't launch good bombardments. That means that for every bomb that lands on a barracks, another nine will fall on residential areas. I can tell you right off that you will not be able to alert the population because if some fascist traitor found out, he would leak it to the soldiers in no time and they would surely take precautions to save themselves from the air raid. Naturally your mother and father live in the city too, and like the others they have no idea of what's coming. One of those nine bombs out of ten that are sure to fall outside of the range of the barracks could easily land right on your house. So tell me: would you call upon the English to bomb your city?'

"'You know, you're nuts,' yells my cousin, 'you're worse than that! I'd rather wait ninety years, if I had to, to free my city!'

"And the officer?" laughed Gilera.

"Now the officer just made a terrible face and unleashed a howl into my cousin's face the likes of which he'd never heard. But actually, Ferdi wasn't fed up only with him, he'd had it with everybody and everything. 'And you call yourself a partisan! All of you call yourselves partisans! You here, and you over there! Why don't you all go back to boot camp? No, why don't you go back to the nursery in heaven! You're a bunch of toddlers who want to do the work of giants!'

"My cousin managed to stand there, he was staring at his feet but he managed to stand there, and meanwhile Ferdi had turned his mad fury against someone else. 'And you call yourselves partisans!' he went on yelling. 'Don't make me die of disgust. We might as well all go home, me included. Or better still, let's all bury ourselves. We didn't come here to eat at the peasants' expense.'

"When my cousin thought he was calmer, he approached him and asked permission to leave. He swore that he wouldn't go home to report to the employment office but that he would just transfer to another formation where they liked him for who he was. But the officer put a hand on his shoulder and in a nearly normal voice invited him to stay on, saying that in the end they'd get along fine, and that my cousin would be fine in his brigade, after all. And in fact, my cousin stayed put with the Stella Rosa. But on the same day of that famous argument, he sent me that famous postcard that said, 'The boss doesn't pay.' I got it a week later because the mails were nearly non-existent by then. But I could read between the lines and that same night I ended up joining the Badogliani."

"Still," Gilera commented, "if your cousin ended up staying, that's a sign that the Stella Rosa is really okay and that the officer finally came around."

"I don't know if the officer came around," Oscar said. "But I can tell you that he left soon after that. One morning he went down to meet up with some others of the same persuasion, but he ran into a fascist patrol at the M—— station. They threw him into jail in C—— where they made all kinds of trouble for him. Just when they were about to finish him off, the Germans arrived, and they wanted him too. The fascists handed him over and hung him up by the neck."

"Holy Jesus, no," said Gilera, raising a hand to his neck.

"They did it on the P—— bridge. They put up a pole near the beginning of the bridge and hung him by the neck on a meat hook."

"Holy Jesus," whispered Gilera.

"My cousin said that somehow the brigade got word, I don't know how, that it took Ferdi fifty-six minutes to die. They hung him up facing the mountain. When they hooked him the sun was turning red and when they finally pronounced him dead the sun had just disappeared behind the mountain. My cousin told me all this the last time I saw him. So it's pretty recent stuff."

"Why? Have you seen him lately?"

"About a month ago," Oscar said. "Remember the last time I asked for leave? I had a date with him. We met at Bonivello, which is exactly half-way between our perimeter and his, so neither of us had to go too far. We went to a restaurant and had lunch at a table by the window where we could watch the road, and while we ate we swapped stories of what had happened to me in the Badogliani and to him in the Stella Rosa. Then at some point in the conversation, I asked my cousin if he was a communist or if he planned to become one, and here's what he said, word for word."

"Tell me, I'm interested."

"Word for word," said Oscar, "here's what he said: 'I'm not a communist and I'll never become one, either. But if anyone, even you, dares to laugh at my red star, I'll rip his heart out.'"

CARLO EMILIO GADDA

The Thieving Magpie

CARLO EMILIO GADDA (1893–1973) Gadda's linguistic inventions, from polylingualism to neologism to unconventional syntax and punctuation, make him one of the most difficult writers for Italians and undoubtedly the most problematical for translators. Still, the novels, *That Awful Mess on Via Merulana* and *Acquainted with Grief* have been superbly translated into English. Gadda's stylistic idiosyncrasy makes him an important point of reference for other writers who have tended towards experimentation. "The Thieving Magpie" exemplifies Gadda's amiable and sometimes puzzling linguistic "divertimenti."

"The Thieving Magpie" is from *I racconti*, 1963.

Signora Campanini was partial to intelligent boys even when their intelligence had taken a bad turn: towards writing, for instance, or even worse, publishing poems. It was her habit to fall a little in love with everybody: rich and poor, fair and dark, painters and poets, gentlemen and servants.

On the other hand, alive and vigilant in her was the instinct for profit and safeguarding what was her own: a mental rigor that prompted her to make obstinate statements, both defensive and offensive, on the most daring outposts of every disagreement – a tactical rigor.

Except that a strange capacity for making an offering – whereupon she would crack the terra-cotta money-box – struggled against the above-mentioned tendency within her; occasionally she would lose track of her money and jewels, usually after some business dispute. Sometimes even her fur coat entered into the game. And then she would misplace a ten-thousand note, or forget her pearl necklace in the "bathroom," only to find it later, lying there on the porcelain wash-basin. At the La Frasca restaurant they tried to rob her mink: and on the train, in Bologna, they actually succeeded. According to the most expensive doctors in the city, beckoned to give consolation as well as consultation, she was schizophrenic: according to others, not doctors (her brothers-in-law, the five brothers of her husband whom she wouldn't admit was dead, out of pride), she was a birdbrain.

No, she was no birdbrain. It was just that for Signora Campanini, life was accomplished through incessant, exciting strategical activities: as soon as one came to her, she would start dreaming up another. Today it was a jar of sauce purchased, with a thousand niceties, at Fagotti's for fifty lire less than Nespola sells it for: tomorrow it was Clemente, the well-known painter, who was supposed to bring her a little bottle of turpentine, gratis, so that she could remove some varnish stains from a dress: the day after tomorrow it was the Vice-President of the insurance company whom Signora Campanini had to phone five times a day on behalf of the gardener, who was expecting a reimbursement of three hundred lire for an accident incurred while shoeing the horses.

Once widowed, she had gone to spend "some time away": a lovely villa, in the middle of a hillock. The wall separating it from the adjoining property is low, gaping, missing those pieces of broken bottles along the top that her more zealous cohorts were in the habit of flaunting: in short, one could either be on this side, or with a little jump, on that. For two years the villa next door had been silent, shutdown: a ghost dwelling: every time the signora thought of it, she'd finger her coral horn charm, just in case. She'd grown accustomed to it and to fingering the coral charm for courage, when one fine morning, the shutters banged: some sleeping bats toppled down from the rotten slates like dead mice: the window panes flashed in the sun, opened: the face of a blossoming girl servant appeared momentarily in the window: and several minutes later, the equally pleasing face of a young man: Lello Citara. Dark, with black, darting eyes, he was, at the time, a teacher in the junior high school: unmarried. The blossoming servant girl didn't go on for long, in her characteristic, dizzying Sanfredina tongue, before the signora found herself acquainted with all identifying information about the young man.

A breath or whim or wind sometimes deposited the poet's handkerchief, or one of his lighter garments, amidst the laurels of the little garden. A ringing followed shortly thereafter: it was Nena, the servant girl, come for the prompt recovery of the handkerchief, the light garment: and a pleasant womanly lingering, a whispering, amidst the withered irises and yet unblossomed dahlias – the spring laurel rustling, and the cypress submitting to the passing wind.

Lello Citara was sometimes invited: the signora's gaze smiled upon him, favored him: there was a burning vibration in her every gracious word, and in his: never had he encountered such cordial favor, nor known that kind of abandon in such a soft armchair. Not even the wall, which came to envy bitterly the gazes of Piramus and Thisbe, and vice versa, could separate their gazes. The painters, and the signora's female friends, were inspired to fantasize, rather foolishly, about that wall and its divisive nature.

Born in a mountain village where hospitality of an intellectual nature is not as common as it is on the terraces along the river, Lello thought of the Campanini salon, with its soft, warm affluence, as some kind of anteroom of glory, and at the same time, of the calm, the clarity of ideas: perhaps of the most poetic of all human "aspirations" – love.

Thanks to the mayor's zeal, the little villa in which Lello occupied two rooms had been transformed into a hospice for homeless migrabonds on uncertain layovers: painters waiting for a studio: some Poles; an unemployed barber; strange fat lizards in search of a hole, a cave.

Could one say that Signora Campanini was a source of positive public relations for Lello? That there were times when she delighted in being the one who had launched him? That little by little she had recruited a most sincere, most propitious female claque to serve him and his poetic fortune?

One day while she was waiting in the garden to give Nena a certain garment that belonged to the poet, she swiftly slipped off the very bracelet that she had already misplaced and recovered twice in two different bathrooms in two different hotels, one at Lido and one in

Rapallo, and set it down on the wrought iron table. A visitor had been announced, a poor man, a swindler: Mister Nespola, before whom she thought it best, for a thousand reasons, not to appear either too rich or overly adorned with diamonds: she usually received him on the spot: and made it a habit to contrast her whining with a bare absence of that enviable dazzle, of which diamonds, and to an even greater extent, rhinestones, are the source. This time she wasted no time before she launched into a discussion, indeed, an argument, with Mr. Nespola: it was a seemingly endless diatribe, an old story concerning some salamis handed over his counter, which in her estimation, were not tasty enough. Meanwhile, in the passion of the argument, she completely forgot about the bracelet. Lello appeared a little later. He distracted her from the anxiety of the argument, and from the subsequent relief of the agreement reached, all to her advantage. But he seemed restless, nervous: the truth was, he was tired: a magazine of rarefied literature had rejected some of his poems: and the National Bank was tardy in sending some back pay from his salary as a substitute teacher, poor thing.

All of a sudden Signora Campanini recalled the jewelery: "The bracelet, my bracelet!" She looked on the iron table: it wasn't there. She called the maids, interrogated them anxiously, rummaged about and made them rummage in the grass, and above all underneath the table, then under the hydrangeas, and in the dahlias. Lello, as unwilling as he was, was also forced to scratch around in the brushwood for a good twenty minutes. Nothing. The rhinestones had disappeared. Lello, more nervous than usual, began to stamp his feet, he flushed, finally he became nauseated. . . . Leaning over like that right after eating, he said. He asked to be excused. Nauseated.

But the signora, already in tears, began to ransack, to investigate all over again: even among the blades of the irises. She seemed to be looking for fleas. Fruitlessly. She burst into tears. She didn't have a handkerchief. She went to get one. Who could have gone off with her treasure? In her own house?

A magpie, perhaps? She gazed up into the air. There was no magpie in sight, just then. She looked at the wall: at that little wall without glass shards, whose mere appearance seemed to offend any legitimate sense of private property. That wretched, crooked low wall separated her from Lello's house. With a jump, Lello could have leapt over it. Some of her friends couldn't bring themselves to deny certain rumors, spread by other friends – in other words that Lello climbed over in the cover of night. And Signora Campanini, in her mental rigor, couldn't help but formulate a hypothesis, a horrendous doubt. Lello? The "mountain boy" whom she had so generously embraced, taken in, launched?

When the police arrived with their jeep, the investigation extended to the little villa and its "dubious" inhabitants. The young man, raising his voice disdainfully in protest, got angry, shouted: such cursing could only get him into trouble with those people. The others, dazed wanderers, fell all at once from their clouds. The barber had been away on a two-day trip. Lello, who was only calmed with difficulty, burst into tears. The bracelet wasn't there. It wasn't to be found. Lello's poetic career came to a halt, and shortly after a collapse. The delicate, if not to say fragile quality of his poems, required a launching, a baptism: a continuous, watchful patronage, or rather, matronage. He'd had the matronage. But since logic takes a single form and doesn't waver, and is the wife of method and the mother of hypotheses (which got the name of logic from her), that precious matronage died on him just when he needed it most.

NATALIA GINZBURG

House at the Sea

NATALIA GINZBURG (1916–) The peculiar tension of Natalia Ginzburg's fiction arises from the flat, naive voice which belies her narrators' acute intelligence. In her autobiographical novels, like *Family Sayings*, which won the Strega prize in 1963, and *Voices in the Evening*, Ginzburg evokes the rhythms of domestic life. Ginzburg's recent biography of the Mazoni family was a bestseller in Italy. "House at the Sea," an early story, is a good example of her lyrical spareness and her capacity to reveal the inner lives of characters who all the while remain obscure to one another, and sometimes, to themselves.

"House at the Sea" is from *Cinque romanzi brevi*, 1964.

I didn't see my friend Walter for many years. Occasionally he wrote, but his silly, illiterate letters said nothing. I was shocked when I heard he had married because when I knew him he had never seemed interested in the women we met. He was strikingly handsome, and many girls fell in love with him, but he rejected them contemptuously. Our other acquaintances didn't like him: I was his only friend.

Five years after his marriage he wrote asking me to go and stay with him, his wife, and his little boy at a seaside town. He hinted at some difficulty for which he wanted my advice.

At the time I was living with my mother. I had a job which paid me next to nothing, so I asked my mother for the money to go. She accused me of being extravagant and inconsiderate and we had an argument. Then I borrowed the money from an uncle of mine and left. I thought about Walter during the trip, and though I was happy about seeing him again, I felt apprehensive, that same tinge of fear and anxiety I had felt whenever I thought of him over the years. I was probably afraid that he would stir up feelings of desire and nostalgia in me and somehow undermine my life, just as I was building it up. I was also curious about his wife. I couldn't imagine what she'd be like and what sort of relationship they could have.

At noon I arrived in a hot, deserted station that had been freshly painted. Walter leaned against the wall, his hands in his pockets. He hadn't changed a bit. He was wearing cotton pants and a white, short-sleeved shirt open at the neck. A smile crossed his large, suntanned face, and he walked toward me and shook my hand. I knew he would greet me mechanically, and that we would not embrace, yet it left me cold. Out on the street, I began questioning him about his problem; swinging my suitcase at his side, he answered in monosyllables that it was a family problem and that Vilma, his wife, had wanted me to come.

When we arrived Vilma was making her way back from the beach with their little boy. She was a tall woman, on the plump side; her black hair was still damp and she had sand sticking to her face. She had on a checked sundress which came just above her knees and was holding a woven straw hat and a red vinyl bag in one hand. The boy looked very small to me though he was supposedly four years old. He was a beautiful child, delicate and pale with thick blond curls to his shoulders.

They had a two-story cottage on the beach. My room was on the top floor and looked out on the countryside, not the beach. The house was full of shade and the pleasant, fresh fragrance of wood and ripe peaches. We had lunch on the porch; the rust-colored linen curtains drifted open in the breeze, revealing a splendid blue of sea and sky and the brightly painted beach cabanas. The little boy didn't want to eat and his mother coaxed in a tired voice while spoon-feeding him. Walter silently crumbled his bread to pieces and stared into space. Then suddenly he blew up and said that the food was awful and that if it tasted better the child would surely eat. The little boy looked from one to the other, his eyes frightened. "Family scenes," Walter said later when we were alone. "Granted we don't get along anymore, but we could at least pretend a little. And things are getting worse – it seems she's in love." I asked him with whom, and he answered me vaguely. "A musician," he said with an unpleasant smirk.

The very day I arrived Vilma wanted to talk to me. It was evening and Walter had slipped out for a moment. She sat down facing me and began to talk so resolutely and openly about herself that it seemed forced; I felt very uncomfortable. She'd been suffering all these years with Walter. I knew him, so this should not have surprised me. She was still young and inexperienced when she married, she said. Watching her, I tried to guess her age. She didn't seem very young; in fact, I would've said she was older than Walter. She had fly-away black hair and narrow, deep-set blue eyes. Despite her longish nose and haggard complexion, she was rather beautiful. "And now I've run into an old friend of mine here. . . Vrasti. He's so refined, such a kind soul. He sensed that I needed help, he's been good to me. I don't see why he should threaten Walter or my little boy, he's just a friend." Her honesty and confidence, instead of flattering me or making me open up too, embarrassed me. She said the problem was complicated by their financial situation and by the little boy's frailty – which required a calm family atmosphere.

Then I met Vrasti. I knew that he usually stopped by every day, but his nearly pathological shyness kept him away when he learned I was there. He was fiftyish, with limp grey-streaked hair and a lean, wrinkled face. He barely spoke; sitting next to Vilma, he fidgeted with the fringe on his scarf and watched her sew. He tried to get the little boy to come to him but he kept running away; then Vrasti grabbed him by the wrist and ran his broken, bitten-down fingernails through the boy's hair.

"An artist, a real artist," Vilma said to me under her breath the first time he came over. "But it's hard to convince him to play."

I asked Vrasti to play but he said no, no, yet it was obvious that he was dying to. Finally, he sat down at the piano and played Mozart dryly and academically, for what seemed an eternity.

Vilma frequently asked him to stay for dinner and he always said no, he couldn't. He obviously wanted to accept but was afraid that she would stop insisting and then he would have to leave. He was clumsy with his knife and fork at dinner and drank like a fish, constantly pouring the wine. Then he babbled in non sequiturs and began trembling. Walter looked away, disgusted. Next to his wife, Vrasti, and the little boy, he seemed oddly young and healthy; he was tall with broad shoulders and solid arms. There was a calm within him that somehow filled the whole room. Vrasti sat at his side with a timid, guilty smile, hardly daring to speak to him directly. But he was friendly and open with me right away.

After several days I felt relaxed and healthy, and I was having a good time. The thought of having to leave dragged me down. I wrote to my uncle and asked for more money, which he sent, though less than I'd hoped for. My mother wrote too, complaining about how I'd left her alone and abandoned my work. I got depressed thinking of work, the city and my mother, and I avoided doing so. I felt as if I'd been away for a long, long time. The others never mentioned my leaving and didn't even seem to remember that they'd asked me for advice. I offered none and nobody brought it up. I had realized that Vilma's love for Vrasti was just a fantasy. She had grabbed onto the only person she thought could save her; maybe at the bottom of her heart she knew how forced and unreal her feelings were and suffered all the more for it.

When I got the money from my uncle, I offered a chunk of it to Walter and he took it. Vilma found out and thanked me, tears in her eyes. She said I'd proven myself a real friend. "I'll never forget this," she said.

I rose early in the morning and looked out my window: I saw the garden, its leafy greens covered with dew, the red and yellow flowers, the long sprawl of fields and distant mountains veiled in a light mist. I went downstairs. The beach was still deserted and the sand, untouched by the sun, was damp and cold. I spotted Walter—he always got up before me—trotting out of the water toward me. All he had on were tight knit trunks, and he looked naked from the back. He lay beside me, stretching his wet, muscular body, and ran his fingers through his hair. An American woman from an important family whose cabana was near ours was infatuated with Walter and always came over to talk when she saw him alone. He was

barely civil to her and walked off. He had named her "the parrot."
He had nicknames for everybody, and he called Vrasti "the old buf-
foon" or "Mr. Stutter." He repeated these names to the little boy to
make him giggle.

Vilma and the boy came to the beach very late. Walter took him by
the neck and dunked him in the water and the child laughed and
screeched with fear. He loved Walter frantically, and Vilma was
clearly jealous.

Then I noticed something strange happening: Vilma stopped in-
viting the musician to dinner and generally seemed indifferent to
whether or not she saw him. Vrasti finally came to this realization
too, and I felt he was suffering over it. She no longer begged him to
play, or tried to stop him from drinking. Once when Walter referred
to him as "Mr. Stutter" in front of her, she burst out laughing.

Everything she did and said seemed an attempt to please me.
When she walked around the house to tidy things, chased the little
boy down the beach, or lay out to sunbathe, I felt she was doing it not
for Vrasti, but for me.

I should have left immediately. But I couldn't. At first I told myself that none of it was true, that I was giving meaning to things that
really had none. Nevertheless, I avoided being alone with her. I
spent most of the day wandering around the countryside with Walter.

During our walks he rarely spoke. There was a steep rock that rose
out of the sea, surrounded by wild Indian fig and palm trees. We lay
down there and watched the sunset; I couldn't imagine what the years
we hadn't seen each other had been for Walter, what he might have
done, believed in or hoped for. But I knew that any question would
have been useless. He, on his part, asked me nothing, and I knew he
wouldn't have been at all interested in anything I could've said about
myself. With somebody else I would've been depressed by this lack
of interest, but with Walter it seemed completely natural. I wasn't offended because I understood better than ever before how different
and set apart he was from others, and why all his relationships took
strange forms which baffled many people, but not me. He was like a
large, isolated plant thriving on the wind that moves its leaves and
the earth that feeds its roots, but on nothing else. And I felt that

Walter's feelings were not caused by his fellow creatures, but by mysterious things which were hidden to us, like the earth and the wind.

Sometimes he talked to me about his little boy and I knew that he loved him. He said Vilma wasn't fit to bring up a child. She got up late and never permitted him to stay in the water or play in the sun without a hat. And then—the way she dressed him up and let his curls grow long. He looked like an actress's son.

Finally I decided to leave and told them. Walter showed neither surprise nor disappointment. But Vilma looked at me with such desperation on her face that my insides shuddered. I had not been loved by many women in my life, so all of this gave me a certain, obscure pleasure. But then I felt ashamed. I'd gone there to clear things up and I'd only complicated things, or maybe done irreparable damage. I went up to my room and began to pack my suitcase. It was night; I'd leave the next morning. Walter had already gone to bed.

Soon after I heard a soft knocking at the door and Vilma came in. She said she'd come to see if I needed any help. I'd already finished, I only had a small bag, I explained. She sat down on the bed and just stared at me while I packed the last of my objects and books. Suddenly she began crying very quietly. I moved toward her and took her hand. "No, Vilma, what's wrong?" I asked. Leaning her head on my shoulder, she hugged me to her and kissed me. I kissed her too. I didn't know what to do, but I felt I loved that woman as she did me. I kissed her whole body.

When I woke the next morning, I was so exhausted that it took a real effort to get out of bed. I felt upset and disgusted. I couldn't leave without telling him what had happened. I never stopped to consider whether it would be better or worse to bring it up. I just knew I couldn't go without talking to him. I saw him lying on the beach, his hands folded behind his neck. During the night the wind had picked up, and the sea was rough. High, frothy waves billowed, one over another, into shore.

He stood when he saw me. "You're pale," he said. We began walking down the beach. I was so humiliated that I couldn't speak. "Why don't you say something? Right, I know. You spent the night with her," he said. I stopped short and we looked into each other's eyes. "Yeah, she told me. She's one of those people with a mania for honesty. She can't live without it. But don't think badly of her. She's just pathetic. She doesn't even know what she wants anymore. So now you've seen how it is between us." His voice was thin, bitter. I put my hand on his arm. "But I don't care," he said, "if you only knew how far away I feel from it all. I don't know what I want either." He gestured weakly. "I, I don't know."

Even Vrasti came to see me off, and all of them—they even woke the little boy—took me to the station. Vilma didn't utter a single word. She looked pale and stunned.

I got on the train and turned to wave good-bye and that was the last time I saw them: the little boy, his curls ruffled by the wind, Vilma, Vrasti waving his floppy hat. Then Walter turned and walked away and the others followed him.

They were all I could think of the entire trip. For a long time after I got back to the city I thought only about them and felt absolutely no connection to any of the people in my life. I wrote to Walter many times but he never answered me. Later, mutual acquaintances of ours told me the little boy had died, Walter and Vilma had separated, and she had gone to live with the musician.

RAFFAELE LA CAPRIA

This Has Nothing
to Do with Me

RAFFAELE LA CAPRIA (1922–) Though his first novel, *The Mortal Wound* (1961), depicting the decadent Neopolitan cafe society, won the Premio Strega and was translated into English, La Capria is not well known to American readers. The long story included here, first published in the magazine *Nuovi Argomenti* (1968) and later worked into the novel *Amore e Psiche*, is a minute and dramatic study of a consciousness watching and analyzing the parts of its world, from the microcosmic to the macrocosmic, split apart. The story gives credence to Pier Pasolini's judgment that "La Capria knows as few others do (perhaps only as Ginzburg) how to narrate daily life. The middle-class apartment, the bedroom, the bathroom with its shaving mirror, the weather, the streets surrounding the house and the office. . . . : but all this without any sort of ordinary narrow-mindedness." "This Has Nothing to Do with Me" is from *Nuovi Argomenti* (nuova serie) 9, 1968.

We had just woken – I from a fitful sleep, and she, well I don't know if she'd slept at all, if the sleeping pills had worked. I was telling her about a dream I'd had, which was connected to the book I'd been reading before going to bed. The book was technically quite sophisticated. The author followed the itinerary Stanley had taken in his search for Livingstone and he described both his own trip and Stanley's, which he'd pieced together on the basis of Stanley's summary. Thus the two journeys were superimposed one upon the other, and what emerged was a continuous comparison of the Africa of the past and that of today, with all the changes that had taken place in the places and people in the interim.

In the dream, I was Africa. Stanley's Africa, which the author described; sometimes I was also Livingstone's Africa, black, formless, and impenetrable. I was trying to explain that Africa corresponded to the three levels of my... but she interrupted me. She announced, in English:

"Mr. Livingstone, *I presume*," turning to me with a bow.

It was obvious that my ideas and dreams were of no interest to her, but I could see that she was trying to provoke me, to offend me, and I didn't understand why.

"Didn't Stanley say that?"

"Would you mind telling me what's gotten into you this morning?"

"He actually said 'I presume?'"

"How should I know?"

"What do you mean, 'how should I know?'"

"I wasn't there."

She let out a little dry, mocking laugh.

"Oh, right, I forgot, you're never there."

"You got up on the wrong side of the bed, didn't you?"

"'*I presume*' is pretty amusing though."

"Stanley had no intentions of amusing. Can you imagine, with that heat? And those four black servants. . . ."

"Come on, will you tell me what he said," she asked me in an irritated tone.

"He said, '*I presume*,' or at least he wrote that. But what difference does it make?"

"It makes a difference to me. What's the pleasure of reading a book if you don't find out what actually happened?"

"And you think that's possible?"

"What?"

"I mean, one never really knows what actually happened."

"Why shouldn't it be possible?"

"Because nobody can ever know what actually happened."

"I don't see your point. What do you mean?"

"I mean nobody ever knows what really happened."

"Then why not just keep quiet and not even pretend to tell a story?"

"One can verify the facts and then make conjectures about the relationships between those facts. Two very complicated things."

"And what about you, for example? What facts have you verified and what conjectures have you made?"

"First tell me what you're talking about?"

"About us."

"What's there to conjecture about?"

"You really don't see anything, do you? During this whole year, you haven't verified one fact or made one conjecture?"

"But what facts and conjectures are you talking about? Will you spit it out already?"

"Okay, it'll be better for both of us. It can't go on like this. If I don't tell you everything, I'll go nuts."

I don't remember anything we said after that.

What happened after that was like a natural catastrophe that comes without warning; and as life is unfolding around you normally, just like any other day, you suddenly find yourself buried, gasping under a pile of wreckage.

She was talking, but it seemed as if another woman, a woman I didn't know, was talking through her, making use of her mouth and that she could do nothing to stop the flow of dark, unnamable things that the other was uttering. She talked with that exasperation that comes after a silence that has been kept too long and accepted too long (by me). She wanted to get to the bottom, to say it's done with. But she could only do that by treating me as her enemy, her worst enemy; and that's what she did. I was completely unprepared, and when one is completely unprepared for an event which he cannot grasp, a strange calm takes hold.

When she had finished there was a pause as between two shocks in an earthquake; we looked at one another silently as if we no longer recognized each other, we observed one another almost with curiosity, surprised that we were both still there, in that bed, apparently unharmed. She searched my eyes for the confirmation that she had really said it all, that it was done now and there was no turning back. She searched my eyes for the same desperation that had given her the courage to speak. But she must have guessed: *I had not heard*. My eyes were blank.

She'd been expecting that, oh, how she'd been expecting it! But as soon as she realized it, after a moment of disbelief, a twitch of fear and fury passed over her, and she threw her head under the pillow, her body shaken by a suppressed moan. "Speak! Say something! React!"

But I kept quiet. I was straining for some reaction that would help me bear this new unbearable situation between us, and this frustrated her somehow. The whole thing, I told myself, was really set off by some words she had spoken in a moment of exasperation. Words are not facts, they are merely sounds that we produce to communicate something that is distinct from the words themselves and that nobody can really define. Even I, if I knew my own mind at that moment, could not communicate it, and even if I did, she wouldn't have understood. And that's usually the case. What I'm doing right now, for example, is trying to understand myself, looking for the appropriate words to express myself, while my wife sits beside me, a thousand miles away from suspecting that I am thus occupied, behind my silence. Perhaps she thinks that I am suffering, and perhaps I am deluded in thinking that I am not. But being so deeply involved in this, central as it is to my situation, prevents me from living it. You can't do both things simultaneously. . . .

"You have nothing to say, then?"

So I assumed the attitude she wanted from me and asked her.

"Where did you go?"

But immediately we both heard the falseness in my voice, that polite tone that comes to my aid whenever I have to react spontaneously to something that's touched a soft spot in me.

"What does it matter where we went?"

Right, what did it matter? I was off on a tangent; I should have been asking more pertinent questions, the questions that others expected, with the tone and the feelings that others expected. But I insisted:

"I want to know."

"He had a studio on Viale della Torre." But she immediately regretted telling me. "What does it matter?" she repeated.

"I thought he'd left? Didn't he move to America, or something, last year?"

"He came back three months ago."

"Three months ago?"

"Yes, three months ago. And the whole thing started up again. Anyone else would have realized it!"

"Ah, now you're making it seem like I was the one..."

"You have no right to be so unaware of everything!"

"You mean, you can lie well."

"But didn't you ever look at me? Don't you have eyes in your head? I left the letters I wrote him right out on the table. Anyone would have realized it."

"I suppose you had to leave your letters out? It wouldn't have been better to talk?"

"You couldn't have not known. And even now you're pretending! You knew, but you didn't want to..."

"I did not know."

Again that silence between us. I tried to figure out *why* I didn't know. I didn't know, did I? I was surprised that I was thinking about myself in the third person, as if somebody else were concerned. But what I was really doing, more than thinking, was formulating sentences, possible definitions: he refuses to really face himself, he deliberately passes superficially over facts which concern him intimately, deliberately because life is more bearable that way. He is so agreeable with everyone, in every situation, that he loses his own identity. His perverted consideration of others, his courtesy, his inability to say no makes him willing prey.

"I realized that you hadn't been happy for a while, I did realize that."

"That I wasn't happy... hah! I was crazy, crazy. I was raving, didn't you realize that? What happened was irreparable. And after that I wanted him, like I said, wanted him with my body and soul. Even when I made love to you, I wanted him. And when I let go, I would cry, do you remember that—because I felt I was betraying him."

"You were always having that dream of the house collapsing on you..."

"You see? You're not even listening to me now, you're thinking about my dreams. But yes, you're right, everything was collapsing. I was desperate, sick and I didn't know how to get out of it. But I tried.

I didn't know who to turn to. . . certainly not to you. . . you didn't notice a thing."

"But I noticed you didn't like the Kamasutra anymore, that you couldn't invent new situations."

"You're the one who should have been inventing something, anything, to help me."

"The atmosphere has to be right for the Kamasutra, I couldn't do it all on my own. . . . "

"You never understand anything, do you? What does the Kamasutra have to do with it? You really believe that everything between a man and woman can be resolved like that, with a little play acting?"

"Why? We had a good time, didn't we? Wasn't it good for you?"

"It was. . . childish!"

"Who said it was childish? Him?"

"You really think that I discussed those things with him?"

"Swear you didn't!"

"I swear."

"But why shouldn't you have talked about it?"

"I didn't talk about it, okay?"

"So you did the Kamasutra with him too, that's why."

"Do you think everyone's like us?"

"Why not, what are they like?"

"Normal people. No Kamasutra."

"Too bad for them. You've become normal too. You have the voice, you speak the words and the good sense of a normal person."

She was all curled up in her nightshirt, still stunned by what she had said. Her knees were drawn up as if she were cold, her eyes bleary from crying. How she had changed, really changed, in so short a time. I thought for a moment of that insinuating voice, the tender childish voice that she used for the Kamasutra. . .

"You're the wood stove, I suppose?"

"Yes, Signora."

"A real country stove?"

"Guaranteed to please."

"Oh, fabulous! Come on, then! Let's not waste any time, let's get comfy. Slip under the covers and warm the bed. Watch while I undress, please, we'll both enjoy it. Brrr!. . . It's so cold! I'm frozen stiff. I can't wait to jump on you and hold you tight. Not many country

stoves end up in a bed like this, but you must know that yourself. . . .
Come on, take your arm out and help me undo my bra. Right, like
this. . . good, or I'll fire you on the spot and have them send me a
more obliging stove, one who knows his place and doesn't start
touching so fast. Your approach is a bit vulgar, yes, a bit careless
and heavy-handed. I hope I can teach you. We need the whole introduction before the approach, the introduction can't be forgotten.
And a lot of inventiveness, and then, finally, you can carry on like a
sturdy country stove should. What are you looking at now? My
boobs, no doubt! I've got you figured out, you know, you're one of
those voyeuristic types, you're not used to city boobs. You like looking through my nightshirt? See how thin the material is, how transparent and fine? Brrr, I'm ready now. What about you, are you ready
to take me. . . ?"

And now *she* was telling me about normal people! Too bad for
them, too bad for her if she had rejected the Kamasutra. And why,
anyway? Right, why? That's what I couldn't figure out.

I was still thinking about it in the bathroom. I stared at myself,
half-shaven, in the mirror, as stunned as I was every morning that
this guy was really me. Sometimes I talked to him and forced him to
respond. But in the ideal mirror, I wouldn't have seen anything,
wouldn't have had anyone to talk to, anyone to answer me, the mirror
would've been blank even as I stood before it. No, I wasn't looking
well this morning and I didn't want to talk, even to myself. But I was
better off than she, that was certain. My defenses were still function-
ing. The lines of my face had not come undone, as hers had. If I was
suffering, I was suffering in perspective, in the future, if you will, because my technique for suppressing the here and now only had an
immediate effect.

"You're not changing your shirt?"

There she was, speaking in her everyday voice, though it was
tinged with sadness.

"My shirt? You're worried about my shirt now? You? Where are
the shirts?"

"Look in the second drawer. What are you doing? Going out?"

"I'm going to buy the paper on the corner of Viale. . . . "

I stopped and looked at her indignantly, as if I'd just realized God knows what: "But it's so near. It's right here, two steps away."

"What difference does it make if it's near or far?" She was trying to maintain a normal tone of voice: "Please take the car. I'm out of cigarettes. Would you stop at the tobacconist's?"

"Sure... just tell me, did he get another car?"

"Who?"

"What do you mean, who? Him."

"No, why do you ask?"

"And what about his name? Why doesn't he change it? Why should he have the *same name as me?* Do you think that's in good taste, given the situation?"

"Do me another favor, will you? Take the kid, because if she's in the house with me this morning, I won't get anything done."

"Fine. But what's your problem?"

"Nothing. I just don't understand you."

"What's there to understand?"

"I'll go get her ready."

She left the bathroom and went into the kid's room. I could hear her: their two voices were indistinguishable, two childish voices. Sometimes during the Kamasutra we both talked like that. But that was... childish. She'd said so.

The kid is like me, especially in the way she becomes distracted. Her eyes will suddenly open wide and drift off somewhere. At first my wife thought it was cute, but now she says it worries her.

When I come home from the office and find her involved in some game or busy with her picture books, she doesn't even notice I'm in the room. She literally doesn't see me, as if I'm not there. And yet she's very attached to me, very affectionate. During this last year when my relationship with my wife was so confusing, if I came home and the kid didn't notice me, I'd suddenly realize how uneasy I was about my life; I actually felt like a figment who may or may not be there, like a phantom. Because my wife looked at me and seemed not to see me too, as if I were made of glass. Her eyes passed right through me. They didn't evade me, they passed through me. I was some third party.

Then I would ask the kid:

"Who am I?"

Slightly surprised, she would raise her eyes from her game.

"You're Daddy."

Fine. At least I knew I was there for her.

Sitting beside me in the car, talking, her voice sounds like my wife's.

"Do you know what microbes look like?" she asked.

"Did they teach you about microbes at school?"

"The teacher drew them on the board. They look like lots of balls or little spiders."

"But do you know how airplanes fly?"

While we waited for the traffic light to change, one passed high above us, trailing a long white stripe in the sky.

"Do they turn them on with an ignition key?"

"Men start themselves up with an ignition key too, did you know that?"

She began to laugh. I pointed to all the men, walking along the identical streets, between the identical buildings where the suburban Roman Sunday was unfolding. What would happen if on some imminent Sunday, just like this one, the whole thing went haywire?

"Look, you see them? They all start up with an ignition key."

"You too?"

"Sure. And even the traffic light. Watch, it's going to change color. The key turns, tells us to go, and we drive on."

We drove. The tobacconist wasn't far from the house if you walked. But it was a circuitous route by car because of the numerous road signs – one-way and closed streets. Right, why had I taken the car? She was the one who'd suggested it. It figured didn't it? And later I always thought it was my idea. I pulled up to the sidewalk and told the kid to stay in the car, not to open the windows. Immediately, she was acting the role of a guard.

The tobacconist was so slow! There were so many people in line this morning, but I had no choice because my wife couldn't go without her cigarettes. She hadn't smoked so much before, but for a while now, it was one cigarette after another. And we couldn't share cigarettes anymore because she preferred another brand, a stronger one now. She was always out, and I always had to go to buy them. She'd sit on the bed, smoking, lost in thought. What was she thinking about? She seemed sick, but with what? She'd gotten over the Asiatic flu.

I first felt it coming over me like a premonition; I was walking between the towering walls of two skyscrapers, a straight sunken canyon that seemed to narrow like a funnel, letting out into a torrid cloud of heat in which all the cars and buses, and all the street noises were drowning. It was June in New York. I was carrying her last letter in my pocket; a lifeless, generic letter which no longer began with the word *love*. Even since the Asiatic flu, that word had vanished from our vocabulary.

The Asiatic flu came to Europe too. When she came to the airport I saw it on her unrecognizable face. She wasn't feeling well, that's how she put it; and the kid was in bed with a high fever, why couldn't I understand that?

And after, whenever I asked her: "What's wrong? Why are you so down?" she kept saying that it was the Asiatic flu, she said that for months and months. It was established that the Asiatic flu was an insidious illness that could hang on and you never knew when it would end. Still it had already ended everywhere else, all over the world, but at our house it hung on, tenaciously. It was a fatal exhaustion, a loss of vitality and enthusiasm, an inertia of the nerves though you remained in a state of tension which prevented you from sleeping, working, getting involved in anything. It was like an inexplicable, resigned desperation. Having felt these symptoms myself in New York, I recognized them now. I knew that if you didn't recognize the condition right away, you'd get used to it, and then perhaps only after the illness had gotten a foothold and you couldn't fight it anymore, would you start to wonder: why do I feel so awful? On the other hand, since these symptoms could not be precisely defined and since they weren't even all that obvious, no definite diagnosis could be made; the fever was so minimal that you scarcely felt anything but a normal, bearable alteration. Perhaps that was why it could hang on so long, so insidiously. . . .

"Which cigarettes?" the tobacconist asked.

I told him and bought a piece of candy for the kid. She was waiting for me in the car with a slightly worried look. She didn't like me to leave her alone. I gave her the candy.

"Be careful, don't swallow it," I said jokingly. "You have to suck it."

"You know, I can swallow pills with water?"

"Good girl!"

"And the last time I got a shot I didn't cry."

"I know."

"In fact, I was laughing, laugh-ing! You can ask mama!"

To get to the newspaper stand, we had to take Viale della Torre. I slowed down a bit. I had driven this wide, tree-lined, quiet street countless times, but now I felt as if I'd suddenly glimpsed another, more squalid aspect of it. I observed the silent buildings, the vacant front doors, the nearly deserted sidewalks, the cars in their marked spaces.

It was a residential street without stores or shops, a lifeless street you passed through. My God, I thought, how can anything ever really happen here, on a street like this, in a city like this? It seemed as if nothing should ever happen in the Eternal City, for eternity. How could I imagine my wife's unfamiliar, mysterious face suddenly appearing in one of these windows; or slipping behind one of these doors, glancing back quickly over her shoulder to check one last time.

"Why are we going so slowly?" she asked me. "It's no fun like this."

"But I thought we were hunting."

"Hunting who?"

"A very dangerous microbe! The Asiatic microbe."

"But how are we going to see it? You can't see microbes."

"I know it's hiding under the seatcovers of a green car, and I'll recognize that car."

"There, there, look! There's a green one!"

"That's not it."

We were at the end of the street; the newspaper stand was on the corner. I got out to get the newspaper, and got a comic for her – Topo Gonzalez, the mouse that moves faster than the speed of thought.

"Listen, let's hunt for Topo Gonzalez instead," she suggested. "It'll be harder that way."

"All right. We'll drive back down the avenue and start the hunt over. But keep an eye out."

She didn't seem very enthusiastic about pursuing the game, and neither did I, at that point. While opening the paper, I had caught sight of a photograph that I couldn't get out of my mind. It showed a row of prisoners, lined up in an open space; they were nude from the waist up, hands bound behind their backs. A soldier in uniform, a pistol in his hand, was shooting them in the temples calmly, one at a time. And then there was that man, the one who was going to take the next bullet. He had witnessed the summary execution of the others in line, had seen them fall one by one, and now it was coming to him, it was his turn. He turned his head to one side so as not to see his executioner, who was already pointing the gun at his head. He was staring at the sky with an indifferent expression, as if he were thinking: this has nothing to do with me, whatever he does to my body, I won't feel it, it's not real, it's a dream, it won't touch me. That indifference toward his own fate, toward what was happening to him, that strange distraction on his face . . .

I was thinking about the photograph, about that detail – the man's expression – and I'd forgotten about the hunting game. She hadn't. As we drove slowly down the avenue in the opposite direction, she observed all the cars parked outside the buildings, attentively. Then suddenly, she stood up and pointed at a green car.

"There it is, you see it?"

That was *it*. And presumably it was parked in front of the building, in front of the door she'd slipped into. I saw the doorman she must have passed, and the windows from which a woman whom I'd never known, the one who belonged to another man, had looked anxiously down into the street. I wondered why I wanted to know precisely where they met, why I had even looked, why I was playing this stupid game. And I told myself that even if you do almost always find what you're looking for, at least your mind is occupied while you're looking.

"Now what do we do?"

Her voice shook me out of my stupor.

"Nothing, what can we do?"

"Isn't that the car?"

"No, I don't think so. Let's go."

"You don't mind?"

"No."

"Then why do you look so serious?"

"Oh well, the game is over, so I'm serious again, right?"

I hit the accelerator and we headed home down the tree-lined avenue at a good speed.

She was sitting on the couch in the living room, smoking, absorbed in thought. Every time I came home, for over a year now, since she'd gotten the Asiatic flu, I found her like that; by now I was used to it. The kid was drawing a picture of a little house. I had the newspaper in my hand.

And then I saw that photograph again, the details of that face, of that prisoner who was about to be killed. . . . He seemed far from everything, absent, as if the situation he was in had no bearing on him, as if it were not him there but another person in his place. The bullet that would crush his brain seemed to be of no importance, nothing more than the passage of a cloud which his eye was following across the sky. I wondered why he was reacting like that. How could he stand there calmly trailing the trajectory of a cloud in the sky? It must have been a normal reaction though because what else could he do if there was absolutely nothing else to be done? And besides, I asked myself, what would happen to someone who reacted normally in the prisoner's situation? To someone who was not just threatened by an executioner, but by Everything, "by the world-as-it-is and by people-as-they-are." How should a person behave when normalcy is a state of emergency, a pistol pointed at his temples, a finger pulling the trigger? Wouldn't it be just as normal for him to disassociate himself from his own life, to somehow distract himself from his usual daily relationships much like the prisoner had?

The kid had been saying she was hungry, my wife had stopped smoking and thinking and had gone to the kitchen to make something; now the three of us sat around the table in the sunlit living room of our little apartment, in a luxurious suburban neighborhood, an apartment which would become all mine when I hit my sixty-fifth birthday, or so I had calculated on the basis of my installment payments. This unspeakably pathetic prospect had immediately made the apartment unbearable to me. But remembering what had happened this morning and seeing my wife's expression, her face blank as a cloud, I was cheered by the thought that it was a most unlikely hypothesis now. I must have smiled at my plate. I looked up and saw my wife's eyes, green, vigilant, waiting; she always looked like that, always stared when she was interrogating me or wanted my approval. But what did she want now? My approval once again? She was capable of that.

"You know," I said to her, "it was easy."

"What?"

"His address. I found it in no time."

"You see?" she said flatly, almost sweetly. "All you have to do is pay a little attention. . . "

"Daddy, why are you always so distracted?" the kid interrupted.

She interrupted our discussions constantly and even talked too much now; the fairy tales I used to make up for her were of no interest anymore. She was so sharp that we had to work to elude her. She vaguely intuited that something was amiss when her mother and I used apparently innocuous words to discuss other things. So when the kid was present and listening attentively, particularly in the last year, our conversations took a strange turn. And then we'd both become so cautious, through sheer habit, that even when we were alone we behaved as if the child were there listening. So we hadn't gone very far in understanding what was happening to us or explaining our feelings. At least until this morning. The Kamasutra was finished—that, yes, we'd been finished with that for over a year; but we'd been stuck, in a state of regression, if you will, that had suited us both. Only before it had been a liberation and now it was the opposite, a continuous reminder of our unhappiness.

"I'm so distracted that sometimes I put a match to my mouth and drop the cigarette," I said.

"And I'm so distracted that sometimes you're here and I don't see you!"

"Today we took a nice ride, didn't we?"

"I didn't like that game."

"What game?"

"We were looking for a dangerous microbe that was hiding in a green car, but we didn't catch it. Tell him, mama, that you can't catch microbes!"

"I didn't like it either, but at least my mind was occupied."

"What a stupid game to play with a child!"

"Everything I do seems stupid to you lately."

"I wanted to go to the geological garden!" the kid said accusingly, imitating her mother's tone.

"Zoological . . ." I corrected.

"No, geological, I said."

"You're wrong. Because geological means something else."

"What, what does it mean? What does it mean?"

"You explain it," I said. "Ever since this kid started going to school, she's unwilling to admit she makes mistakes, she thinks she knows it all. She corrects me!"

"Geological *is* right."

I saw that my wife would have preferred to be alone; our chatter was annoying her, but she had to put up with us. That's the law of the nuclear triad; a circuit of contagious sensitivity, a perverse den of emotions, a kind of group immaturity, a destructive intimacy. Someone is always on your back. You can't desert that little formation, exile yourself in your own autonomy, you can't mind your own business, even for a moment. You don't have your own business because it's always divisible by three.

"A hideous and pretentious building," I began again, "with a doorman, no less! How do you have the nerve to walk in with a doorman standing right there? Someone might recognize you . . ."

"But what are you talking about? What building?"

"You know perfectly well."

"Please, leave me in peace, stop tormenting me. I already feel bad enough without your help."

"Oh really, I should leave you in peace?"

"Yes please."

"But I'm not at peace. And I intend to go back to that building to clear this up. Without the kid, this time!"

"But I want to come!" the child protested.

"You won't find anyone there anyway," she said almost begrudgingly.

"Why not?"

"He's getting ready to leave . . ."

So that's what she'd been thinking about while I was talking to her. I would have liked to be leaving too, going out into the vast world to live my own adult life, uninterrupted, where I wouldn't be infantalized anymore by my responsibilities to the pathetic trio, where I'd be alone and out of the formation at last. . . .

"And where is he off to this time? India?"

"India? What does India have to do with anything? How did you come up with that?"

"Why? Couldn't he be going to practice yoga in India?"

"You know, I don't understand you. He's not going to India and he doesn't practice yoga, so what do you mean? You're confusing me."

"No, you're confusing me, and you're doing it on purpose. You even confuse people's names. Is it normal to pick someone who has the same name as me? Think about it. What a fantasy! Tell him to change it, will you?"

"I only said that he was leaving. . ."

"The last time he was leaving for America. He's a lucky man — he's always leaving!"

"This time he's really leaving."

"Ah, how do you know?"

"He told me. I told him what happened this morning."

"Oh, as soon as I left, you called to alert him, is that it?"

"Of course."

"Who's going to India?" asked the kid.

She let out a sigh of exasperation as if to make me see the absurdity of the situation.

"Who's going to India, huh?"

"Topo Gonzales," I said to distract her.

"I asked him to leave," she said, "and he agreed to do it for me."

She was trying to play the role with dignity, she was using all her energy to stay in control at the table, but her hands were trembling.

"It seems that Topo Gonzales has a noble spirit."

"Don't call him Topo Gonzales. It's not right, considering the circumstances."

"Right, right, calling him by my name is better."

"Mama, are you still afraid of mice?" the child asked in a superior tone. She was not.

"Terribly," I answered. "But not in the least afraid of Topo Gonzales."

"*Stop it!*" she screamed.

None of us, not even she, was expecting a shriek like that. We all jumped. But then she caught hold of herself and smiled.

She pretended to smile. She took the child's hand on the table and squeezed it in her own to make up for the outburst.

"I'm sorry, I can't stand talking about mice, you know."

"I'm not afraid of mice, right daddy?"

"That's true, and why be afraid anyway? They're the ones who are afraid, they run away."

I was despondent, humiliated. Why was I acting like this?

"It's also true that you've become quite a big mouth, my love. And if someone talks so much, how can he eat?"

She was caressing her, as if to lighten the atmosphere, but then the telephone started ringing in the bedroom. She stopped short, her eyes darted as if she were looking for a way out, and she stood up.

While she stood there not daring to move, as if paralyzed, the telephone went on ringing.

"That's him," she said to me.

"So go ahead. Go on!"

The kid had started talking again, she was telling me something, laughing. She touched my arm. . . . "And so?"

"So what?"

"See how distracted you are!"

She kept on talking, but I was watching the door where my wife had disappeared; I couldn't hear anything. Then I saw her come staggering back in, white as a ghost. Thinking she might fall, I rushed over to hold her up.

"What is it? What's wrong?"

"I feel sick."

She whispered something about the kid, and leaning on me like a dead weight, she went limp. I was holding her by the shoulders, but she'd suddenly become extremely heavy. I helped her lie down on the couch. She was trying her best to stay in control.

"It's passing," she said, "it's getting better. I'm sorry."

She lay there motionless on the couch, her eyes closed.

The kid had gotten up from the table and was watching her curiously as she munched on a bread stick.

"Why don't you go to your room and draw another pretty little house for us?" I said to her. "You can see Mom's very tired."

"But I haven't finished my fruit yet!"

"Okay, finish your fruit and then go to your room."

"All right, but you play with me while she's resting."

"If you don't sit down at the table right away, I'm going to get really mad."

Offended, she walked over to her chair.

I went to the couch.

"He'll come back as soon as I call him, he kept saying that. But I don't understand anything anymore."

"What don't you understand?"

"This morning I said. . . horrible things. And now I don't even know why I said them, why I'm acting like this. I feel cut off from everything, from everybody, cut off from myself."

Crying silently, she folded her arm across her face.

"Take me to bed, please. . . I don't want to be seen in this state."

I took her to the bedroom, turned off the light and lay down beside her.

We lay there motionless in a kind of stupor in the dark, each lost in our own thoughts and trying to shake them, for a long time. So long in fact, that out of exhaustion or whatever, without even realizing it, we fell asleep. Or if we weren't truly asleep, some strange waking sleep. . . .

In fact in that darkness, I heard, or thought I heard, or perhaps I dreamed that complicitous, seductive, voice calling to me softly, as in the Kamasutra.

We seemed to be sleeping, but perhaps we were talking out loud in our sleep because even the child heard and came to knock on the door. And then suddenly there she was, lying on the bed between us.

Words in Commotion

TOMMASO LANDOLFI (1908–1979) Landolfi, who is often compared to
Poe, Kafka, and Russian writers whom he translated – like Gogol and
Dostoevesky – worked outside of all movements and schools of his time. Comparable only to Carlo Emilio Gadda in his verbal acrobatics and inventions but
closer to Buzzati in his vision, Landolfi's grotesque and irrational vision renders
everyday life into the surreal, the fantastic, the horrific. He was an important
model for other Italian writers like Calvino, who edited the most recent volume
of his selected stories. Landolfi, misanthrope, dandy, and obsessive gambler,
narrates in a voice that modulates from the whimsical, to the acerbic, to the
cruel. The two stories here exemplify these divergent narrative tendencies.
"Words in Commotion" and "Gogol's Wife" are from *Le piu belle pagine di
Tommaso Landolfi*, 1981, and *Words in Commotion*, 1986.

In the morning when I get up, naturally I brush my teeth. Thus,
today I thrust the brush with half a squiggle of toothpaste into my
mouth and brushed vigorously; and then with my mouth still full of
foam, I sucked a gulp of water from the faucet. I'm saying this to
point out that I did everything as usual.

I rinsed my mouth and spit. But now, instead of the usual disgust-
ing mixture, out came words. I don't know how to explain this: not
only were they words, but they were alive and darted this way and
that in the sink which, luckily, was empty. One slid, nearly disappearing down the drain, but it caught on and saved itself. They
seemed sprightly and happy, though a bit silly; turning around as
rabbits sometimes do in cages, or otters caught in rapids, they then

decided to climb up to the mirror. Not really the mirror: they wanted to cling onto the brackets, and I don't know how but they managed quite well. And then I realized that they were also conversing, or actually shouting in terribly high-pitched voices, which were nevertheless faint to my ears. They danced, played games and curtsied on the brackets as if they were on a stage, and then they began to gesture, so that I understood they wanted to talk to me. I strained my ears and leaned my face close so that I could hear without struggling; and when I focused my eyes, I began to recognize some of them. I really should say, single them out or read them because I knew some words that were somewhat similar; in any case, I saw the words Locupletale and Massicotto and Erario and Martello, among others.

"We're words," began Locupletale, who seemed to be in command.

"I can see that," I answered.

"We're words and you're one of them."

"Them who?"

"One of those people who deal with us and misdeal us. That's why it's fair that it's you we're turning to for justice. In these times of revenge, of redefinitions and other such re's, it seems strange that we, alone, are left out. But now that we're all showing up together, you're in trouble: in short, we demand a redistribution."

"What redistribution? Of what, you fools?"

"Of meaning, to begin with. Does each of us mean something or not?"

"I would say so, even if some novelists or journalists may not think so."

"All right, listen. Take me, for example: I'm Locupletale, and what do I mean?"

"More or less, you mean pertaining to wealth."

"Sure, because you know; but what if you didn't know?"

"What a question!"

"No, look, I do mean what you said, but do you think it's fair? I should really mean pertaining to a brook or generally to flowing water."

"But why?"

"By God, Lo-cu-ple-ta-le: do you have a tin ear?"

"Uhm. But to begin with, you may not even exist. I know locupletare, locupletazione, locupletatissimo, but you. . . ? And if you do exist, you're so rarely used, so what are you complaining about?"

"I do exist, I exist! And the fact that I'm rarely used doesn't mean anything."

"Tell us," another leaped up, "I'm Magiostra: so what do I mean, then?"

"How should I know?"

"Good, I mean if you're one of them; but so much the better, actually. I mean, take a rough guess. What do you think I sound like?"

"I don't know. . . something like a straw hat?"

"No, no! You're thinking of Maggiostrina; forget words that sound similar or things will get even more complicated. You have to try to look at me without any particular idea in mind. So just guess the first thing that comes into your head: what do I mean?"

"Then I'd say some kind of tent or lodge."

"You see?"

"What?"

"Actually, I represent a very large strawberry. You think that's fair?"

"And me," a third interrupted, "how would you size me up? Because you can do this in reverse, too. Look, then: I'm Martello, isn't that an utter outrage?"

"What you're saying is Greek to me!"

"What's a Martello: maybe you know that? Well, never mind – a hammer should be called something other than Martello."

"Oh, and what should it be called?"

"It's obvious: Totano."

"I see what you mean, but I don't see how this concerns you, you in particular. You're Martello, and if you're saying that a hammer should be called Totano instead, you're sorely mistaken, because in that case, you would be a squid and not a hammer; you're only a word, you wretch!"

"You don't understand anything at all," interrupted Totano herself. "It's so simple: we two want to switch meanings, so that at least this matter would be settled, isn't that right, Martello?"

"Not at all, sweetheart!" screamed Martello. "What would happen? You'd be fine, that's for sure, but I would end up designating some kind of cuttlefish. . . uugh! You're kidding yourself, honey: Martello can only mean some sort of. . . of tree, that's it. Something vegetal."

"Calm down," I said. "One thing's for sure, two females and a goose make a market in Naples!"

"What do you mean two females. The proverb says three females."

"And you two are making enough confusion for three. Wait a second: you, Martello, didn't you say you'd rather be called or rather be, Totano?"

"Not at all, what are you, a real nitwit? I only said that the object, a hammer, should be called a squid, which makes a hell of a difference."

"Oh, for Pete's sake, you're making my head spin. And so?"

"So what?"

"So nothing. I certainly can't exchange my meaning for Totano's, even though Totano should take mine. Do you understand?"

"No."

"In other words, I give up and should rightly give my meaning to Totano, but I don't want hers to exchange, hell, no! I want someone else's."

"Whose, for example?"

"For example, hers; see over there, Betulla."

"And what about her?"

"Who, Betulla? She'll take someone else's since hers — birch — doesn't suit her anyway; let's say she'll take Trave's and mean beam."

"What, what," squealed Trave hearing herself named. "What are you, nuts? You mind your own business, and I'll mind mine."

And they were off and arguing.

"I, Iridio," began another with an air of importance, "can only mean a file, it's obvious."

"And do you expect me to take your name and saddle myself with a meaning like iridium?" Lina rebutted. "Going by your rule, I can only mean something very soft, hardly a metal, let alone such a hard one. At best I could switch meanings with Guanciale or Cuscino and mean pillow or cushion. . . . "

Anyway, by now they were all screaming and squeaking at once; I felt as if I had a handful of pins in my ears. I lost my patience.

"But will you tell me what's gotten into your heads, you scamps?" I yelled. "Now watch what a neat little thing I'm going to do now so we'll all be equals."

"What are you doing, what are you doing?" they jeered.

"Wait a minute."

Blind with rage, I ran into the kitchen, got an empty bottle, then went to the studio for a sheet of paper and pencil, and came back.

"Now I'm going to list all your meanings very neatly here, then I'll throw you all into this bottle, and finally I'll let you out one by one. That way, whoever gets it gets it: the first to come out will take the first meaning, the second, the second, and so on. You will take them and be content, like it or not. Come on, let's begin."

They didn't want to cooperate and put up a struggle, trying to befuddle me, but I forced them to explain themselves point by point. But they didn't want to be caught, to say the least, and fled every which way, so I caught and squeezed them in my cupped palm; and then holding them between the thumb and index finger of my other hand, I finally managed to bottle them all. They seemed like trapped mice, they were screeching so. When they were all inside the bottle, I let them out one at a time, as planned; and each one, as I said, had to be content with the meaning she got. As soon as they got out, they fled, God knows where, and I lost sight of them. And that's the end of the story.

Right, but now there's one big problem. Because each of them took a meaning and kept it, and that's fine: but precisely who took what meaning? That's the problem. I don't know if I'm explaining myself; do you understand the question? It was all done on friendly terms, in good faith; but in the confusion of the moment, I didn't think of noting down how the various meanings were exchanged and assigned; and I was left with nothing to show for it, no documentary evidence. So now, to sum up, they know what they mean, but I don't. It's awful.

Besides, I'm a little worried. Yes, I said God knows where they went when they got out of the bottle: but surely they are somewhere in the house, and you'll see, sooner or later, they'll jump all over me again.

There's just one thing I'm happy about: now, I finally understand the meaning of the expression "to rinse your mouth out with words."

Gogol's Wife

Thus confronted with the complex question of Nikolai Vasilyevich's wife, I am overwhelmed by hesitation. Do I have any right to reveal something that nobody knows, something that my unforgettable friend himself kept hidden from everyone (and with good reason) and that will undoubtedly serve only the most evil and foolish interpretations? Not to mention the many sordid, sanctimonious and hypocritical souls who will be offended, and perhaps some truly honest souls too, if they still come that way? Do I have any right, finally, to reveal something before which my own sensibility shrinks, when I am not inclined toward a more or less open disapproval? But, after all, precise duties are incumbent upon me as a biographer: and seeing that each and every piece of news about such a lofty man might turn out to be precious to us and to future generations, I would not wish to entrust it to transient judgment, in other words, to conceal something that could only eventually, if ever, be judged sanely. Because who are we to condemn? Have we been granted the right to know not only the needs of these outstanding men, but also the superior and general ends to which their actions (which we may consider vile) correspond? Certainly not, since fundamentally we understand nothing of such privileged natures. "It's true," a great man said, "I pee too, but for altogether different reasons."

But dispensing with all that, I will come to what I know undeniably, what I know without a shadow of a doubt about the controversial question, which I can prove in any case to be otherwise, at

least I dare hope; thus, I will not summarize any of that, since at this
point it is superfluous to the current phase of Gogol studies.

Gogol's wife, it must be said, was not a woman, nor was she a human being, nor a living creature of any kind, nor an animal or plant
(as some have insinuated); she was simply a doll. Yes, a doll; and
this well explains the bewilderment, or worse, the indignation of
some biographers, who were also personal friends of our Man, and
who complained they had never seen her although they frequented
her great husband's house quite often; not only that, they had "never
even heard her voice." Hence, goodness knows what dark, disgrace-
ful and perhaps even abominable complications they may have in-
ferred. But no, gentlemen, everything is always simpler than one
might believe; you never heard her voice simply because she could
not speak. Or more precisely, she could only speak under certain
conditions, as we will see, and in all those cases, except one, only to
Nikolai Vasilyevich. But let me dispense with useless and facile
refutations, and let us work toward the most precise and complete
description possible of the being or object in question.

Gogol's so-called wife, then, looked like a common doll made of
thick rubber the hue of flesh, or as it is often called, skin color, and
was nude regardless of the season. But since women's skin is not always the same color, I should specify that hers was generally somewhat fair and smooth, like that of some brunettes. It, or she, was in
fact (but must this be said?) of the female sex. Indeed, let me add
immediately that she was highly fickle in her characteristics, although obviously, she could not change her sex. Yet without a doubt
she could appear thin, almost flat-chested and straight-hipped, more
like an ephebe than a woman, on one occasion, and on another, exceedingly buxom, or to put it plainly, plump. She frequently
changed her hair color as well as the other hair on her body, sometimes to match and sometimes not. Thus she could also alter other
minute particulars, such as the placement of moles, the color of her
mucous membranes, and so on; and even to a certain extent, the actual color of her skin. Therefore, ultimately, one must ask oneself
what she really was, and if he should speak of her as a singular being;
yet, as we shall see, it would not be wise to insist on this point.

The reasons for these changes were, as my readers must already have guessed, none other than the very will of Nikolai Vasilyevich. He would inflate her accordingly, change her hairstyle and other body fuzz, anoint her with oils and touch her up in various ways in order to obtain the closest possible version of the type of woman that suited him that day or that moment. Indeed, he sometimes amused himself by following the natural inclination of his fantasy, manipulating her into grotesque and monstrous forms. Because clearly, beyond a certain air capacity, she only became deformed, but she would appear equally hideous if the volume remained too low. But Gogol soon tired of such experiments, as he considered them "basically disrespectful" of his wife, whom he loved in his own way (as inscrutable as it might be to us). He loved her, but one might ask precisely which of her incarnations he loved? Alas, I have already indicated that the rest of the present account might provide some sort of answer. Oh, dear, how could I have just stated that Nikolai Vasilyevich's will governed that woman! In a limited sense yes, that is true, but it is just as certain that she soon became his tyrant rather than his slave. And this is where the abyss, or if you will, the jaws of Tartarus, open. But let us proceed in an orderly manner.

I also said that Gogol obtained an approximation of the woman that suited him from one occasion to the next. I should also add that in those rare cases when the resulting form completely incarnated his fantasy, Nikolai Vasilyevich fell in love, "in an exclusive manner" (as he put it in his native tongue), which actually created a stable relationship for a certain period, that is, until he fell out of love with her appearance.

I must say that I have come across only three or four instances of such violent passions, or as the unfortunate expression goes today, crushes, in the life, or might I say the married life, of the great writer. Let us add right away for the sake of expedience that several years after his so-called marriage, Gogol even gave his wife a name; it was "Caracas," which, if I'm not mistaken, is the capital of Venezuela. I have never been able to comprehend the reasons for such a choice: the eccentricities of lofty minds!

As for her overall shape, Caracas was what is known as a "beautiful woman," well-built and proportioned in all her parts. As remarked earlier, even the smallest characteristics of her sex were where they should have been. Particularly noteworthy were her genitalia (if this word can have any meaning here), which Gogol allowed me to observe one memorable evening; but more about that later. This was the result of an ingenious folding of the rubber. Nothing had been overlooked: the pressurized air inside her and other clever devices made her easy to use.

Caracas also had a skeleton, though a rudimentary one, made perhaps from whalebone; special care had been taken in the construction of the rib cage, the bones of the pelvis and the cranium. The first two systems were more or less visible, as one would expect, in proportion to the thickness of the so-called adipose tissue which covered it. If I may quickly add, it is a real pity that Gogol never wanted to reveal the identity of the artist behind such a beautiful piece of work; indeed, I never understood the obstinacy of his refusal.

Nikolai Vasilyevich inflated his wife through the anal sphincter with the aid of a pump of his own invention, somewhat similar to those that are held in place by the feet and which are commonly seen in mechanics' garages; in the anus there was a small movable valve, or whatever it is called in technical jargon, comparable to the mitral valve in the heart, such that once the body was inflated it could still take in air without losing any. To deflate it, one had to unscrew a little cap located in the mouth, at the back of the throat. And nevertheless... but let's not jump ahead.

And now I think I have covered all of the notable particulars of this being — except to remark upon the stupendous row of little teeth which graced her mouth and her brown eyes which, despite constant immobility, feigned life perfectly. Good Lord, feigned is not the word for it! Indeed, one really cannot say anything legitimately about Caracas. The color of those eyes could also be modified through a rather long and tedious process, yet Gogol rarely did this. And finally I must speak about her voice, which I had occasion to hear only once. But first I must touch upon the relationship between the spouses, and here I can no longer proceed randomly, or answer everything with the same absolute certainty. I could not do that in good conscience, for what I am about to relate is too confusing, inherently and in my own mind. Here nevertheless are my memories, as chaotic as they may be.

The first and indeed the last time I heard Caracas speak was on an intensely intimate evening spent in the room where the woman, if I may be allowed this verb, lived; nobody was permitted to enter. The room was decorated in somewhat of an oriental style, had no windows and was located in the most impenetrable corner of the house. I had not been unaware that she spoke, but Gogol never wished to clarify the circumstances under which she did. There we were, you see, the two, or three of us. Nikolai Vasilyevich and I were drinking vodka and discussing Butkov's novel; I remember that he digressed from the topic a bit and was insisting on the need for radical reforms in the inheritance laws; we had nearly forgotten her. And then in a hoarse, meek voice like Venus in the nuptial bed, she said point-blank, "I have to go poop." I gave a start thinking I had misheard, and I looked at her: she was sitting propped against a wall on a pile of pillows, and on that day she was a soft, gorgeous blonde, and rather fleshy. Her face seemed to have taken on an expression bordering on maliciousness and cunning, childishness and scorn. As for Gogol, he blushed violently and leaped onto her, thrusting two fingers down her throat; and as she began to get thinner and, one might say, paler, she took on that look of astonishment and befuddlement that was truly hers; and at last she shrunk to nothing more than a flabby skin covering a makeshift framework of bones. In fact, since she had an extremely flexible spine (one can intuit how this made for more comfortable use), she nearly folded in half; and she continued to stare at us for the rest of the evening from that degrading position on the floor where she had slid.

"She is either being nasty or joking," Gogol muttered, "because she doesn't suffer such needs." He generally made a show of treating her with disdain in the presence of others, or at least with me.

We continued drinking and conversing, but Nikolai Vasilyevich seemed deeply disturbed and somehow removed. Suddenly he broke off, and taking my hands in his own, burst into tears. "Now what," he exclaimed. "Don't you see, Foma Paskalovic, I loved her!" It must be mentioned that, short of a miracle, none of the forms Caracas took was reproducible; she was a new creation each time, and any attempt to recreate the particular proportions, the particular fullness and so on, of a deflated Caracas would have been in vain. Therefore, that particular plump blonde was now hopelessly lost to Gogol. And indeed, this was the pitiful end of one of Nikolai Vasilyevich's few loves which I made a reference to earlier. He refused to provide any explanation, he refused my consolation, and we parted early that evening. But he had opened his heart to me in that outburst; from then on he was never as reticent, and soon he kept no secrets from me. This, parenthetically, was a source of infinite pride.

Things seemed to have gone well for the "couple" during the first phase of their life together. Nikolai Vasilyevich appeared to be content with Caracas and slept in the same bed with her regularly. He continued to do this up until the end as well, admitting with a timid smile that there could not be a quieter or less tiresome companion than she; nevertheless, I soon had reason to doubt this, judging mostly from the state I sometimes found him in when he awoke. Within several years, however, their relationship became strangely troubled.

This, let me caution once and for all, is merely a schematic attempt at explanation. But it seems that around that time the woman began to show an inclination for independence, or should I say, autonomy. Nikolai Vasilyevich had the bizarre impression that she was assuming a personality of her own, which, although indecipherable, was distinct from his own, and she seemed to be slipping, if you will, from his grasp. It is true that a continuity was finally established among all her diverse and varied appearances: there was something in common among all those brunette, blond, auburn and red-haired women, among the fat, thin, withered, pallid and ambered ones. In the beginning of this chapter, I threw some doubt on the legitimacy of considering Caracas a single personality; nevertheless, whenever I saw her I could not free myself of the impression that, incredible as it may seem, she was essentially one and the same woman. And perhaps it was precisely this which prompted Gogol to give her a name.

It is another thing again to try to establish the nature of the quality common to all those forms. Perhaps it was no more and no less than the breath of her creator, Nikolai Vasilyevich. But truly, it would have been too peculiar for him to be so detached from himself, so conflicted. Because it must be said immediately that whoever Caracas was, she was nonetheless a disturbing presence, and let this be clear, a hostile one. In conclusion, however, neither Gogol nor I ever managed to formulate a vaguely plausible hypothesis concerning her nature. I mean to "formulate" one in rational terms that would be accessible to everyone. I cannot, in any case, suppress an extraordinary incident which occurred during this period.

Caracas fell ill with a shameful disease, or at least Gogol did, although he had never had any contact with other women. I will not even try to speculate on how such a thing happened or from whence the foul illness sprung: I only know that it happened. And that my great unhappy friend sometimes said to me, "So you see, Foma Paskalovic, what was in Caracas' heart: the spirit of syphilis!" But at other times, he blamed himself quite absurdly (he had always had a tendency for self-accusation). This incident was truly catastrophic for the relations between the spouses, which were already confused enough, and for Nikolai Vasilyevich's conflicting feelings. He was thus obliged to undergo continuous and painful cures (as they were in those days). And the situation was aggravated by the fact that in the woman's case, the disease did not initially appear to be curable. I should also add that for some time Gogol continued to pretend that by inflating and deflating his wife and giving her a great variety of appearances, he could create a woman immune to the infection; however, as his efforts were not successful, he had to cease.

But I will shorten the story so as not to bore my readers. Besides, my conclusions are only becoming more and more confused and uncertain. Thus I will hasten toward the tragic denouement. Let it be clear, I must insist upon my view of this: indeed, I was an eyewitness. Would that I had not been!

The years passed. Nikolai Vasilyevich's disgust for his wife grew more intense even though there was no sign that his love for her was diminishing. Toward the end, aversion and attachment put up such a fierce battle in his spirit that he came out of it exhausted and ravaged. His restless eyes, which normally reflected a myriad of expressions and often spoke sweetly to the heart, now nearly always shone with a weak light, as though he were under the effects of a drug. He developed the strangest manias accompanied by the darkest fears. More and more frequently he talked to me of Caracas, accusing her of unlikely and astonishing things. I could not follow him in this, given my occasional dealings with his wife, and the fact that I had little or no intimacy with her; and above all given my sensibility (which is extremely narrow in comparison to his). I will therefore limit my references to some of those accusations without bringing in any of my own personal impressions.

"You understand, don't you, Foma Paskalovic," he often said to me, for example, "you understand that *she's getting old?*" And, caught between unspeakable emotions, he took my hands in his, as was his manner. He also accused Caracas of abandoning herself to her own solitary pleasures although he had explicitly forbidden it. He even began to accuse her of betrayal. But his discussions on this subject ultimately became so obscure that I will refrain from reporting any others.

What appeared certain is that toward the end, Caracas, old or not, was reduced to a bitter, argumentative and hypocritical creature who was subject to religious obsessions. I don't rule out that she may have influenced Gogol's moral attitude during the latter part of his life, an attitude known to all. In any case, the tragedy befell Nikolai Vasilyevich unexpectedly one evening while he was celebrating his silver anniversary with me – unfortunately one of the last nights that we spent together. Exactly what had brought it on just then, when he already seemed resigned to tolerating just about anything from his consort, I cannot, nor is it my place to, say. I do not know what new occurrence may have come about in those days. I am sticking to the facts here; my readers must form their own opinions.

Nikolai Vasilyevich was particularly agitated that evening. His disgust for Caracas seemed to have reached an unprecedented pitch. He had already carried out his famous "vanity burning," that is the burning of his precious manuscripts – I dare not say whether or not at his wife's instigation. He was in an agitated state of mind for other reasons too. As for his physical condition, it grew more pitiful by the day, reinforcing my impression that he might be drugged. Nevertheless, he began to speak rather normally of Belinskij, whose attacks and criticism of the *Correspondence* was causing him concern. But then he broke off suddenly, crying out, "No, no! It's too much, too much. . . . I can't stand it anymore!. . . " as tears streamed from his eyes. And he added other obscure and disconnected exclamations which he failed to clarify. He seemed to be speaking to himself. He clapped his hands together, he shook his head, and after having taken four or five faltering steps, he leaped up only to sit back down.

When Caracas appeared, or more precisely, when he moved to her oriental room late that night, he began to behave like an old, senile man (if I may make such a comparison) whose fixations have gotten the better of him. For example, he kept elbowing me, winking and repeating nonsensically "Look, there she is, there she is, Foma Paskalovic!. . . " Meanwhile she seemed to be watching him with scornful attention. But behind these "mannerisms" one could sense genuine repulsion, which I suppose had surpassed tolerable limits. In fact. . .

After a time, Nikolai Vasilyevich seemed to pull himself together. He burst into tears again, but I would almost call these more manly tears. Once again, he wrung his hands, grabbed hold of mine and walked up and down muttering: "No, no more, it's impossible!. . . How could I. . . such a thing?. . . Such a thing. . . to me? How can I possibly bear *this*, endure *this!* . . . " and so on. Then, as if he had just then remembered the pump, he leaped on it suddenly and made for Caracas in a whirl. Inserting the tube in her anus, he began to inflate her. Meanwhile he wept and shouted, as if possessed: "How I love her, my God, how I love her, the poor dear!. . . But I must blow her up, wretched Caracas, God's miserable creature! She must die," alternating these phrases endlessly.

Caracas was swelling. Nikolai Vasilyevich perspired and wept as he continued to pump. I wanted to restrain him, but I didn't have the courage, I don't know why. She began to look deformed, and soon she took on a monstrous appearance; yet up until then she hadn't shown any sign of alarm, being used to such pranks. But when she began to feel unbearably full, or perhaps when she realized Nikolai Vasilyevich's intentions, she assumed an expression which I can only describe as stupid and befuddled, and even imploring. But she never lost that scornful look of hers; though she was afraid and nearly begging, she still did not believe, could not believe, the fate that lay ahead for her, could not believe that her husband could be so audacious. Moreover, he could not see her because he was standing behind her; I watched her fascinated, not moving a finger. Finally, the excessive internal pressure forced out the fragile bones of her cranium, bringing an indescribable grimace to her face. Her belly, thighs, hips, breasts, and what I could see of her behind had reached unimaginable proportions. Then suddenly she belched and let out a long whistling moan, both phenomena that could be explained, if you will, by the increasing air pressure which had suddenly burst open the valve in her throat. And finally, her eyes bulged out, threatening to pop out of their sockets. Her ribs were spread so wide that they had detached from her sternum, and she now looked like a python digesting a mule. What am I saying? Like an ox, an elephant! Her genitals, those pink and velvety organs so dear to Nikolai Vasilyevich, protruded horrendously. At this point, I deemed her already dead. But Nikolai Vasilyevich, sweating and weeping, murmured, "My dear, my saint, my good lady," and continued to pump.

She exploded suddenly, and all at once: thus, it wasn't one area of her skin that gave out, but her whole surface simultaneously. And she was strewn through the air. The pieces then drifted back down at varying speeds depending on their size, which were very small in any case. I distinctly remember a part of the cheek, with a bit of mouth, dangling from the corner of the fireplace; and elsewhere, a tatter of breast with the nipple. Nikolai Vasilyevich was staring at me absent-mindedly. Then he roused himself, and possessed by a new mania, went about the task of carefully collecting all those pitiful little scraps that had once been the smooth skin of Caracas, all of her. "Good-bye, Caracas," I thought I heard him murmur, "good-bye, you were too pitiful. . . . " And then he added quickly, distinctly, "Into the fire, into the fire, she too must burn!" and he crossed himself, with his left hand, naturally. Once he had gathered up all those withered shreds, even climbing onto all the furniture so as not to miss any, he threw them straight into the flames in the fireplace, where they began to burn slowly with an exceedingly unpleasant odor. Indeed, Nikolai Vasilyevich, like all Russians, had a passion for throwing important things into the fire.

Red in the face, wearing an expression of unspeakable desperation and sinister triumph, he contemplated the pyre of those miserable remains; he grabbed my arm and clutched it violently. But once those shredded spoils had begun to burn, he seemed to rouse himself once again, as if suddenly remembering something or making a momentous decision; then abruptly, he ran out of the room. A few moments later I heard his broken, strident voice addressing me through the door. "Foma Paskalovic," he shouted, "Foma Paskalovic, promise me you won't look, *golubcik*, at what I'm about to do!" I don't remember clearly what I said, or whether I tried somehow to calm him. But he insisted: I had to promise him, as if he were a child, that I would stand with my face to the wall and wait for his permission to turn around. Then the door clattered open and Nikolai Vasilyevich rushed headlong into the room and ran toward the fireplace.

Here I must confess my weakness, though it was justified, considering the extraordinary circumstances in which I found myself: I turned around before Nikolai Vasilyevich told me to. The impulse was stronger than me. I turned just in time to notice that he was carrying something in his arms, something he hurled into the flames, which then flared. In any case, the yearning to see which had irresistibly taken hold of me, conquering every other impulse, now impelled me toward the fireplace. But Nikolai Vasilyevich stepped in front of me and butted his chest against me with a force I did not believe him capable of. Meanwhile, the object burned, giving off great fumes. By the time he began to calm down, all I could make out was a heap of silent ashes.

Truthfully, if I wanted to see, it was mainly because I had already glimpsed, but only glimpsed. Perhaps I best not report anything else, or introduce any element of uncertainty in this veracious narration. And yet, an eyewitness account is not complete if the witness does not also relate what he thinks, even if he is not completely certain of it. In short, that something was a child. Not a child of flesh and blood, of course, but something like a puppet or a boy doll made of rubber. Something that, in a word, could be called Caracas' son. Could I have been delirious too? That I cannot say; yet this is what I saw, however confusedly, with my own eyes. But what sentiment was I obeying just now, when I refrained from saying that as Nikolai Vasilyevich entered the room, he was muttering, "Him too, him too!"

And now I have exhausted all that I know of Nikolai Vasilyevich's wife. I will relate what became of him in the next chapter, the last chapter of his life. But any interpretation of his relationship and his feelings for his wife, as for all others, is another matter altogether and a good deal more problematical. Nevertheless, I attempt that in another section of the present volume and refer the reader to it. In any case, I hope that I have cast sufficient light on this controversial question, and that even if I have not laid bare the mystery of Gogol, I have clarified the mystery of his wife. I have implicitly refuted the nonsensical accusation that he ever maltreated or beat his companion, and all the other absurdities. And fundamentally, what other intention should a humble biographer like myself have if not to serve the memory of the lofty man who is the object of his study?

Bakarak

LUIGI MALERBA (1927–) Malerba is a humorist, a satirist of the human condition – whether of the peasant life portrayed in the stories of *La scoperta dell'alfabeta* or the more familiar urban, industrial settings of *Dopo il pescecane* (from which the two selections here are taken). Malerba's satire seems to spring not from antipathy but from solidarity, not from an impulse to condemn but from the impulse to chuckle at common foibles. He writes in a spare, conversational style that on the surface appears glib but is actually scrupulously paced to create a laconic effect. He is a writer of novels, stories, children's books and film scripts. "After the Shark" and "Bakarak" are from *Dopo il pescecane*, 1966.

It was Bakarak himself who had me fired. Bakarak is a Swiss professor who owns a Diet Institute carrying his name. Now I'm standing here on the street, and my thoughts are rising up to the third floor, passing through the window and finding Bakarak in his office, where I know, at this very moment, he is leafing through the pornographic photographs in that famous Swedish magazine.

Can a nurse with eighteen years of experience have a theory about diet? It would seem not, in Bakarak's view. And yet, I was the first person in the world to observe the effects of words on the human organism. Words act on the involuntary nervous system and the endocrine glands. Unfortunately, though, I need help from a professor to formulate my theory scientifically. Not only did Bakarak refuse to help me, he also had me fired. He will regret it. Not that I am planning to hurt him, or to kill him, but my thoughts will pursue him everywhere, they won't leave him alone for a moment, even at night.

My theory arose from direct observation of the subjects, it didn't come out of thin air like so many other theories. The first case I documented in my notebook was the famous writer of a famous novel. This writer had come to Bakarak and said, "I feel fat, I feel like I'm going to explode." In fact, he did have swollen cheeks, he had to struggle to keep his eyes open because fat was growing around them.

"My wife is going to leave me unless I drop at least fifteen pounds. She told me, 'If you don't drop at least fifteen pounds I'm leaving you for another writer.'"

Bakarak put him on a perfectly balanced diet, one day meat, one day vegetables, one day cheese, one day pasta, one day freedom, and so on back to the beginning. The writer lost a little, about a pound.

"I can't write anymore," he said, "with all this fat around my eyes. I feel like I'm going to explode, my mind is drifting, my wife is drifting." He was really desperate.

How does one come upon scientific discovery? Through science? No, not always. Sometimes, or almost always, one comes upon it through intuition. I already had an idea in mind. I went out and bought this writer's novel, a love story that had been a great success. It was beautiful, sentimental, psychological. There are love stories in which love is hardly ever named, but here it was mentioned continually on all two hundred and seventy-seven pages.

Impossible, I thought, it's such a common word. But actually, no, *love* is one of those very common words which normal people hardly ever use, a rarely spoken word, generally speaking. This writer, on the other hand, didn't speak of anything else, he said it and used it in all the interviews and newspaper articles publicizing the book. I went back through the book page by page. He had written the word one thousand seven hundred and twenty-two times. He had even put it in the title.

Like all inventors who sacrifice themselves for their theories and who sometimes give up an arm or a leg for their love of science, I too wanted to test out my theory on myself. I sat down at the typewriter and wrote *love love* for three days running, I wrote and said *love love* out loud. Naturally, I had shut the windows so that my neighbors wouldn't hear. By the third day I felt swollen, as if I were about to explode, explode then and there. "Good," I said, "we're on the right track."

I realized that even people who read the book would gain a little weight. I told Bakarak that I had the flu and shut myself in the house for another three days to read and re-read the book. The truth is, I just scanned the page and let my eyes stop on the word *love* because, as I said, it spoke of nothing else.

Finally the scale read five more pounds. "Now I get it," I said to myself. "I've got it."

A few days later, I made the first vague reference about the connection between certain words and the endocrine glands to Bakarak. "Shut up, you imbecile," he said. Bakarak was on familiar terms with me, and now and then he would call me an imbecile. It was only a manner of speaking, otherwise I wouldn't have stood for it. Then he had me fired. He will regret it.

I went around interviewing other subjects and then went home to work on my dictionary. A red mark alongside the words with a positive effect on the endocrine glands, a green one next to the ones with a negative one – because I had discovered that there were also words that worked the other way around, as inhibitors. Writers generally vary their vocabulary without even realizing it, thereby creating a balance. But in some cases, if they abuse certain words, they can actually put on a good deal of weight and they can become pathologically obese.

A written word has a greater effect, acts upon the endocrine glands more powerfully than a word spoken or read. The word that is sung can have a detrimental effect on the organism. Almost all the words in an operatic work have a positive effect, which is why opera singers are so fat. Thin opera singers are a rarity.

Words with a negative effect are rarer. I began to list some: *literature, structure, anthropology, score, treatise*. In all these words, one can easily note the frequency of certain consonants, like the combination of *t* and *r*. I found that *t* alone, as in the word *then*, which on first glance would appear to be neutral, had a positive effect. Indeed those who frequently write the word *then* get fat. And so on for *senti-*

ment, tact, cot, contact, pentimento. On the other hand, *tetralogy, orthography, tragedy, instrumental, parameter* are words with negative effect because *t* is combined with *r*.

Some words act in assonance with a certain person more than with another. Naturally there are many neutral words which have no effect at all on the endocrine glands.

These were the first rules that I noted down day by day in the notebook for my *Dietetics Grammar*, the title I had chosen. One might note that this title has one word with negative effect and one with positive effect, it is a neutral title, in other words.

I would have completed my *Dietetics Grammar* by the end of the year if Bakarak had not continually put a monkey wrench in the works. Naturally, this *Grammar* was only to serve as a foundation for the theory, and each individual case would be considered one by one, just like a medical treatise, which is not made by theory alone but requires single cases.

After I read his novel, I was no longer able to contact that writer. He refused to come to the phone; perhaps Bakarak had advised him not to speak to me. Then I wrote him a letter and I told him, "Leave *love* alone, let *love* go, it will be better."

I made one last try with Bakarak, I wrote him a letter, too. He answered, saying that he wanted nothing to do with me, that my theory would make a dog laugh. His answer doesn't surprise me. I am going to frame it to document the difficulty of making scientific progress. That way Bakarak will remain nailed there on the wall, in all his shame, at the entrance of my new Institute.

Two other professors refused to have anything to do with me. I have the impression that it might have been Bakarak who turned them against me. But I'm not giving up, I'm forging ahead like a rhinoceros. I could kill Bakarak, but I prefer to follow him with my thoughts. Against thoughts Bakarak cannot defend himself, thoughts can pass through walls and windows, enter the third floor studio, enter his bedroom. I'll ruin him, I'll ruin you, Bakarak.

To compile my *Grammar*, I needed the assistance of a linguist, a scholar of the Italian language. After studying the effect of words, I must study the effect of sentences, that is, of words combined with other words. And after the *Grammar,* I want to write a *Dietetics Syntax,* too.

I've found a scholar who has shown interest in my discovery. He is not a linguist in the true sense of the word, but he knows everything about languages, he attends many conferences and writes many articles. I actually convinced him by making him gain two pounds. He was extremely run down, unbelievably thin. I found some words in his book that were repeated many times: *structuralism,* for example, *structural anthropology,* et cetera. I attended one of his conferences and he said *structuralism* seventy-four times. I told him, "Try to forget that word, let *structuralism* be for a while, for six months."

"What will I do," he said, "if you take *structuralism* away from me? I'll be ruined," and I said, "Please, there are so many topics." Then he gave a series of conferences on love and gained five pounds in fifteen days. He also wrote many articles on the same topic and everyone said, "See how clever, how original." Now he has actually gained too much, but he will certainly collaborate with me when I open my new Institute.

As for Bakarak, my thoughts will pursue him everywhere, even in death.

After the Shark

Naturally, they don't know what I have in the drawer. They come to my office, sit down across from me, and speak at their ease. I listen, interjecting only when I think it's appropriate, depending on the conversation or sometimes on my feeling for the person, and then I say yes or no. Actually, I could just let them speak and then simply give that yes or no, but I don't want to abuse my authority. In fact, I am the person who decides upon all the projects that are presented to me. I was appointed by the president of the Company, or in old-fashioned words, the boss. Thus, there is the boss, who does nothing, above me, and then there's me. Everyone else is an employee and has no say whatsoever.

I keep a pistol in my desk drawer, a .775 caliber Beretta which I obtained lawfully and have a license for. I've never used it, but I've been on the verge of doing so many times. I don't know what my visitors think when they sit facing me and see me opening the desk drawer and reaching in. One day a famous architect, a Swiss from Zurich, stopped talking and waited for me to take my hand out and shut the drawer. There was a sort of challenge between us, me and my visitor, to see who would hold out longer. I went on clutching the handle of the Beretta in the drawer, and he sat there, mute, facing me, staring me down, probably for three or four minutes, which seemed three or four hours. Fortunately, I stopped myself in the nick of time. I let go of the handle, took out a pack of cigarettes and snapped the drawer shut. While I was lighting the cigarette, the architect began to speak again. I rejected his project in the end, and I may have lost a fine opportunity, but so what?

In all those cases, I was split into two people. I've heard that this kind of disassociation happens to unbalanced individuals in particular, but I, on the other hand, am known for my balance. I was appointed the manager of a large construction company with shares in the stock market, I have a family, friends, and I was nominated for the Knights of Work. It is a well-known fact that the Knights of Work are nominated directly by the President of the Republic on the recommendation of a highly qualified committee. The newspapers have written about me both as an industrial leader and as a private individual, and nobody has ever called my balance into question. But as I was saying, at those moments I was split into two people: the first was saying shoot shoot and the second was saying for God's sake don't do it. Fortunately, the second me, the one saying for God's sake don't do it, always won out.

I said I have been on the verge of shooting many times. Truthfully, not more than ten times. But almost every time an architect was sitting in front of me. I am calm around businessmen, bankers and financiers. Architects, on the other hand, always make me suffer. Perhaps because I feel their disdain for me. They all consider themselves geniuses and artists, and they speak to me as if I were someone who has money but no head on his shoulders. As if it didn't take a head to manage a huge company! Naturally, I've never taken it up with them, partly because none would have had the courage to tell me openly what they think of me. But I could feel their disdain. They didn't know it, but I was reading their minds like an open book.

Now I am horrified to think what would have happened if I had shot. First of all, my interviewee, the architect, would have been a stiff because I'm a dead shot, I love sports, I hunt on the land and sea, I mean underwater. Given my social position, a colossal scandal would have broken out, first page news. One split second of weakness could have shot my career to hell and put the Company into a crisis. Our Company is a real financial power. It can easily absorb inflation, the devaluation of the dollar or the lire, and all the other insidious afflictions of the economy, but I don't know what would hap-

pen if one of its managing directors killed an architect sitting across
from him in his office. I already know what the papers would write
and what my enemies would say. But I can assure you that my height
has nothing to do with this even if, now that I think about it, every
time I was closest to shooting I happened to be sitting across from architects who were taller than average. But this might be purely coin-
cidental.

Things changed after the shark. As I said, I'm a sportsman and I
love hunting, especially hunting underwater. It was a very noisy
summer and I fled Rome every Friday afternoon and returned Sunday evening or sometimes even early enough Monday morning to be
in the office by nine. I drove to Circeo, where I went straight from the
wheel of my Mercedes to the wheel of my motorboat and headed offshore with Angelo, my driver. Driver in so many words because I
never let him drive, I am always the one who drives whether we are in
the car or in the motorboat. He says, "But what are you paying me to
do if you always drive?" I laugh and give him some odd job, some
personal errand. And anyway, I pay him to keep me company. Sometimes I ask him to drive home the people who come to my office and
when he gets back, I make him tell me everything they said in the
car, word for word, just like a tape recorder. Angelo has an incredible memory.

So that Saturday we go out in my motorboat and when we're offshore I take the gun and dive in holding my breath, I mean, without
my tank, and sink about forty feet. Usually at that depth you run into
groupers. Instead, that day I ran into the shark. As I'm looking down
into the depths, I suddenly feel something like a stone on the back of
my neck. I turn around and I see that monstrous tail disappearing. I
don't lose my head. I begin to rise, but then before I can surface, he
turns around and heads for me again. Help. He approaches, his jaws
wide open, all I can see are the triangular teeth angling in toward my
head. And at that moment I simply think to myself, okay, now he's
going to eat me. It's not true that when you're face to face with death,
you think of your family and the things you don't want to lose. I've
talked to others who experienced similar situations, I mean people
who have been face to face with death, and they all said they had

really asinine thoughts like I did when I thought okay, now he is going to eat me.

Naturally, I didn't even make a move to shoot him with the spear gun because I knew that a beast like that would only be annoyed and nothing else. Something told me to give him a little smack on the snout with the barrel of the gun instead. I don't know why I did it, but I just touched him and it worked, the shark turned around and swam off again. The second time around I really realized what kind of beast I was dealing with. Help.

I finally resurfaced a couple of feet from the boat. I let out a yelp, took four strokes and next thing I knew I was clutching the wheel. Angelo said he saw me leap out of the water like a dolphin. Then I sat there for five minutes without saying a word.

That week I resumed my work at the office. I had brought my underwater gun with me and propped it against the wall behind the desk like an umbrella or a decorative object. The people who come to my office look at it, but nobody asks me anything about it because they know that if I get started about underwater fishing I'll never stop and I'll bore them silly. It seems that nothing is more boring than hunters recounting their conquests, whether on land or sea. If they only knew the risk they were running, they would have rather listened to my stories.

I remember that week I met with an old American architect who is world famous, a kind of walking monument, one of those people who I can use as a cover when I am involved in some project that might stir up controversy. If I were using the name of some big architect, I could even build a little villa in Piazza del Popolo, if you will, or a skyscraper in front of the Duomo in Orvieto. That poor old man spoke slowly and calmly, not dreaming of what I was thinking. I was thinking, now you're going to be a stiff. Sometimes I think in the language of underwater hunting. For a moment while he was talking, I thought I saw triangular teeth like the shark's. I grabbed one hand by the other, I mean, the right by the left, to keep myself from picking up the gun and shooting him in the mouth.

The next Saturday I went back to Circeo and headed offshore to the same spot where I had met the shark. I brought a barrel of ox blood and a sack of entrails which I tied to a large harpoon, and I threw it into the water. Then I poured the ox blood overboard and read newspapers and magazines while I sat there waiting. Every now and then I interrupted my reading to chat with Angelo, to gossip about the Company employees. All the hours of the morning went by until one, when we had sandwiches and beer.

It was around three when I got groggy and thought about taking a half-hour nap. Suddenly we heard a crack and the motorboat began to slip backwards. "This is it," I said to Angelo. We began to pull the capstan and after a few seconds there, the shark surfaced and came toward us. A beast like that could even overturn a heavy motorboat like the Tritone, without any problem.

This time I had brought an arsenal with me. I picked up a gun loaded with the kind of bullets you use to hunt boar and I got ready to shoot the shark between the eyes. I was out of my mind with the pleasure of it. Angelo said something to me but I didn't hear a word, the only thing I saw was the eyes and mouth of the architect turning to pulp with every shot. I kept shooting for so long that its body over-turned in the water, its stomach facing the sun. At this point, I laced a second harpoon into him and took off in fourth, the boat dragging him in our wake. Now I'll stop because I don't want to bore like those hunters who talk about their conquests.

I dragged the architect's body to shore and gave it out to the fisher-man in Terracina who will sell it as dogfish for more than thirty thou-sand lire. Since that day I have gone on expeditions in Sardinia, in the Red Sea and the Persian Gulf, I even went all the way to the sea of Haiti which is as packed with architects as it is with sardines. I kill about twenty architects a year with Angelo, who always accompanies me on my conquests though he never puts a foot in the water since he can't swim. Naturally, I always keep the pistol in my desk drawer at the office, but now I never get an urge to shoot the sharks who come to me with their projects.

A L B E R T O   M O R A V I A

Blocked

ALBERTO MORAVIA (1907–) Italy's most celebrated and well-known
novelist for decades, Alberto Moravia established himself with his first, ground-
breaking novel, *Gli indifferenti*. With its explicit condemnation of the Roman
bourgeoisie under fascism, this book is said to have anticipated the stance of
post-war neorealism as well as the themes of Sartre's existentialism. The collections of stories which followed like *La bella vita* and the novel *Agostino* confirmed Moravia's singular gift as a storyteller. Moravia has called himself a
novelist of "imbroglio," and in fact, his plots are sometimes mechanistic to a
fault. In his later work, he claims that psychological analysis and Marxism have
helped him to portray contemporary life. Yet some critics think his openness to
the ideological and cultural fashions explains the inconsistency of his work.
Nevertheless, his recent novels, *Time of Desecration* and *1934* are evidence of
his tendency to experiment and develop. Also important is his work as a journalist, travel writer, film and literary critic. Along with Enzo Siciliano and
Leonardo Sciascia, he edits *Nuovi argomenti*, Italy's leading literary magazine.
The piece included here is from a collection of stories narrated by female characters; thus the title – *Another Life*. "Blocked" is from *Un' altra vita*, 1973.

I never married, having realized early on that people who think
about love continually like me should keep away from marriage. Instead of getting married, as many girls do so that they won't have to
think about love anymore, I took up a profession as an airplane stewardess; working, I can support myself and think about love whenever
I want without answering to anyone. I fly the Middle East route daily;
and while I'm doing the usual things like serving meals, making sure

seatbelts are fastened, helping mothers with whatever problems they may have, a solicitous smile on my face, I think about love. Or else I think of the lovers I have had, or those I will have. But this doesn't mean that I'm a woman with promiscuous tastes. On the contrary, I'm almost completely inhibited. In fact, it's because I rarely fall in love and men rarely fall in love with me that I think about love so much. At thirty, as beautiful as I am, I've only had a few big affairs. But to make up for it I've done nothing but think about love.

Sometimes I think the fact that my romantic impulses are blocked may be a result of the profession I have chosen. I could be wrong, but somehow I remember being more sure of myself before I was a stewardess. Being a professional stewardess has turned me into a rootless person who doesn't know what to call home, who hardly ever speaks her native language, who mostly lives above the clouds, in the endless lovely weather of great heights. But the truth is, to love and be loved, one must have roots. The peasant bound to the farmhouse and fields loves and is loved; the shopkeeper does so between her shop and her home. But what roots can one put down in the sky? Sure, the saints, who always do the opposite of us sinners, can. But how many of us are saints?

One night in Beirut recently, again thanks to my endless, inane preoccupation with love, I accepted a dinner invitation from a pilot from my airline named Marco who has been after me for quite some time; I went to see whether he, by some chance, had what it takes to become "the man in my life," as the expression goes. I want to describe this guy Marco, if only because he was my ideal man; nevertheless, things went as they went.

So Marco was one of those very personable men, whose strength, even if it's a bit excessive, is balanced by some opposite trait: he's athletic but has mild manners; pugnacious but melancholy; wellbuilt but timid. In awkward moments he even stammered, which is something that I like and arouses my affection.

We went to an Oriental-type restaurant with waiters in costume and Arab-style furniture, we sat in a little courtyard with a marble tub and a spurting fountain. We ordered the special and then sat looking at one another. The situation was clear: I was there to hear him say that he loved me and even that he wanted to marry me; but precisely because it was clear, I was baffled. Utterly lacking romantic impulses, with a lovely body which always turns off on occasions like these and refuses to give me any sort of sign, the idea that Marco was about to declare his love forced me to ask myself the fundamental question, so to speak, uncomfortable as it was: in other words, did I or didn't I like him? I looked at him, aware as I did that I was frowning in bewilderment, turning my lovely stewardess' face into a carnival mask; and the more I looked at him, the less I felt sure. Now I told myself: "Yes, he's it, he's really it," and then, "No, he isn't, God no, not him, not even by a long shot." Marco must have realized something because he whispered: "What's wrong? Is something wrong?"

"No. But let's not sit here so quietly. Let's talk."

"Actually, I have something to tell you."

And then panic overtook me. "Only one thing? Let's talk about lots of things. Tell me about your home town. Tell me where you were born. Talk about your family."

He agreed unwillingly; and I was disappointed because I had imagined that he came from some little village somewhere, who knows why, and actually he was born in Milan, and then to add insult to injury, he described it in a colorless and summary manner, like the man of few words that he really was. Meanwhile, however, he tried to let me know rather pitifully that he loved me by ogling me with these gazes full of insistent and obtuse melancholy; meanwhile, I was feeling more and more unnerved under that persistent gaze of his. Then the waiter brought a plate of mussels; while trying unsuccessfully to open one that was closed, I broke a fingernail. And that's when I exploded: "You see this oyster? Well, thanks to you, I'm like this oyster tonight: closed, hostile, secretive."

"But really, I . . ."

"Really, you came here tonight to tell me that you love me. Don't deny it, I know. And to let me know it, you stare at me like a frustrated dog. Well, I don't like it, I really don't."

"Don't like what?"

"Your way of showing a woman that you like her."

"You tell me how to behave then."

I let out a little unpleasant laugh. And then, God knows why, I decided to teach him the very thing I know nothing about. "And meanwhile, no looks, no smiles, no touching my hand, in other words, no coming on. Nobody does that anymore. You have to think in terms of mathematical eroticism."

He was stunned. "Mathematical eroticism," he repeated. "What is mathematical eroticism?"

Now that I'd started, I answered: "It's eroticism that skips the preliminary phases – glances, compliments, smiles and that sort of thing. It's like a mathematical operation: I like this woman, she likes me; therefore, we should put our mutual pleasure together and total it, I mean, do precisely what we must do."

"And what is it?"

"It."

He plunged into a meditative silence; he was probably finding this mathematical eroticism a bit hard to swallow. We finished eating with hardly a word; and then I said dryly that I was tired and he paid. And since the hotel was nearby, we walked there, still in silence. I got the key from the desk clerk, but by then my confusion was so great that even the doorman noticed the frown of indecision contorting my face. I was thinking that I should put Marco to the final test, and I asked him to take me up to my floor. Once inside the elevator, I drew back and leaned against the wall; but inside me, a voice was hollering, "Come on, jump on me! What are you waiting for!" But nothing happened, which was lucky because if he had "jumped on me" as I wanted, my absurd and inevitable response would have been a stiff smack in the face.

The elevator stopped; biting my lower lip in fury, I got off and walked, my head down, towards my room. Marco caught up with me and I turned quickly to find his mouth almost pressed to mine, and then we finally kissed. That kiss was worse than mediocre, in fact I managed to think to myself "He's not it, he's definitely not it." When we pulled away from one another, I gazed over Marco's shoulder down the corridor, towards the two elevators. One, ours, was going down, but I saw that the doors of the other were just opening and a man, who'd obviously seen us kissing, was looking at me. He was a middle-aged blond with short hair and a forelock; his face was flushed and he had blue, slightly sinister eyes. Small but well-built, he was wearing a pair of bright blue pants and a sailor shirt with anchors on it: a sailor.

Then, perhaps for the first time in my life, the instinct I never thought I had made itself known, loud and clear. I whispered to Marco: "There are people here, go, I'll see you tomorrow." And I gave him a handshake that nearly pushed him backwards. Marco ran off, intoxicated with happiness, and I leaned over to put my key in the door. But my hand was trembling with that instinct that had finally been awakened; I was still struggling to insert the key in the door when I heard the sailor approaching me from behind. I thought, "I hope he really saw us and comes on strong." Then a chubby red hand covered with blond hair slid over mine, took the key and slid it easily into the lock. The door swung open, the man shoved me into my room, closed the door behind me and turned on the light.

Mathematical! It had all happened just like it should in a, yes, mathematical operation. But as I saw the man with the blond forelock coming towards me in his blue pants and shirt with anchors on it, his hands tensing to seize me and a smile that revealed his teeth, the instinct all but completely vanished and I shouted: "Don't come near me!"

Confidently, he shook his head and took another step forward. I then backed up to the bathroom door, I quickly leaned into the bathtub, grabbed the shower head, turned on the faucet and pointed it at him. It was a very modern hotel: the jet of water was quite powerful. Like a real sailor who is accustomed to sea waves, he stood implacably, his face scarlet and hard, while the jet of water drenched him. Then he stepped backwards, slowly and calmly, as if to reassure me. And speaking in English, he said: "I'm sorry, I assumed..."

I too answered in English: "That since that other guy kissed me, you could go to bed with me? That's it, isn't it?"

"I suppose so."

"Well, get out, get out now! Otherwise I'll start screaming."

And then, I don't know why, he asked me where I was from. And I told him, pointing the shower head toward him all the while. To be polite he said he liked Rome very much, made a little bow and left.

Now I was alone. Marco had been timid and romantic, and I didn't like it. The sailor had been "mathematical," which I didn't like any better. I walked over to the mirror and looked at myself. "You're blocked," I said.

A Pair of Glasses

ANNA MARIA ORTESE (1916–) Ortese's work was described by the critic
Bontempelli as a kind of "magic realism." However, it is hard to label, rich as it
is with varied tendencies – from the naturalistic, lyric, fantastic, to the expressionistic. The celebrated story "A Pair of Glasses" exemplifies how Ortese renders reality – in this case the squalor of post-war Naples – by filtering it through
the protagonist's heightened perceptions and feelings – with the grotesque effects of a distorting mirror. She has won Italy's two most prestigious literary
prizes, the Premio Strega and the Viareggio. Her highly acclaimed novel
L'iguana (The Iguana) was recently published in English translation.

"A Pair of Glasses" is from *Il mare non bagna Napoli,* 1967.

Don Peppino Quaglia stood near the threshold of the basement
apartment, singing "Ce sta' o sole... 'o sole!"

"Leave the sun to God," his wife Rosa answered, her soft, vaguely
cheerful voice rising from within where she was laid up in bed with
arthritic pain, complicated by heart disease; and addressing her
sister-in-law, who was in the bathroom, she added: "You know what
I'm going to do, Nunziata? I'll get up later and take the soaking
clothes out of the wash."

"Do as you please, but I think you're crazy," Nunziata answered
from the little cubbyhole, in her dry, sad voice. "With the pains that
you have, one more day in bed wouldn't hurt you!" A silence. "We
have to put down that other poison, I found a cockroach in my sleeve
this morning."

And then Eugenia's calm, quiet voice called from the bed in the rear of the room, a veritable grotto with its low ceiling vault strung with spider webs:

"Mama, today I get my glasses."

There was a kind of secret jubilation in the little girl's subdued tone; she was Don Peppino's third-born (the first two, Carmela and Luisella, were with the nuns, and would soon don the veil, convinced as they were that this life is a punishment; and the two small ones, Pasqualino and Teresella, still lay feet first, snoring in their mother's bed).

"And smash them too, I bet," her aunt insisted, even more irritated now, from behind the door. She made everybody pay for the displeasures of her life, most importantly the displeasure of being unmarried and of being subjected, as she saw it, to her sister-in-law's charity, although she never failed to mention that she offered this humiliation to God. She had put a little of her own savings aside, however, and since she was not really mean, she offered to buy glasses for Eugenia after the family had discovered that she couldn't see a thing. "And what they cost!" she added now. "Eight thousand lire in hard cash." Eugenia heard water running in the basin and pictured her washing her face, squinting, her eyes full of soap, and she didn't bother to answer.

Anyway, she was much too happy to bother.

A week ago she and her aunt had gone to an optometrist on Via Roma. There, in that elegant store full of shining tables and a marvelous green reflection that rained down from the curtains, the doctor had tested her eyes, making her read entire columns of letters printed on a card, some as big as boxes and others as tiny as pins, while he changed lenses. "This poor child is nearly blind," he finally said to her aunt, as if in commiseration. "She must never take these glasses off again." And then, while Eugenia sat waiting anxiously on a stool, he quickly placed another pair of lenses in a white wire frame on her face and said to her: "Now look at the street." Eugenia stood, her legs trembling with excitement, and could not hold back a little shout of joy. Well-dressed people, so many of them, passed before her on the sidewalk, and they were crystal clear even if smaller than usual: ladies in silk suits and powdered faces, young men with long hair and colorful sweaters, an old man with a white beard and reddened hands clasping a cane with a silver handle; and in the street, beautiful automobiles that looked like toys, painted shiny red or light green; and green trolleys as big as houses. Across the street, the elegant stores whose windows shone like mirrors (sales clerks in black smocks were polishing them) were so full of fine things that Eugenia's heart swelled. There was a cafe with red and yellow tables outside, and young girls with golden hair sitting cross-legged laughed as they drank from tall, colored glasses. Above the cafe, balcony doors stood ajar, as it was already spring; the embroidered curtains blew, revealing blue and gold paintings, heavy gold and crystal chandeliers that glittered. Amazing! Enthralled by all that splendor, she had not followed the conversation between her aunt and the doctor. Her aunt, standing at some distance from the glass counter in her brown Sunday dress, now broached the subject of the price with a timidity that was unnatural for her. "Doctor, don't forget to give us a good price, we're poor people..." And when she had heard "eight thousand lire," she nearly fainted.

"For two pieces of glass? What are you saying? Jesus Christ!"

"You see, when people are ignorant, they never reason things out. But if you give this child two pieces of glass, tell me, won't she see better? She has nine diopters in one eye, and ten in the other. And if you want to know the truth, she's nearly blind."

While the doctor wrote down the child's first and last name, "Eugenia Quaglia, vicolo della Cupa, Santa Maria in Portico," Nunziata walked over to Eugenia, who still stood in the doorway of the store, adjusting the glasses with her damp hands and looking about eagerly. "Look, look, my lovely girl. You see what this luxury is costing us! Eight thousand lire, did you hear? Eight thousand in hard cash!" She could barely breathe. Eugenia had turned completely red, not so much at this reproach, but at the gaze of the cashier who had been looking at them while her aunt announced the family's poverty. She took off the glasses.

"But how can she be so young and so myopic already?" the cashier asked as Nunziata signed the receipt, adding "and wrinkled too?"

"My good lady, there's not a pair of bad eyes in our house, this is just a stroke of bad luck that came... along with all the others. God rubs salt in our wounds...."

"Come back in a week," the doctor said, "The glasses will be ready."

Eugenia tripped on the stairs as she was leaving.

"Thank you, Aunt Nunzia," she said after a while. "I'm always so rude to you and you're so nice to buy me glasses."

Her voice was trembling.

"Listen, my dear, it's better not to see the world than to see it," Nunziata answered with sudden melancholy.

Eugenia did not even answer her this time. Aunt Nunzia was often strange; she cried and shouted over nothing and said so many ugly words. On the other hand, she went to mass conscientiously; she was a good Christian, and whenever some wretch needed help, she was always there, with a full heart. Eugenia didn't have to worry.

From that day on, Eugenia lived in a sort of rapture, waiting for those blessed glasses that would allow her to see every single person, every little thing in its minutest detail. Until now, she had been enveloped in a fog: the room where she lived, the courtyard that was always hung with clothes, the *vicolo*, spilling over with colors and noises—all of that for her was covered by a thick veil: the only faces she knew well were those of her intimates—her mother especially, and her brothers and sister because they often slept together. Sometimes when she woke in the night, she would look at them in the gaslight. Her mother slept with her mouth open, and Eugenia could see her broken, yellowed teeth; and Pasqualino and Teresella were always dirty and covered with boils, their noses full of mucus: when they slept, they made a strange noise, as if they had beasts inside them. Once in a while, Eugenia caught herself staring without really knowing what she was thinking. She felt confusedly that beyond that room, forever filled with its dripping clothing, broken chairs and stinking toilet, there must be beautiful light, sounds, things; and the moment she had put the glasses on, the revelation struck her: the world outside was beautiful, quite beautiful.

"Respects, Marchesa. . . ."

It was her father speaking. She saw his tattered shirt, his back moving out of the doorframe.

"You must do me a favor, Don Peppino. . . ," the marchesa said now in a placid, indifferent voice.

"Whatever you want, tell me..."

Eugenia wriggled out of bed without a sound, slipped into a dress and went barefoot to the door. The sun, which entered the ugly courtyard early every morning through a fissure between the buildings, came towards her in all its purity and splendor, illuminating her little old woman's face, her strawlike, disheveled hair, her small, coarse wooden hands with their long, dirty fingernails. Oh, if only she had glasses now! The marchesa was standing there with that majestic and kindly air that so enchanted Eugenia, wearing a black silk suit, a little lace scarf, her white hands covered with jewels; but her face was not clear, it was an oval, a whitish stain. Two violet feathers quivered above it.

"Listen, you must do the child's mattress again... Can you come up at around ten-thirty?"

"Gladly, gladly, but I wouldn't be ready until this afternoon, Signora marchesa..."

"No, Don Peppino, it must be done in the morning. People are coming this afternoon. You can work out on the terrace. Don't make me beg you, do me this favor. They're ringing the bells for mass now. Call me at ten-thirty."

And without waiting for an answer, she walked away, carefully avoiding a yellow stream of water that was spilling down from one of the terraces into a puddle on the ground.

"Papa," Eugenia said, coming up behind her father as he headed back inside the basement apartment. "The marchesa is so good, isn't she! She treats you like a gentleman. God will reward her for it."

"A good Christian she certainly is," Don Peppino answered, implying another meaning beyond Eugenia's understanding. Exploiting the fact that she was the landlord, the Marchesa D'Avanzo made the people in the courtyard serve her continually; she would give Don Peppino a pittance for the mattress; and Rosa, who waited on the marchesa even when her bones burned, was always at her beck and call to bring clean sheets. It's true, the marchesa had cloistered the girls, saving two souls from the world's perils, which are numerous for the poor. But she charged three thousand lire, and not one less, for that basement space where everyone had gotten sick. She loved to repeat, with a certain cool tone, "I would do it with all my heart, I would, it's just the money that's missing. These days, Don Peppino, you're a gentleman, and you should be grateful that you have no worries, thankful that providence has given you such a situation, has saved you. . . . " Donna Rosa felt a sort of adoration for the marchesa and her religious sentiments: whenever they saw one another, they spoke continually of the other life. And though the marchesa didn't put much credence in it, she didn't say so; she exhorted the mother of the family to be patient and hope.

"Did you speak to her?" Donna Rosa asked anxiously from the bed.

"She wants me to make a bed for her nephew," said Don Peppino, annoyed. He had taken the tripod stove, a gift from the nuns, outside to heat some coffee and now came back in for water. "I won't do it for less than five hundred," he said.

"That's a fair price."

"And who's going to pick up Eugenia's glasses?" asked Aunt Nunzia, coming out of the bathroom. She was wearing a shirt, a skirt whose hem was down, and slippers. Her pointed shoulders, grey as rocks, poked through her shirt. She was drying her face with a napkin. "I can't go and Rosa is sick. . . "

Nobody noticed Eugenia's large, nearly blind eyes filling with tears. See, maybe she wouldn't have her glasses for another day now. She sidled up to her mother's bed and let her arms and forehead fall on the blanket with a pathetic gesture. Donna Rosa reached a hand out to caress her.

"I'll go, Nunzia, don't get worked up. In fact, it'll do me good to go out."

"Mama!" Eugenia kissed her hand.

At eight, there was a great commotion in the courtyard. Rosa had just stepped out; in the stained, too-short black coat without shoulder pads, she was a tall, gaunt figure whose legs stuck out like wooden sticks. She held a shopping bag on her arm for the bread she'd pick up on her way back from the optician. Don Peppino was sweeping the water out of the middle of the courtyard with a long broom, a useless effort because the tub leaked constantly, like a spring. The courtyard was hung with the clothes of the two families upstairs: the Greborio sisters on the first floor, and the cavaliere

Amodio's wife, who'd had a baby two days early. In fact, the Greborio's maid, Lina Tarallo, was making a terrible racket as she shook out the carpets on the balcony. The dust, mixed with real filth, drifted down and gradually settled like a cloud over those poor people. But nobody paid it any attention. Then suddenly shrill screams, cries broke out: Aunt Nunzia was calling upon all the saints to be her witness: she was cursed, and all because Pasqualino was bawling and screeching like a devil to go with his mother. "Look at him, look at this demon!" screamed Aunt Nunzia. *"Madonna bella,* have mercy on me, let me die, let me die now if you can, because only thieves and bad women are fit for this life." Teresella, who was smaller than her brother because she was born the year the king fled, sat in the doorway smiling; every now and then she would lick a crust of bread that she found under a chair.

Eugenia was sitting on the steps of the doorkeeper Mariuccia's apartment, looking at a page from a children's magazine which had fallen from the third floor. She had her nose to it because that was the only way she could read the words under the colored figures: a little blue river in the middle of an endless meadow, and a boat going. . . going. . . who knows where? It was not in dialect but in Italian, so she didn't understand much. But now and then she would laugh for no reason.

"So, today you're going to get your glasses?" said Mariuccia, leaning over her shoulder. Everybody in the courtyard knew because Eugenia could not resist telling, and also because Aunt Nunziata had found it necessary to announce that she was the one in the family who would spend her own money. . . .

"Your aunt is giving them to you, eh?" added Mariuccia, smiling good-naturedly. She was a small woman, almost a dwarf with a man's face, full of whiskers. Just then she was brushing the long black hair which reached her knees: one of the few attributes that attested to the fact that she was a woman too. She brushed slowly, her sly, kind, mousey eyes smiling.

"Mama went to Via Roma to get them," said Eugenia with a look of gratitude. "We paid eight thousand lire for them, you know, in hard cash. . . . My aunt is," she was adding, when Nunziata appeared in the doorway of the cubbyhole and screeched furiously: "Eugenia!"

Pasqualino stood behind her with a terrible grimace of disdain and surprise on his face, all red and dazed. "Go to the tobacconist and buy me two three-lire caramels from Don Vicenzo. And come back right away!"

"Yes, Aunt."

She took the money in her fist, without another thought of the magazine, and walked out of the courtyard swiftly.

As she entered the tobacconist's, she grazed by Rosaria Buonincontri's yellow basket. Rosaria, the Amodio's fat maid, was wearing black but her legs were white, and her face flushed, calm. "Tell your mama to come up for a moment today, Signora Amodio has a message for her."

Eugenia recognized the voice.

"She's not home. She went to Via Roma to pick up my glasses."

"I have to get a pair too, but my fiancé doesn't want me to."

Eugenia did not grasp the meaning of this prohibition. She answered ingenuously:

"They really cost a lot, you have to take care of them."

They entered the hole that was Don Vincenzo's store. People were waiting and Eugenia was pushed backwards. "Move up... you really are blind," Amodio's maid commented, with a kindly smile.

"But now your Aunt Nunzia is giving you glasses," Don Vincenzo cut in, winking with a playful, complicitous air when he overheard. He wore glasses too.

"At your age," he said, handing her the candies, "I could see like a cat, my grandmother wanted me around all the time because I could thread needles at night... but now I'm old..."

Eugenia nodded vaguely.

"None of my friends wear glasses," she said. Then turning back to Buonincontri, but speaking for Don Vincenzo's benefit as well: "Only me... I have nine diopters in one eye and ten in the other... I'm practically blind!" she stressed gently.

"See how lucky you are," Don Vincenzo to her, laughing; and to Rosaria: "How much salt?"

"Poor thing!" said Amodio's maid after Eugenia had gone, all contented. "It's the damp that ruined her. It nails us down in that house.

Now Donna Rosa has pains in her bones. Give me a kilo of coarse salt and a package of the fine type."

"You've got it."

"What a morning we have today, eh, Don Vincenzo? It seems like summer already."

Walking back more slowly than she had come, Eugenia began to unwrap one of the candies without thinking and stuck it in her mouth. It was lemon-flavored. "I'll tell Aunt Nunzia that I lost it on the street," she decided. She was happy, she didn't care if her nice aunt (who was so good to her) got angry.

What a great day! Maybe mama was returning now with the glasses all wrapped in a package. . . . Soon she would be wearing them, she would. . . . A fury of slaps pounded her head, a real avalanche. She felt as if she were crumbling; futilely, she raised her hands to defend herself. It was Aunt Nunzia—who else?—furious that she was late, and right behind her Pasqualino was throwing a tantrum because he didn't believe the line about the candies anymore. "I'm dying! Here, blind, ugly thing!. . . And I give you everything I have for this kind of gratitude! You'll end up a good-for-nothing, that's what you'll be! Eight thousand lire it cost me! These demons. . . they're killing me!. . . ."

She let her hands drop to her sides only to burst out into tears. "Suffering virgin, Jesus, for the wounds you suffered, let me die."

Now Eugenia was crying hard too.

"Oh, Aunt, forgive me. . . Aunt. . . "

"Uh. . . uh. . . uh. . . ," Pasqualino grunted, his mouth gaping.

"Poor thing," said Donna Mariuccia walking over to Eugenia, who was trying to hide her blotched, tear-stained face from her aunt's anger. "She didn't do it on purpose, Nunzia. . . , calm down." And to Eugenia: "What did you do with the candies?"

Eugenia answered softly, hopelessly, holding out the remaining candy in a dirty hand. "I ate one. I was hungry."

Before her aunt could attack the child again, the marchesa's voice called down softly, calmly, from the third floor, where the sun was shining.

"Nunziata!"

Aunt Nunzia lifted her embittered face which resembled the one at the end of her bed, the Madonna of the seven afflictions.

"Today is the first Friday of the month. Offer your prayers to God."

"Marchesa, you are so kind! These children make me commit so many little sins, I am losing my soul, I . . . ," and her head collapsed into her pawlike hands, the skin brown and scaly as a laborer's.

"Your brother isn't home?"

"Your poor aunt, she buys you a pair of glasses and this is how you thank her . . . ," Mariuccia said to Eugenia who was still trembling.

"Yes, signora, here I am," answered Don Peppino, emerging from behind the apartment door that had half-concealed him; he'd been fanning the fire under his lunch with a piece of cardboard.

"Can you come up now?"

"My wife went to get Eugenia's glasses. . . . I'm watching the beans . . . would you mind waiting?"

"Then send up the little girl. I have a dress for Nunziata. I want to give it to her."

"God will reward you. We're ever so grateful," answered Don Peppino with a sigh of relief, because this was the one thing that would calm his sister. But looking over at Nunziata, he realized that she was not cheered at all. She went on crying her heart out, and her lament had so stunned Pasqualino that the child had fallen into a silence of fascination, a small sweet smile on his face; he was licking the mucus that dripped from his nose.

"Did you hear? Go up to the marchesa's, she wants to give you a dress," Don Peppino said to his daughter.

Eugenia's eyes were fixed on something in the air, seeing nothing: opened wide, they focused and focused. She started and got up quickly, obediently.

"Tell her, 'God will reward you,' and stay outside the door."

"Yes, Papa."

"Believe me, Mariuccia," Aunt Nunziata said when Eugenia was out of earshot, "I adore that child, and afterwards I regret slapping her, God only knows. But believe me, when I have to struggle with kids the blood goes right to my head. I'm not young anymore, as you can see . . . ," and she touched her sunken cheeks. "Sometimes I feel like a mad woman. . . ."

"On the other hand, they also have to let off steam," answered Donna Mariuccia, "they're just innocent souls. They'll have plenty of time for tears. When I look at them and think they'll become like us . . ." She went to fetch a broom and pushed a cabbage leaf over the threshold, "I really wonder what God is up to."

"You're giving it away brand new!" said Eugenia, pressing her nose to the green dress, spread across the kitchen sofa while the marchesa went to look for an old newspaper to wrap it in.

Signora D'Avanzo was thinking that the child could not see at all if she didn't realize the dress was ancient and darned all over (it was her dead sister's), but she said nothing. Only when she returned with the newspaper did she finally ask after several seconds:

"And the glasses your aunt gave you? Are they new?"

"They have gold wires. And they cost eight thousand lire," Eugenia answered in a breath, moved again at the thought of the privilege that had touched her. "Because I'm nearly blind," she added bluntly.

"In my opinion," said the marchesa, wrapping the dress in the newspaper gently and then opening the package again because a sleeve was sticking out, "your aunt could've spent less. I've seen the best eyeglasses for only two thousand lire at a store on Ascenzione."

Eugenia blushed. She realized that the marchesa was displeased. "Each in his own range, we must all limit ourselves. . . ." She had heard her say so many times when Donna Rosa brought up the clean wash and lingered to lament the family's financial straits.

"Maybe they weren't any good. . . . I have nine diopters," Eugenia answered timidly.

The marchesa raised an eyebrow, but fortunately Eugenia didn't see.

"I'm telling you, they were good," Signora D'Avanzo insisted, her voice hardening slightly. Then regretting it, she said more gently, "My dear child, I'm saying this because I know your family's troubles. With that six thousand lire, you could buy bread for ten days, you could buy . . . why, why should you need to see well? With what is around you!. . . " There was a silence. "To read? Do you read?"

"No, Signora."

"But I've seen you with your nose in a book sometimes. So, you're a liar too, my child. . . . That's no good. . . . "

Eugenia did not answer this time. Feeling utterly hopeless, she fixed her nearly white eyes on the dress.

"Is it silk?" she asked stupidly.

The marchesa looked at her pensively.

"You don't deserve it, but I want to give you a little something," she said suddenly, and she walked toward an armoire of white wood. Just at that moment, the telephone, which was in the hall, began to ring, and instead of opening the armoire Signor D'Avanzo went to answer it. Eugenia was so discouraged by those words she had barely heard the old woman's consoling hint; and as soon as she was alone, she began looking – as best as she could – all around her. There were so many beautiful, fine things, just like the store on Via Roma! And there, right before her eyes, was an open balcony covered with vases of flowers.

She went out on the balcony. So much space, so much blue! The houses seemed to be covered by a blue veil, and the vicolo below looked like a well with so many ants coming and going. . . like her family. . . . What were they doing, where were they going? They came out and went back inside little holes, carrying large crumbs of bread: that's what they were doing, they had done it yesterday, they would do it again tomorrow, and forever. . . forever. So many holes, so many ants. And all around, nearly invisible in the great light, was the world as God had made it, with wind and sun, and further away, the great, clear sea. . . . She stood there thoughtfully, resting her chin on the grating, with an expression of pain, of dismay that made her ugly. The marchesa's voice called out, calm, pious. In her hand, her smooth ivory hand, she held a little book covered with black pasteboard and gold letters.

"These are the saints' reflections, dear girl. You people today don't read anything, and that's why the world is changing. Take it, it's my gift. But you must promise me that you'll read a little every night. Now that you've got glasses."

"Yes, Signora," Eugenia replied quickly as she took the book, blushing once again because the marchesa had found her on the balcony. The signora gazed at her, pleased.

"The Lord wanted to save you, my child!" she said, going to get the package with the dress and handing it to her. "You're not pretty, quite the contrary, you already look like an old woman. The Lord chose you above others, precisely so that you wouldn't get into trouble. He wants you to be saintly, like your sisters!"

Because Eugenia had been long prepared for a life lacking in joy, albeit unconsciously, she was not really wounded by these words, but she was disturbed nevertheless. And it seemed to her, if only for a moment, that the sun was less bright: even the thought of the glasses failed to cheer her. She stared vaguely, her eyes nearly dark, at the faded green of Posillipo that stretched into the sea like a lizard.

"Tell your papa," the marchesa went on, "that we won't be doing anything about the child's mattress today. My cousin called, and I have to be down at Posillipo all day."

"I was once there too," Eugenia began, coming alive again at the sound of that name and gazing out toward it with a look of enchantment.

"Oh, really?" Signora D'Avanzo was indifferent; to her the name meant nothing. Then, moving with all the majesty of her person, she walked to the front door with the child, who lingered, turning back to stare at that luminous point until the door closed gently behind her.

It was as she was stepping off the last step into the courtyard that the shadow which had momentarily darkened her forehead lifted, and her mouth opened in a cry of joy as she caught sight of her mother returning. Her familiar shabby figure was easily recognizable. She threw the dress down on a chair and ran toward her.

"Mama, my glasses!"

"Slow down, child. You'll knock me down!"

Immediately a small crowd gathered around them. Donna Mariuccia, Don Peppino, one of the Geborios who had stopped to rest on a chair before tackling the stairs, Amodio's maid who had just come in, and of course, Pasqualino and Teresella who were screeching to see too, their hands outstretched. Nunziata was observing the unwrapped dress with a crestfallen expression.

"See Mariuccia, this looks like pretty old stuff to me. . . . It's all worn out under the arms," she said approaching the group. But nobody paid her any attention. Donna Rosa was taking the wrapped case from the collar of her dress, opening it with the utmost care. Like a sort of radiant insect with two big, big eyes and two curved antennae, it lay shining in a blurred ray of sunlight, as Donna Rosa extended her long, red hand into the circle of those poor admiring people.

"Eight thousand lire for a thing like this," said Donna Rosa, gazing religiously but with a sort of remorse at the glasses.

Then silently she placed them on Eugenia's face; ecstatic, the child raised her hands to push the antennae carefully behind her ears. "Well, do you see us?" she asked, nearly moved to tears.

Arranging them with her hands, as if she were afraid someone would grab them away, her eyes half-closed and her mouth half-open in an enraptured smile, Eugenia took two steps backward, stumbling into a chair.

"Congratulations," said Greborio's maid.

"Congratulations," said Signora Greborio.

"She looks like a teacher, doesn't she?" said Don Peppino, delighted.

"Not as much as a thank you," said Aunt Nunziata, looking bitterly at the dress. "Even after all this: Congratulations."

"She's afraid, my dear," murmured Donna Rosa, walking towards the door of the apartment to put down her things. "This is the first time she's ever worn glasses," she said, looking up at the first floor balcony where the other Greborio sister stood gazing down.

"Everybody looks so little," Eugenia said in a strange voice that sounded as if it were coming from under a chair. "And very, very black."

"Of course, it's a double lens. But do you see well?" asked Don Peppino. "That's the important thing. She's wearing her glasses for the first time," he repeated, turning to Sir Amodio who was passing by with an opened newspaper in his hand.

"I warn you," said Amodio, after having stared at Eugenia for a moment as if she were a cat, "the stairs have not been swept. . . . I found fish bones in front of the door!" And he walked off, all but hid-

den behind the newspaper, bent over an article about the proposed
law for pensions that concerned him.

Eugenia walked to the front door to look out into the Vicolo della
Cupa, her hands still on the glasses. Her legs were shaking, her head
spinning, all the joy had gone out of her. She wanted to smile, but her
whitened lips were turned down in an idiotic grimace. Suddenly,
there were so many balconies—two thousand, one-hundred thousand; the vegetable carts rushed towards her, the voices filling the
air, the cries, the sound of the whip, all filled her head at once as if
she were sick. Staggering, she turned back towards the courtyard,
and the terrible impression grew: the courtyard she saw now, a slimy
funnel pointing up towards the sky, had leprous walls and decrepit
balconies. There were black arches over the ground floor apartments
and circles of bright bulbs around Our Lady of Sorrows; the pave-
ment was white with soapy water and cauliflower leaves, scraps of
paper, garbage; and in the middle of the courtyard, that group of tattered, deformed Christians, their faces pocked by poverty and resignation, turned their eyes toward her now, full of love. They began to
twist, to blur, to grow. Through the two bewitched circles of her
glasses, she saw them coming at her all at once. But it was Mariuccia
who realized that the little girl was not well and pulled off her
glasses. Whimpering, Eugenia had doubled over and vomited.

"They made her sick to her stomach!" yelled Mariuccia, feeling
her forehead. "Go get a coffee bean, Nunziata!"

"Eight thousand lire in hard cash!" Aunt Nunziata cried with fury
in her eyes, as she ran to the basement apartment to take a coffee
bean from a bottle on the credenza; and she raised the new glasses
into the air, as if to receive some explanation from God. "And now
they're not even right!"

"It's always like this the first time," Amodio's maid said to Donna
Rosa calmly. "You shouldn't be alarmed; she'll adjust to them with
time."

"It's nothing, child, nothing, don't be afraid," but Donna Rosa's
heart tightened at the thought of how unfortunate they were.

When Aunt Nunziata came back with the coffee, she was still
screaming, "Eight thousand in hard cash!" while Eugenia, who had
turned white as a ghost, gagged uselessly, for there was nothing left

inside her. Her bulging eyes were nearly crossed from the strain, and her tear-stained, ancient face appeared stunned. She leaned against her mother and shook.

"Mama, where are we?"

"We're in the courtyard, that's where, child," Donna Rosa said patiently, and the flickering smile of pity and awe that shone in her eyes suddenly brightened the faces of all those wretched people.

"She's half-blind!"

"She's half-stupid is what she is!"

"Let her be, poor thing, she's just shocked," said Donna Mariuccia, her face grim with compassion as she walked back into her own apartment which looked darker than ever.

Only Aunt Nunziata was still wringing her hands:

"Eight thousand lire!"

G O F F R E D O   P A R I S E

Woman

GOFFREDO PARISE (1929–) In his early work Parise is primarily a critic of the middle class, a satirist of narrow-mindedness and conformity. *Il prete bello*, from this period, was a best seller in Italy and was translated under the title *Don Gastone and the Ladies*. The critic Giacinto Spagnoletti called Parise "a fiction writer capable of profound emotional repercussions, intent upon knowing and defining the world he lives in. . . . " In his recent *Sillabario I* and *II*, written over a ten-year period, Parise has become a writer of what he called "poems in prose," short, crystalline pieces which succeed in portraying the texture of human transactions or of the decisive moments in a life that come to seem inevitable. *Sillabario II* was published in English under the title *Solitudes*. Goffredo Parise won Italy's two most prestigious awards, the Premio Strega and the Viareggio. "Caress" and "Woman" are from *Sillabario I*, 1972.

One day a woman skiing swiftly and playfully in a great valley between the Tofane peaks in Cortina noticed a man who was standing utterly still and alone in the midst of that white space without wind or shadow; he had black eyes and wore a black ski mask called a mephisto. An instant passed and then she went back to leaping down through the freshly fallen snow, but everything was not as it had been before and she felt strange.

At the bottom of the valley, she took off her skis, put them in a red jeep (she was wearing red, too, and had short, curly red hair) and drove home. As soon as she arrived, she heard the children squealing and the telephone ringing: thinking it might be the man in the mephisto, she shuddered slightly, but when she picked up the telephone, it wasn't he but a friend. She said so many things to her so quickly that she was stammering and didn't really know what she was saying. At the dinner table, she babbled to her husband and hugged him twice without knowing why, she kept getting up to talk to the governess and then to the children who she took into her arms one at a time and kissed and then sat back down.

Several days passed, the weather darkened. It grew cold again, and on a morning of a dense but delicate snow – a strange thing for that month – the woman, dressed in a white fur jacket and white lambswool cap, was passing under the bell tower holding her children by the hand when she saw the man again: instead of the mephisto, he had an old leather flyer's cap on his head. He was with a blond curly-haired man in a military vest and a very beautiful woman: the three of them were laughing, and the woman could see from their white teeth that they were happy together and she felt a twinge of pain and envy. At that very instant, the man saw her too, stopped laughing and looked at her so intensely and enigmatically that she couldn't take her eyes off him and finally had to turn away.

The sun returned and a warm spring wind began to melt the snow. The woman continued to go skiing, now and then she thought about seeing the man with the mephisto again, but whenever she thought she saw him, it wasn't he. Then at a dinner party with a lot of people, she actually did see him and was introduced, though she didn't catch his name, but later she found herself seated next to him.

"You ski very well," said the man giving her that enigmatic look (his eyes were very black and their whites were very white), "like a boy."

In an uncertain voice, the woman said: "That's not a compliment."

"Oh yes it is," said the man. "Your mannerisms, your skin, even your voice, are like a boy's."

"Why, what kind of voice do I have?" She felt timid; perhaps she should be offended?

"A slightly hoarse voice."

"Do you like it?"

The man looked at her, then said: "Very, very much," and vanished without saying goodbye.

From that moment on, the woman felt like a boy and began talking without interruption, interrupting everybody like children do. Her cheeks were always red, her heart pounded and she gestured with her hands. That night the woman, who always slept profoundly and tranquilly, thought about the man's strange words again, then she thought about him and tried to picture his face before her in the darkness: he had very black, arched eyebrows and a hard mouth with almost no lips, yet there was something extremely fragile about him, about his way of moving, like a person who is sad or sick.

The next morning the woman telephoned him and said quickly: "I want to say two things: first, will you come skiing with me, and second, you're invited for dinner at my house tonight. Can you come?"

"Sure, little boy," the man said, and they met; she loaded her skis, poles, and boots in his car and they headed out. The telephone call had filled the woman with anticipation, and she slid down into the seat, stealing sideways looks at the man when he wasn't looking, but twice he caught her looking and smiled; the woman, intuiting that her curiosity was quite apparent, said: "You know, I was very curious to meet you."

The man looked at her silently for a long time, he looked at her forehead, her eyes, her mouth, her cheeks and then said: "I was even more curious. I've been watching you for a month."

The woman blushed and said nothing. Finally she said: "Why is that?"

"Because you're like life."

Many things blurred in the woman's mind and heart but among all those things she recognized fear.

They stopped near the ski lift, but neither made a move.

"What do you want to do?" said the man. "Do you want to ski?"

The woman didn't have the slightest desire to ski, she only wanted to ask the man a lot of questions, to find out as much as she could about him, but she said: "Whatever you want, you choose."

The man hesitated for a long time, making little grunts of indecision, smiled, and was silent again while he gazed up at the great slope in the sun, then said: "Forget skiing, let's go for lunch somewhere. But you decide where."

Feeling happy, the woman said: "I usually know where I want to go, but today I don't. I don't even want to think about it. I'd rather you decide."

The man suggested several places half-heartedly and the woman was glad because she'd already decided where to go. She said: "Let's go to the Casetta Rossa. Do you know it?"

"I don't, but let's go there," the man said. The woman thought that he had known her choice all along and added quickly: "But if you'd prefer somewhere else. . ." But the man interrupted her, laughing, and said: "No, little boy, we'll go to the Casetta Rossa," and ruffled her hair.

"Why are you calling me little boy? Would you stop calling me little boy?" said the woman. The man laughed and repeated in a calm, happy voice: "Little boy, the little red-haired boy never sits still, and he's shy, too."

The woman had an urge to play the game, to contradict, to argue.

"I've never been shy in my life, I'm thirty-five years old and I have two children. And a husband."

The man laughed: "No, you are thirteen years old, you're terribly shy, and you have no kids and no husband."

"Are you always this sure of everything?"

"No, but now I am."

They ate at the Casetta Rossa which was sunken amidst the snow with its crystals and glare. She felt shy, just as the man had said, and therefore a great hunger came over her and she ate a huge plate of spaghetti, a big veal steak with polenta and drank a great deal of wine and two glasses of grappa. On the way home she sang and when the man stroked her face with the back of his hand, she grabbed it and rubbed his knuckles hard against her cheek.

The woman got home, slept a bit, gave instructions for dinner and slipped into the bathtub where she sang and talked to herself. Her husband heard her and said: "What's wrong with you, are you nuts?" and the woman answered: "No, sweetheart, I'm not nuts."

She got out of the bath and went to the closet. Perhaps she should wear a long dress: but when she tried it on, she felt ridiculous—like a married woman with two children, and ridiculous. She tried on a miniskirt and saw that her legs were pretty but not gorgeous and in any case, they were not a tall woman's legs. Not like the woman she'd seen laughing in Mephisto's company. She thought Mephisto was a nice name and she laughed to herself thinking that she would tell him. Then she put on black crepe pajamas and found herself even more ridiculous than before. Then a pair of tweed pants with a soft red satin blouse and black patent leather shoes. Nothing, nothing, and nothing. When a pair of plaid pants caught the corner of her eye, she suddenly saw (as if he were telling her) what "bad taste" was, and she blushed. She tried on a deerskin skirt and a shirt with little white and light blue checks. That wasn't bad, but it wasn't good either, and feeling exhausted, she threw herself down on the bed, naked and distressed.

She heard her husband spraying himself with perfume: the sound of the spray, the perfume, and the fact that her husband used perfume, all displeased her. Even the idea of having a husband and two children displeased her, but most of all the husband she had displeased her. (Asking her if she was "nuts" – what a fool!) At that moment, something told her to put on the satin shirt and a pair of pigskin pants, which she did. Then she looked at herself from all angles in the mirror (pressing her lips together twice) and realized that she really did look rather boyish. And with that thought, two very fat tears fell onto the blouse with little light blue checks.

Caress

One winter evening in 1937 in a cold and poorly lit Italian city of numerous porticos and barricaded churches, a tall man with a long overcoat and a wide-brimmed fur hat which gave him a sinister shadow, climbed the stairs of a damp house, advanced through the darkness to a door and rang the bell, which let out an uncertain trill.

A youngish woman lived in the apartment with her seven-year-old son and two elderly relatives whom the child called grandparents. The woman usually answered the door ready to go out, as the visitor expressly wished, (the man always appeared at eight on the dot), or on occasion they went into a small drawing room furnished in wicker and sat there talking.

The boy had only seen the man twice before and each time the man had given him ten lire for his bank; he could remember nothing about him except that every night his presence "in the other room" had kept him in suspense. "That's him," one of the two relatives would say; then doors would close, and time would pass as if the two old people and the child were waiting for something. Often during these suspended hours, the old people talked about the visitor (they always called him "he," thinking the boy wouldn't understand) in tones of near veneration. And usually, the old woman speculated on what sort of behavior the family should show him: whether they should greet him or not, whether they should go in and ask him a question. With time, the figure of the invisible visitor who took his mother out or stayed with her behind closed doors in the quiet house, and the two whispering relatives, entered the child's nightly thoughts, and began to frighten him.

One night the man went to the small wicker sitting room, but when the two old people followed him in, the child knew that his life would change. He knew it because he saw his "grandpa" through the glass doors of the kitchen crying and caressing the man's hand and his "grandma" standing on tiptoe to embrace him with excessive emotion. Then he, too, was called into the sitting room (they had been dressing and tidying his hair up to the very last moment) and as he walked out between the high, narrow walls of the dining room, he felt like an apparition of himself that would be out of place from then on.

The boy neither said a word nor took a step forward; his relatives urged him to "say hello to the gentleman," and he said "Good evening" and even smiled. The visitor answered in kind, calling him by name, but the boy, being too young and inexperienced to see into his soul, saw only shiny black hair on a very long head.

There was a pause: the lights in all the lamps flickered, and everyone except the child raised their eyes when the "grandma" said: "The lights went out yesterday too."

She opened the glass doors of the cupboard (a faint glare flashed before the boy's eyes and vanished in a corner of the ceiling), took out a bottle, and poured a dark liquor into four glasses that the boy only then noticed had already been arranged on a doily on the table. The woman passed out the glasses and everyone sipped the liquor silently. Then the "grandma" said to the boy in a seemingly severe tone of voice: "Thank the gentleman; do you know what he's doing for you?"

The boy didn't speak, didn't move, but stood awkwardly at attention with his hands spread against his velvet shorts.

"Don't say that," the man interrupted, "I don't want to be thanked by anyone. . . ." And just then the boy's mother began to cry silently.

"See, you've made her cry," the "grandpa" said, turning to his wife and shaking his head in disappointment.

"But being thankful . . . ," his wife began, stopped short by the visitor's glance. Then there was another long pause: the man patted the woman's hand several times as she was still crying, and from one of the numerous landings in the house, a wheezing male voice called out "Tilde...," two or three times, and at the nearby convent of Canossian nuns, the bells began to ring.

The adults started to speak again of renting a new house with a garden that had a fig tree, where the visitor, the woman, and the child would go to live, and of a trip ("Venice will do, Venice will do fine," said the old "grandpa") whereupon the old woman poured another glass of *nocino* which the man took with a little laugh.

The boy was still standing at attention. His mother approached him, took him by the hand and leading him towards the visitor, said:

"Don't you have anything to say to him?"

The boy wondered what he should say, and then remembering the two previous encounters and the ten lire, he said, though with great shame: "The ten lire."

The old relatives looked confused but his mother blushed and said: "He remembers the ten lire that you gave him for his bank last year," and she smiled. But the man did not smile; from the top of his long shiny head, he looked the child straight in the eyes, stood up, took a ten lire piece from his pocket and handed it to the boy, who had extended his hand. The child then went out, turned on the light in a room with two very old walnut beds, and standing on tiptoe to reach the marble top of the dresser, managed to grab the metal bank and a small yellow plush dog. He glanced at the dog, dropped the coin into the bank (which he put to his ear and shook) and went back to the drawing room.

"He went to put it in his bank," remarked the "grandma," but the visitor was already standing, his big fur hat in his hand, to go out with the young woman. He said goodnight to everyone and then stopped beside the boy and said: "Remember little fellow, you'll never have to ask for anything."

The boy, full of fear, took a small step backwards and stood at attention once again; then the man stepped forward, leaned over him, and caressed his cheek with a shiny grayish hand: "From now on, call me 'Uncle,'" he said.

Publisher's Reader

GIUSEPPE PONTIGGIA (1934–) Modern architecture, the impersonal space where business is transacted in advanced industrial societies, is usually the backdrop for this Milanese writer's fiction. Within this space the individual performs a function, plays a role – and in doing so, loses some essential sense of himself. So, as the protagonist in "Publisher's Reader" reads through manuscripts, searching for a "publishable" work, he seems to lose his literary instincts and commits an ironic oversight. What this oversight means is left an open question, a question that goes to the heart of what literature is, and whether it can be translated. Pontiggia's approach to his material is that of understated satire. "Publisher's Reader" is from *La morte in banca*, 1979.

On a dark November morning, a man came out of a building and headed for the subway station. He was wearing a grey coat and a hat with a broad brim. He had on dark glasses and was holding a small black briefcase in his right hand.

The man emerged again in a piazza surrounded by skyscrapers and a low church. He turned down an avenue whose perspective dissolved to a grey fog. He walked down the sidewalk, jammed with the shiny hoods of cars, and finally stepped into the doorway of a building.

The inside of the elevator lit up as soon as he set foot in it. The door opened on the fifth floor. The word "forward" was written above a gold plate. The man took several steps into a silent waiting room.

"The editor is waiting for you in his office," a secretary said to him, appearing in a doorway.

"Here are the manuscripts you'll be reading," the editor said.

They were carefully piled one on the other. "They're novels by new writers," he continued. "Just give them a look. Only take them home if they interest you."

He walked into a room of books: books on the table, on the shelves, books piled in dirty rows along the walls, books on the radiator and in a corner of the room, books spread out on the window sill.

Sitting down, he spread the pen, eraser and notebook of shiny white paper before him. He laid the manuscripts on the table. Then he pulled the first manuscript out of a red folder. He began to read, adjusting the loose sheets.

A pier on a lake, a man and a woman in a room, description of the objects, their lovemaking, panoramic description of the hotel as seen from above, as if in an aerial photograph, a tiny hotel on an immense lake; returning to the room *she suddenly lowers her eyes and says to him*, some more images, the lake glinting and still, then him leaving the small hotel to go to town on foot on the straight road.

He didn't read the remaining chapters through. The action always took place in the hotel. The relationship between the two became a relationship of three towards the middle until a new couple was formed at the end. The chapters had a geometric shape to them, and some of the dialogues, which were always connected to the same images (the magnolia that grazed the window, the lake's horizon), were identical.

He wrote:

"The error, as usual, is in the end. Here the ending relies on narrative to try to make an erotic device believable, and vice versa."

He erased "end" and substituted the word "premise." He looked at the window, re-read the sentence and erased it.

He wrote:

"The story is not interesting: it's the usual triangle." But that wasn't true: the story was interesting. What stories are interesting if not the usual ones?

He began to write:

"Static effects, something between a Dreyer film and Robbe-Grillet's catalogue of objects."

Men with two phalluses appeared in her dreams, and each time she hesitated before choosing. The psychoanalyst explained that the number was a compensation for her husband's indifference and that her hesitation suggested pleasure but also remorse about the way she was compensating. It was obvious nevertheless that this mental compensation was not enough, and in fact on page 83 she walked out onto a tree-lined avenue with a fellow worker and the betrayal was consummated on page 105.

Now she dreamed of being followed by a wolf and the psychoanalyst explained that it was a compensation for guilt. These dialogues, inserted abruptly into various scenes – a train trip, lovemaking in the woods, a dinner under a pergola in summer – interrupted the action.

The author narrated in the first person. The book had no conclusion, but perhaps the conclusion was the book itself. It had an unassuming confessional tone.

It was entitled *Personnel Office,* and the plot was this: each chapter was named for the employee who was its subject and began with his curriculum vitae (place and date of birth, civil status, residence, qualifications). This was followed by a narrative section in which the author's voice weaved a counterpoint to the bureaucratic one: "The employee as object," it had said in the preface, "thus becomes a man again,"

"Indifferent personality who lacks interests," for example, was a young man with literary ambitions who often vanished into the bathroom with a book of poetry in his pocket. Meanwhile the shadowy private life of an inspector was illuminated by the streetlights on an outlying avenue in a homosexual district.

But the tone hit the falsetto range too often. The author, who was most likely describing his co-workers, had invented grotesque names for them.

He wrote:

"Sometimes the curricula, edited from the corporate point of view, are preferable."

A rather unusual touch: the trattoria menu was transcribed with the prices. The tormented protagonist who was low on money, reflected for a long time, evaluating the taste, caloric value and cost before choosing: it was a shame that the fried shrimp was expensive and the lasagna within reach but not enough to eat, a small green parallelepiped. He entered places wafting with smoke and odors and slinked out after having left the waiter a minimal tip. He walked down half-lit passages, climbed grimy stairways, the dawn filtered into furnished rooms, his eldest colleague was sarcastic and he was hard put to respond to his comments. The author had not even omitted his first prostitute, approached in an alleyway on a rainy night, and the uncertain pleasure which seemed consummated by a third party. This was told well, precisely, but it was a repetition of the same old story, as if to say winter follows autumn.

The author smiled at himself too often and asked the reader's complicity. Thus it became difficult to give it. It was a flat, unending narration which could have gone on ad infinitum.

Dear Publishing House:

In sending this first novel to you, I would like to make two points, which I believe are essential, to the committee of readers. First: let there be no mistake about the first-person narration (it's not me). Second: Proust. I would be grateful if this name goes unmentioned in my regard. Even if it's the first to come to mind, I'm convinced it's all wrong.

"How far has our reader gotten?" said the editor from the doorway. "Shall we go for a cup of coffee?"

They stepped out in the sooty air filled with impalpable rain.

"You end up losing a sense of proportion," said the reader. "You get accustomed to shoddy work."

"Oh, dear," said the editor.

"But don't worry, one doesn't become too easy. If anything, the opposite happens."

He added: "The mistakes discourage you, and you end up looking for them so you can finish sooner."

They entered a small bar and stood by the counter.

"Nevertheless," said the reader, "you can learn from mistakes too. They contain a misunderstood truth, and that in itself is interesting."

"What do you think the most serious error is?" asked the editor.

"Perhaps writing a bad ending."

The editor shook his head. "The outcome depends completely upon the means at one's disposal."

"But the ending is also a means of writing successfully, don't you think?" Looking towards the door, he added, "The problem isn't only what one finds, but also what one is looking for."

He went back into the room.

He sat down at the table and opened another manuscript.

He began reading again.

What do you say to a classroom of people watching you? This was interesting. Like the fact that the professor, at the beginning, was looking elsewhere. What he saw in front of him was a wall he had to scale and his first words were sounds.

Only after several minutes did the words acquire meanings: at that point, the students looked at him and he at them.

His questions also became an important theme: asking about the divinities of the ancient world or the meaning of a funerary inscription and giving grades for this.

The author did not play games or allude to things.

However, this part ended quickly. The rest turned into a parody aimed at a sole target: the "Vittorio da Feltre" school on Via Farneti.

There were several specific mistakes, for example, the misuse of capital letters. The office manager became The Manager, and the protagonist's son, The Son. They lived in a world of roles and there was no hope of escape.

He wrote:

"Reality never becomes symbolic here while the symbols become the only reality."

He erased the first sentence and the "while." Why on earth should reality always become a symbol?

He left the words: "The symbols become the only reality."

The Skyscraper, the Client, the Interpreter.

He wrote:

"Life is sacrificed to abstraction."

But sometimes life took revenge. Like when the Sun and the Moon appeared with capital letters and geography textbooks turned up inexplicably on city streets.

"Five years of war seen through a soldier's eyes."

But the word "soldier" was already a mistake, and so he wrote the word "man" above it, then erased this too: the narrator was merely a young man who had tried to survive the war. And what had he seen? The train of recruits leaving the town on a July afternoon without clouds; the courtyard sloping down from the barracks, the fog which wafted into the room through a cracked window pane, at night, then the unexpected light and the face of the lieutenant who punished him. At the front, he had only learned this: one shot meant the end of the world for him, but the world would go on without him.

Like all reminiscences of war, his rarely erred because he didn't have time to notice anything false. Reading, "Today, the 2nd of July, I leave for the front," one had no doubt that he was indeed leaving. But one pictured a photograph yellowing at the margins, a daguerreotype.

A man walking in a train station, entering a vaporous Turkish bath, then newspaper headlines were followed by rallies, stock quotations, sequences from psychedelic films, protest marches. Demands for ransom were followed by intimations of kidnapping, long distance business phone calls, sunsets, trees lining a river, dinner with the other woman in the frame of the semi-oval window.

"I've tried to give our times a face," the author had written, "which explains the title—*Alienation*."

But the narrator's problem was more complicated: how to reject his wife without anxiety or to get rid of her without risk. The wife was superimposed over the Mideast, world hunger, the revolution.

"An imagined crime," the reader wrote "postponed by a literary undertaking."

The last manuscript had no title and was more voluminous than the others. He could open up to any page and have a look.

A suffocating heat lay over the street. The crowds, the sight of falling plaster, bricks, scaffolding . . . the unbearable stench from the taverns, which were numerous in that part of the city, and the drunks one came across at every turn, though it was a workday, somehow gave the scene a revolting aspect.

But immediately after:

Hero . . . chestnut hair and dark eyes.

He leafed through the manuscript quickly. Lapses of an expressionistic nature (*Crucify me, Judge, but when you crucify me, take pity!*) alternated with effective moments of tension. (*His heart was pounding violently. But the stairs were completely deserted.*)

Although the Slavic setting was disturbing, it was difficult to shake off certain images – intense, visionary images of the city: the twilight, the crowds, the streets. The dreams were told with such precision they seemed taken from Freud.

"And now his dream: he takes the street, with his father, that leads to the cemetery; both of them pass before the cemetery."

He stood and went to the window. He looked out the panes at the milky fog, then returned to the table and sat down.

He opened again to page 30.

I sought sadness, sadness and tears, at the bottom of this glass, and I found them there, I savored them.

He closed the manuscript again.

"Nothing then?" the editor asked, raising his eyes.

"No," answered the reader, sitting down.

He added: "Only the last one gave me some second thoughts."

"In what sense?"

The reader hesitated.

"It has a certain atmosphere," he said, "and there are some striking passages."

"But do you think we should publish it?"

"No," answered the reader, looking at him. "It's not convincing. There are too many errors, too much melodrama. But he's a writer worth keeping an eye on in the future."

"Can I see it?"

The reader handed him the manuscript and the editor glanced at it with a look of surprise.

"But you weren't supposed to consider this," he said, "how on earth did it end up with the others?"

The reader raised his arms.

"Don't tell me you didn't realize this is a translation?"

"No," the reader replied, staring at him. "I didn't catch it."

He added "I'm very tired this morning."

He asked: "A translation of what?"

The editor was staring at him incredulously.

"Why, it's *Crime and Punishment*," he said.

V A S C O   P R A T O L I N I

Vanda

VASCO PRATOLINI (1913–) A native of Florence, which is often the setting for his fiction, Pratolini most often portrays the struggle of working-class lives through a lyrical realism and a remarkable expression of empathy. His involvement in the resistance was reflected in both *Il quartiere* and *Cronache di poveri amanti*. However, it was *Metello*, the first in the trilogy *Una storia d'Italia*, which spurred a debate among critics, some claiming that it marked the crisis of neorealism and others a movement into realism. He is also known for his portraits of women, as in the story presented here, "Vanda." In 1957 he won the Premio Feltrenelli for his whole body of work. "Vanda" is from *Diario sentimentale*, 1956.

Vanda had black eyes with a point of gold within; her hair was blond. I never managed to tell her I loved her. I didn't even know her name was Vanda. It was she who finally stopped one morning in the middle of the bridge; she waited until I had the courage to take two more steps toward her. "This is obsessive," she exclaimed. "You've been trailing behind me like a shadow for a month. Say what you have to say and then let's forget it."

"What?" I said, "What are you talking about?" Just then a woman holding a little girl by the hand and forcing her to repeat some lesson passed by; still half-asleep, the child was babbling conjugations of the verb to be: "*Sii, siate, siano.*" The two of us burst out laughing; it was a way to break the ice. Vanda placed a hand on the parapet and leaned over, and I did the same. I looked down at the river. It was green and the water was so high it nearly reached the large windows of the silversmiths' workshops. I pointed towards the middle of the river: "Look at that man in a kayak." It seemed the most important thing I had to say to her.

"Obviously he has nothing better to do," she said. "I'm jealous." At the end of the bridge, the statues of the four seasons turned their backs.

We were eighteen years old; I was an apprentice at a newspaper; she was a salesgirl at a fashionable shop where she earned seven lire a day. She lived with her father and her grandmother, and her father was a marshall who collected unpaid bills. We met on the bridge, every day for a year. Her house was on the other side of the river, on the Spring and Summer side. We had coffee at the bar; they had brioches fresh out of the oven, and we would buy one and split it; she dunked her half and nibbled at it, sucking the coffee out before biting into it; she scolded me for finishing my half all at once. I would walk her to the store; I lingered there a bit while she found some excuse to re-organize the window display so she could wave goodbye again. We would walk across the bridge at noon and then again in the evening. The days were reflected in the river as it flowed below us: yellow and turbid when the water was high, in January; it carried tree trunks and the overturned carcasses of boars, having flooded the countryside; the silversmiths would appear at the windows to check the water gauges. Then in the longer days of sun, islands emerged from the gravel, the weir dried out and naked children played there all day long. Right under the bridge the water quickened slightly and ran so clear that you could see to the bottom. But in spring the water was green; whenever we stopped there in the evenings, Vanda would sing, her elbows resting on the parapet, her face framed by her hands as she stared at the river, singing. "Love," I said to her, caressing her, but she never seemed to hear. "You like the river better than me," I said. Then summer came, people sat along the parapets, bands of mandolin players strolled up and down, the watermelon stand appeared in its spot just beyond the bridge.

It was 1938; the Spanish communists had lost Brunete, a husband had murdered his wife, the government had passed the race law, but these were all distant facts for us, mere newspaper headlines. What mattered to us were those hours on the bridge, our walks down the boulevards and her father's refusal to meet me.

"I'll convince him, you'll see," Vanda said. "Anyway, he has nothing against you, he just thinks we're too young." She grew more womanly every day, and taller. And as time passed and we learned to kiss, things changed. She became restless and began asking questions, even about the most insignificant things, anxiously, as if she lived in a continuous nightmare which would come back to her from time to time and overwhelm her. "This is obsessive," she would say then as she had that first day. "Why are the lights going on so late? Why did you have your hair cut today? Why has the moon been full for so many nights?"

I dreamed of our home, and of us married, and of a radio with headphones and a tuner, shiny as a toy. That June I gave her an amaranthine handkerchief; in the cool evenings, she would wear it around her neck on a white suit. "I didn't want to fall in love. I ran over to you that first night so that you would leave me alone."

"I know," I would answer foolishly and laugh. Then I would ask: "And when you are going to tell me the secret? Don't you know that you can't scare me anymore, I love you too much for that," I asked her.

"Not yet." She looked at me gravely, and all I could do was kiss her.

She seemed paler, more and more distracted, uneasy. "Your responsibilities at home tire you out too much," I told her more than once.

"Do you really love me a lot?" she would ask, caressing me. Then one night she said: "But if you really love me so much why don't you try to see who I really am? I'm going to wait until you do to tell you the secret."

"I know everything about you, you're like the air I breathe. I can read you like an open book," I told her.

"Oh, you fool," she said, with a tone of affection and discomfort in her voice that I couldn't get out of my mind. We were leaning on the parapet; it was windy and the park was deep in fog; the parallel lines of lamps vanished in it. The river was a moving black mass that emerged from beneath the arches; you could hear it breaking continually against the pillars. Vanda said: "It's obsessive. You keep saying, 'I know, I know, I know.' But you don't. You don't know anything. Why am I blond? I shouldn't be. Do you know that?"

"You're blond because you are," I said.

"I shouldn't be blond. It's obsessive. And I love you too. Why do I love you? You must know why, so let's hear it. Why? I don't know. I only know that I love you and that I can't figure out why." There was a strange calm about her; the sense of her words were disordered, but not her voice; her voice was actually full of tenderness, the tenderness of someone who has been wronged and wants to forgive. "Sure, you know everything," she repeated. "You also know that the river ends up in the sea. But you can't know that I've never seen the sea. You see, I'm twenty years old and I've never seen the sea, I've never even been on a train. Did you know that?"

"You dope," I said, "was that the secret?"

She had her elbows on the parapet and she leaned her head into her hands: "Oh, now you think that's the secret? It's obsessive."

I put my arms around her and turned her face toward me: then I realized that she was crying. I put my finger on a tear and wet her lips with it. "Listen," I told her, "the sea is salty like this." I kissed her cheek. "On Sunday we'll go to the sea. We'll even take the train. We'll go early enough to come back the same night. We'll find an excuse for your father."

"We don't have to," she answered slowly, looking out into the river. "My father's gone away for a while."

"Did he go to visit relatives?"

"Yes," she said.

As I was walking her home, she turned back toward the statues of the seasons on the bridge, then said: "What is spring doing here at this time of year? Can you tell me that? She punched my chest affectionately before she put her mouth to mine; but her eyes were wet with tears again. I dried them with the handkerchief.

That night my mother came into my room, waking me. "I just came to see whether you closed the window," she said. "Do you hear that storm?" It was a downpour and the rain, blown by the wind, beat in gusts against the glass. "Tomorrow the river will be high," my mother said as she left. The next morning the sun was shining on the bridge; and that new air that comes after a storm swept through the streets and across the facades of the houses.

The river had risen to the silversmiths' workshops, their large windows closed with iron shutters. I waited for Vanda and she didn't come; I wandered through the market without finding her; then I thought that she might have caught cold in the chill of the previous evening. I decided to go up to her house. When I knocked, a thin woman who was getting on in years answered the door; she wore glasses on a pince-nez and a faded, light blue housecoat. She was drying a food container with a towel. "Vanda's not home," she said discourteously in an irritated tone. "She must have gone out very early. A nurse has already been here twice looking for her, but she's nowhere to be seen."

"A nurse? Why?" I asked.

"Her father had a more violent episode . . . this time it seems . . ."

I was still standing in the doorway, and I was so bewildered that I only managed to say, "Why, is her father sick?"

The woman laid down the container and the towel on a nearby table and rearranged her housecoat. "You're not from the police, are you?" she asked.

"No," I said, "I'm a friend."

"Oh, please forgive me. Yes, they come nearly every day. You see, Vanda's father had a breakdown three months ago, after they fired him from his job because he's Jewish. It was the desperation that got him."

"And what about Vanda?" I asked.

"I have no idea where she could've gone," answered the woman. "Maybe she's gone to look for a loan. You know, we do our best to help out since she lost her job too, but we're not exactly swimming in money ourselves. . . ."

Then two days later, way down near the mouth of the river, the water gave back Vanda's body.

FRANCESCA SANVITALE

Jolly and Poker

FRANCESCA SANVITALE (1928–) Since her debut in 1972 with the novel *Il cuore borghese*, Sanvitale has established herself as a writer of ideas, a writer who reflects the myriad influences and tendencies of Italian literature and culture of the 1960s and 1970s. Enzo Siciliano wrote that in Sanvitale's work, "The narrator is compromised in what is expressed; and that compromise is manifested explicitly: if the novel is a fiction, the need that induces one to write the novel is not a fiction." Sanvitale is particularly effective in rendering psychic states – of anxiety, of disillusionment, and of hopelessness. Her characters and plots seem almost secondary, as if they were mere vehicles for the expression of feeling. However, in *La realtà é un dono*, Sanvitale's first collection of stories, she seems to take a slightly different stance towards her characters and their states of being, that of a muted irony. "Jolly and Poker" is from *La realtà é un dono*, 1987.

He opened his eyes to distract himself and stared at the sun shining on the waves; but once again his own voice repeated, accusingly, insistently, that he would never ever get used to being alone.

He knew the man who inhabited his mind and used his voice to speak; a just, implacable type who pointed a finger, coldly condemning him for his vile weaknesses, and sometimes for some secret crime. This had happened on other occasions, even when he was a schoolboy. But today the voice derided him to prove that it was he himself who had yearned all his life for the very thing he couldn't bear: he had pursued and found his own ruin.

"Get out, get out!" he'd tell the persecuting ghost whenever he left friends, or work, or when closing the door behind him, he found himself in the safety of his own house. Since he'd left his wife five years ago, he had gotten into the habit of repeating these words for solace.

Now he stared out at the bay of Mazzaro and saw nothing special; one reef right in the middle, another farther out. The wind rocked the motorboats at anchor, and the waves curled white on the middle reef. Behind his shoulders extended a perfumed, tropical garden.

He wasn't stupid enough to really think that the promontory of Mazzaro, the bay of Isola Bella and Taormina, with its hibiscus and oleander, was nothing special, but the nothingness of his anxiety seemed to turn everything white, dissolve it and enclose it in a transparent bag.

Mary, the English girl he'd met, was sitting within the circle of space in front of him. He moved to one side, trying to indicate her lack of consideration. Unsuccessfully, because the woman's very character prevented her from acknowledging the negative feelings that she inspired. He found her casual manner offensive.

No sooner did he make these observations than a strange thing happened; he saw Jolly three-dimensional and alive, superimposed on the water. He opened his eyes wide: it really was Jolly, his dog, his adored puppy, his anxious love. He turned his gaze back to the beach and another Jolly, belly to the ground and tongue hanging, in the distance, in search of an invisible prey.

His attention was drawn back to the waves but a third Jolly, panting and gasping, sat directly between him and the sea.

There is no logical explanation for the advent of memories; yet when it struck him that our lives are spent treading above an unknown abyss, that we are forever looking over the edge of a volcano, he felt frightened.

Then realizing that two tears were running down his cheeks, he felt even more frightened. And to think that he had once pursed his lips in disdain at his wife who knelt beside a dying dog that trembled even as its paws had gone rigid; sobbing, she'd murmured "poor dog, poor dog" in a monotonous and desperate tone. Yes, he had felt great scorn for that disproportionate pain of hers. "What about me?" he had shouted silently, "What about me? Do I matter less than a dog?"

He hated these servile animals who lacked reason. He didn't want one underfoot. He had never changed his opinion. But then one day, thanks to a dog, his life changed.

On a work trip he'd visited his old friend Antonio and had begun watching a dog and her two puppies. Mechanically, without thinking, he had taken one onto his lap.

The puppy raised its brown and white spotted snout and stared at him: damp pupils, full of innocent questions, had wrenched his heart and put him under a spell of sorts, and he had remained motionless in that position, eyes fixed on those other trembling eyes.

Then the eyes disappeared between folds of skin and burrowing into his lap, the puppy fell asleep. He wrapped his arms around the body that quivered as it breathed, and they sat still like that, now dog and owner.

He named him Jolly because he had come to him, through circumstances unexpected, fatal and revolutionary, beyond all calculation.

He returned to Rome from Bologna. The long trip was quiet and strange. Inside, something appeased his heart and filled the time. He had driven slowly, but Jolly was frightened; he hid his snout between his paws and whined. Then Jolly vomited and took care of his needs several times. Without losing patience, he had pulled in at every road stop to clean the seat, attached the leash to the collar and slowly, slowly walked Jolly around, talked to him, encouraged him, told him that soon he would have a comfortable basket and so on. Jolly, standing perfectly still on his soft paws, turned his snout upwards, begging with his gaze and his whole miniature body to be defended and loved.

At six months, Jolly could leap up and lick a visitor's nose to express contentment and hospitality. He yelped furiously and ran so enthusiastically that he seemed to be laughing.

When his father, who was sick and tired and on the brink of death came to visit him, he would sit down with a sigh with eyes only for Jolly, who leapt all around him in a chaotic saraband, or crouched on the floor, blinking and wagging his tail.

"Circus dog!" the old man cried, shaking his head, and he'd stare deep into the dog's eyes, hypnotizing him. And every time the dog made a move, he'd repeat this remark, ad infinitum, as if it were not only the definition of a bastard race but of a destiny, of ruin.

Now he wondered what his father meant. A stray dog? An artistic dog? The definition said it all, signified an irreparable evil, a destiny; but not what actually came to be.

His life had changed. He couldn't say *how*, but for the worse. In compensation for the solitude that had lifted, now a weight burdened his heart. His pain over the relationship gave him no freedom. He didn't *really* think of anything else. When he was in his office, Jolly, who he'd left alone in the house, pursued his thoughts, and when he went to the movies with friends there was no break from the remorse he felt – nothing calmed him. What is he doing now? he would wonder. Is he howling? Is he barking, disturbing the neighbors? Is he dirtying the bed or the rug? He couldn't bring himself to shut Jolly in the garden; why, he didn't know. But he knew that his fears had been farsighted.

He sensed that Jolly wasn't a dog like other dogs. He had hoped that the difficulties would be smoothed out by training, but instead his efforts had not brought any relief. In fact, the urgency with which he had devoted himself to the work of taming Jolly damaged their relationship. He advanced forcefully like an owner should and Jolly withdrew. He forced him to be meek and servile as he imagined all dogs were, and Jolly disobeyed openly; he would take all the beatings and then immediately take possession of the forbidden divan. He would cower at the sound of hollering and then do the same thing in the very same place several hours later.

But this dog loved his master, yearned for him, wanted to stay by his side, moaned at the foot of the bed, clawed at the door whining when he left. And he did this not like a humble dog who loves his master but like a zealous gypsy, with all the exuberance of the gypsy's bastardly nature.

The days passed, and now Jolly was nearly a year old, yet he had not succeeded in changing him at all. In the name of love, Jolly took noisy revenge for his absences, though he was quick to lose the battle, and panting, beaten, would retreat to a corner. For all his mysterious charm, he was a dog out of a nightmare.

"He must've been so cute," exclaimed Mary after he began telling her the story.

They were sitting on the stones, near the transparent, frothy waves that lapped at their feet.

He observed her furtively: like all single women past fifty who are unattached, she was full of good will. But he wouldn't fall into the trap. He had realized straight away that she was odd: from her endless, meaningless little gestures; and the disjointed discussions that flowed back to her like streams of water that vanish in the soil and continue to flow there; in her obsessive attention to a body that no one looked at, convinced that one could unexpectedly stumble upon sex like the philosopher's stone.

Now Mary listened to him as she would have listened to any other man, open to whatever might happen, open to life in general: that was how he saw it. Anyway, now that his story was told, it was a good thing that the dog had gone out of his thoughts and vanished once and for all, leaving him in peace.

But now he continued, "My father died. Jolly and I were left alone. I'm not going to tell you everything that happened during that time. But the worst part was the anger I felt – things kept taking turns that escaped me. You know what I mean, right? All right, we can't control death, agreed, but we should at least be able to control life! And yet, we can't even control the most minuscule, insignificant shred of life! So we can't control anything. Everyone assured me that dogs are faithful, you can count on them, and yet that's not always so."

He stopped and drew close to Mary's face. He lowered his voice. "Do you know what I mean, dearest Mary? I mean a dog can also reject his master, and I assure you, it's an awful experience." He paused because he was so upset now that he couldn't breathe.

"They say no dog will urinate on his master's bed. But he did, yes he did." He lay back on the stones and took a breath. Then more calmly, he concluded: "The veterinarian, who had quite a struggle to give him an injection, burst out laughing and said, 'He really is a bastard.'"

He closed his eyes and took in the sun. Mary sat motionlessly, looking out at the reef of Mazzaro, then, standing, she adjusted her bathing suit on buttocks that drooped slightly and entered the water with graceful movements: she had a good stroke and was pleasant company. The lines of her body seemed to trace, in a generous and uncertain line, the old line of the slender, and from what he could see, lovely girl she had been. He preferred women who remained thin as they aged; they had deep wrinkles and more class.

But all that was even further from him than Jolly. He was better off when he didn't try to love. Although he might've made an exception for an adolescent, flat as a child or a boy.

He forgot Mary and pictured instead the garden of his house and the odious lawyer who had brought the other bastard to the identical garden facing his from above.

Together, he and Jolly had stood stone still for one long moment, staring at the new dog, the same size as Jolly, who stared back at them between two bars of the railing. He barked, wagged his tail, then froze, waiting.

Jolly broke the silence and stillness with a violent sidestep. Then a frenetic barking broke out between the two. The two dogs, in a disordered, furious, parallel race, a crazy zig-zag, ran and heeled as if to invisible commands, frozen eye-to-eye on paws trembling with excitement, snouts thrust forward.

Either they had been moved by an electrical current, struck by recognition, or by love. Jolly stood with his snout turned up and would not listen to reason. Indeed, from that moment on, he understood that his influence had come to an end. Meanwhile, he heard the owner of the other dog, calling, "Poker, Poker!"

So it had all been a prank, an insulting joke at his expense. Was there some message intended for him in all of this? He didn't know and couldn't figure it out. Plunged into a whirl of deductions, his once tranquil life was lost for good. The experience had turned it upside down.

He raised himself onto his elbows. Mary was beside him, drying off in the sun, apparently with great pleasure. Had he kept on talking while she was swimming, or had he continued the story in his head? It didn't matter. He could behave however he wished around Mary.

"No one can imagine what I've gone through. They'd run off together no matter what we did to keep them apart. Poker risked suicide, leaping off the embankment. The lawyer and I agreed to put up a barbed-wire fence, and they'd wound themselves on it. We penned them in, and they overcame all the obstacles and escaped, bounding down the hill in a wild, precipitous run. They showed up only to eat. They managed to find their way into other people's gardens, like real vagabonds. It was always me, me, who went to claim the two bastards, and I had to apologize for Poker as well.

"Then the lawyer disappeared. He left the dog shut in the garden all day long. He had caught on that I, I was always the one who would prepare something to eat for both dogs, run home from the office to look for them, to check up on their pranks and troublemaking. At that point I called my friend Antonio for advice. He said, 'Don't let the two dogs stay together, they're still too young. They could become wild and then Jolly won't recognize you anymore.' But the damage was already done."

He stopped. He breathed heavily as he relived that calamitous time that had been so full of anxiety for him.

Mary listened gravely without interrupting, as if she was trying to reconstruct, find the missing pieces of this rushed and piecemeal story.

Some thought made him wrinkle his forehead before he continued, commenting, "They say homosexuality is practiced among dogs. I think that was the case here, even though I never caught them mounting each other. Perhaps they were too young. It seemed more like love, a connection. What do I know? – some sort of inseparable belonging, a need."

They sat in silence. Now he felt weary somehow, and he imagined that Mary shared this feeling. The waves were calmer now, the wind had died down, and the sun was too hot. The wind at Taormina comes and goes abruptly.

"Even at night, I'd have to go looking for them with a flashlight, at the risk of being taken for a burglar! Then one fine day, the whole affair – which all the neighbors knew about – came to an end. Poker and Jolly never came back."

"Oh, I'm so sorry for you, I'm sorry!" exclaimed Mary.

"Yes," he nodded, "just like that: they vanished for good. And what happened? Nobody ever found out. Maybe poachers got them in the valley or in the field. That's what the doorwoman thought. Or they wandered so far from home that they couldn't find their way back. Maybe they escaped on purpose. Or maybe someone who didn't want to be bothered anymore killed them."

"I'm so sorry," Mary said again, "You must have felt so alone."

He looked up and stared at her with a peculiar little smile on his face.

"Ah, no!" he said. "I was actually relieved. That damned dog disappeared like a bad dream disappears. I started to live again, I had peace again. I swore that I would never again have a dog, never again."

"And you stuck to that?" Mary asked, completely bewildered.

"Of course," he responded with certainty, "I stuck to that."

They sat in silence again. After a while Mary stood up and said she would see him tomorrow. He was rather irritated that she didn't wait to hear the end of the story: how he had cried over Jolly, how he felt his absence more acutely as the days passed, and how he suffered ever since from an unnerving sense of remorse, an uneasiness, as if he really were guilty of something; as if he had pushed Jolly towards Poker because he was incapable of loving him; as if by provoking his escape, he had killed Jolly himself. It had even occurred to him that perhaps Jolly preferred death to his company. Even in the end, something about the whole affair somehow escaped him.

Parlor Game

LEONARDO SCIASCIA (1921–1989) A chronicler of the society and culture of his native Sicily, Sciascia combines the novelist's gifts of imagination with the historian's rigorous attention to fact. In much of his work, beginning with his first novel *Le parrocchie di Regalpetra*, Sciascia analyzes life in Sicily, and the mechanisms of its society and culture. Sciascia's characteristic technique is his adaptation of the detective story to his own particular ends, which are instruction and accusation. At the same time, he frustrates the reader's expectation of the conventional detective fiction. His essays, which are essentially another form for his social and literary commentary, are also considered important.

Much of his work has been translated into English. "Parlor Game" is from *Il mare colore di vino*, 1973.

The door swung open unexpectedly as he hesitated at the doorbell. "Come in, I was expecting you," the woman said with a trill in her voice, smiling as if a moment she had desired, awaited with emotion and joy, had finally arrived. Thinking there must be some mistake, he tried to anticipate the consequences. Confused, almost shocked, he stood immobile in the doorway. Undoubtedly, he thought, she was waiting for someone, someone she didn't know or barely knew or hadn't seen for many years. And then she wasn't wearing glasses, and she usually did, he knew that.

"You were expecting me... ?"

"Of course I was... but please, come in," she trilled again.

He entered, taking three steps on the ceramic tile floor, a reproduction of an old nautical map. He moved heavily as if through mud.

He turned toward her; still smiling, she had already shut the door and was pointing to an armchair.

He attempted to correct the error, to find out what was going on. "But exactly who were you expecting?"

"Exactly?" she echoed, her smile ironic now.

"You see, I . . . "

"You what. . . ?"

"I mean, I think. . . "

"That I'm mistaking you for somebody else?"

She was no longer smiling. And she looked younger. "No, no, it was you I was expecting. It's true I'm not wearing glasses, but I only need them to see things up close. I recognized you at the gate. Now that you're right here, perhaps I do need my glasses: that way neither of us will have the slightest doubt."

Her glasses were resting on an open book, the book on the window sill. Waiting for him, intently listening for the creak of the gate, she had begun reading, but she'd read only a few pages. A ludicrous curiosity about the book, about what she had chosen to pass the time waiting, overcame him. But why on earth should she have been waiting for him? Had he fallen into a trap? Had he been betrayed? Or had the man who sent him suddenly repented?

Strange as it was, the glasses in their thick, heavy frames made her appear even younger: dilated by the lenses, her eyes had a look of astonishment, of fear. But she was neither astonished nor afraid. She even turned away, as if to challenge him. She opened a desk drawer and took out some papers. When she turned back and approached him, she had a fan of photographs in her hand. "They're a little blurred," she said "but there's no doubt. This one was taken at eleven o'clock on the twentieth of June on Via Mazzini: you're with my husband. This other one, at five in the afternoon in Piazza del Popolo, on the twenty-third of July; you're alone, you've just parked and you're locking the car; and your wife's here too, in this one. . . . Do you want to see them?"

Her tone was ironic but not malicious, almost distracted. He finally felt ready to do what he had to do. But he couldn't; from what little he had figured out, he knew he could not do it now, should not. He nodded, yes he wanted to see them. Handing them to him, she

stood watching with the slight, gratified eagerness of someone showing photographs of her family, her children, and waiting to be com-
plimented. But the man felt paralyzed; his perceptions, thoughts,
and movements were slow, distant, hopelessly sluggish. And then,
there came a compliment, banal and bold. "You're photogenic, you
know." And in fact, the picture wasn't so blurred as to conceal his
identity, while his wife and the commander's could have easily been
confused.

"Make yourself comfortable," the woman said, pointing to a
nearby armchair: and he let himself sink down, as if his very existence were caving in. Then she said, "Would you like something to
drink?" and without waiting for his answer, she took two glasses and
a bottle of cognac. He found himself sitting across from her, glass in
hand, as she sipped and regarded him with amusement. He drank
and looked about like someone coming to: the house was nice. He
handed back the photographs.

"She's a pretty girl, your wife. Are you aware that she looks like
the Princess of Monaco? But with this photograph I could be wrong.
Am I wrong?"

"Maybe not."

"Ah, so you never realized it!" And she let out that hideous, gur-
gling laugh. "Are you in love with her?"

He didn't answer.

"Don't think I'm being indiscreet, I'm not asking for curiosity's
sake."

"Then why are you asking?"

"You'll see. . . . Are you in love?"

He pushed the question away with his hand.

"I must assume that either you don't want to answer or you have no
feelings toward your wife."

"As you like."

"I'd like a precise answer." She said this severely, threateningly,
then in a persuasive, knowing tone. "Because, you see, first, I have
to know whether or not you can take it."

"First?"

"You've already answered my question."

"I don't think so."

"Yes you did. I said: first, I have to know whether or not you can take it; and you didn't ask me what you would have to take, what I would reveal about your wife, about your love for her. . . . You responded instantly to that 'first.' 'First?' you asked. So you're not worried about your wife but about yourself. Right. That's fine."

"Then I'll ask you now: what will I have to take?"

"What I'm going to tell you."

"About my wife? And you're worried about whether I can take it?"

"About your wife. And I was concerned about your reaction because we two are destined to a long, solid friendship, and we will have to let a lot of things ride. As long as you agree, of course."

"But my wife . . ."

"I'll get to that. Just tell me: are you following?"

"What?"

"These photographs, the fact that I was expecting you: do you follow?"

"No."

"Don't disappoint me: if you really don't my hopes are dashed. And so are yours."

"Mine?"

"Yes, definitely, yours too. Didn't I tell you we would be friends? Then tell me honestly: do you understand? And don't be afraid to talk openly, there's no hidden microphone, no tape recorder running. You can check if you'd like. Anyway, I'm about to offer you a job that's simple, quick, profitable – and without risk. Not to mention that I'm saving you from certain, immediate danger. So you must admit that, at the very least, I have the right to know how intelligent you are. . . . So: do you understand?"

"Not everything."

"Naturally . . . , but just tell me what you do understand."

"I understand that you know."

"A quick and comprehensive answer. Now would you like to know how I figured it out?"

"Yes, I'd like that."

"We'll be wasting time, but you should know. . . . But what time are you due to meet my husband? You'd better tell me right off because our whole future friendship hangs on your meeting with my husband this evening. What time is it set for?"

"But we're not supposed to meet."

"Aha, you still don't trust me. I know my husband perfectly well: it's impossible that he didn't make an appointment with you tonight. What time is it for?"

"Twelve-fifteen tonight."

"Where?"

"On a little country road about twenty-five miles from here."

"Fine, we have time . . . , but maybe it would be better if you asked me the questions now. . . . "

"I wouldn't know where to begin. I'm rather confused."

"Really? I expected you to be more on the ball, a man with swift reflexes, immediate ideas. But perhaps the reason for your shock and confusion lies in the fact that my husband told you nothing about me, about my character or capacity to intuit his most secret thoughts. After fifteen years of life together, a man like him is an open book for a woman like me. And a very silly, very boring book. What do you think?

"About what?"

"About my husband?"

"Judging from the situation I'm in now, I'd say he's an imbecile."

"I'm happy to hear you say that . . . , but you could have figured out what an imbecile he is a lot sooner. I can see, though, how you might have been dazzled by his presence, his way of doing things, continually flaunting his authority and money in that shrewd way of his, that nonchalance. . . . And he does have money, don't worry. Anyway, I fell for it myself. Not that I'm sorry about it: my only regret is that I married for love rather than calculated gain. But I would have married him in any case, and my adjustment was immediate. And it wasn't that I . . . I so much adapted but actually indulged in a situation that allowed me to express my whims and my scorn at the same time, a situation that offered me everything a woman could want, including scorn for the man she lives with. And now the imbecile comes along to upset the balance!"

"But I can't agree that he is the total imbecile you say: in this case, well yes, no doubt he acted foolishly, carelessly. But he's a self-made man, at least that's what he said, that's what everybody says, and he's become very rich, very powerful. . . ."

"Your idea of the self-made man comes straight out of a romantic novel or an American how-to-succeed manual. Aside from my husband, I know a fairly vast circle of self-made men, and I can assure you that all of them were made by others, who in turn were made by circumstances, coincidences and underhanded deals that may have made history but will always remain fortuitous and pathetic. In the last war, my husband fought in the fascist militia along with Sabatelli, who then became minister of public works: they both volunteered. Need I say more? And you can't imagine what an idiot Sabatelli is. In a well-ordered, honest society where people don't cheat and where ability and merit stand for something, the kindest fate would have carried them to the doors of public office, as doormen, and the cruelest behind the bars of a prison. But instead. . ."

"Instead they're rich, powerful and respected. . . , but you invited me to ask the questions. May I?"

Stopped short in her oratory flight, she nodded yes, but she was vexed, cross.

"I have many questions, but the most important is this: why were you expecting me tonight, in particular?"

"Because today at the table my husband asked me if I planned to spend the evening out, at the movies or at a friend's house; he said that he would be coming back late, very late, from a board of directors meeting. And he's already had two other meetings of the kind this summer, so the third had to be the right one. Right for him, fatal for me. That's not even to say I know him profoundly, but anyone on familiar terms with him knows that he's totally devoted to this superstitious idea about the perfection of the number three. Not to mention nine, which he actually swoons over. So, the third meeting, the third day of the month, and you arrived at nine sharp. He told you to ring the bell at nine sharp, didn't he?"

"Yes, but I thought. . ."

"That it was a detail calculated by his organized mind. But you have no idea how badly organized his mind really is, assuming he actually has one. And I must add, the fact that you're a mathematics professor certainly played a role in his decision to entrust you with such a delicate, and I dare say risky, mission. He barely knows the multiplication table, so he cultivates this conviction that his own robberies, in fact all successful robberies, draw upon a sublime mathematics. In some bank robberies, he actually hears the music of the spheres; you know, the ones you read about in the papers that are perfectly timed. And when they're flawed, he studies the reports to find their weaknesses and errors, and then he imagines them perfected. He did that in one case. It was a crime you must remember too, several years back, a famous trial. My husband was so excited over it that he went so far as to send one of his employees to hold a seat in the courtroom for him in case he had time to come; and on several occasions he did have the time. But while he was looking for the mistakes that had brought the accused to the bench, he was making one himself. Today, if you. . . . I mean, if things had gone according to plan, at least ten people would have remembered his interest in that trial, especially the employee who held a seat for him and one of the judges who knows him well and smiled at him from the bench now and then."

"So that was when you became suspicious?"

"No, even before; but his passion for that trial made me realize that his intentions were becoming a precise plan."

"And then you went to a detective agency?"

"It was time-consuming and costly, but as you can see, it was worth it. For several years, the agency only reported his infidelities. What a laugh: his infidelities! After a few months of marriage, I couldn't have cared less. He had always bought women and he went on buying them; by marrying he bought me too, figuring that he could pay the price, as high and long-term as it was."

"And he couldn't?"

"Evidently not."

"I mean, why couldn't he?"

"It was my fault, of course. I did everything I could to distance him from me, to push him into the margins of my days and nights, an extremely narrow margin, just an endless stream of checks. . . . No, I didn't have other men. Or rather, only once, when my husband began to disgust me. And that time it was just an experiment. But the experiment failed. So don't get any ideas in your head."

Enraged, he searched his mind for a rebuttal.

"Don't be offended. I know I'm not beautiful or young, you might even say I'm an ugly old woman. But what I meant is that you might think you could get to all my money, rather than a part of it, that you could use my living body after you've used my husband's corpse. So I want things to be clear between us from here on in."

"So you admit that your husband isn't all wrong."

"I don't admit anything; and if you're still at a point, if we're at a point, where you still want to weigh the merits of our two plans of action on the archangel's scale, the execution of my husband's plan against mine, that's your business. But it's bad business to use the scale in matters like these. I mean that kind of scale. You . . . ," and she broke into a complimentary smile, "are a small, greedy crook: take on more than you can handle, and you'll end up with nothing."

"I'm not a crook."

"Oh really?"

"No more than you are."

"That's right. And much less than your wife, I dare say."

"Maybe. But how do you know?"

"I'm inferring from what I know. Don't you know that your wife, shall we say, sees other men?"

"That's not true!"

"Oh, yes it is true. Don't be angry. After all, what can these men your wife sees take away from her? You're an attractive couple, you get along, you want the same things, you never argue, the neighbors think well of you. . . . The first report the agency sent me says truly sweet things about you: she's twenty-two, teaches in a nursery school, is very beautiful, lively, elegant; he's twenty-seven, a substitute mathematics teacher in a junior high school, is likeable, serious; they're in love and very happy. . . . The second report, and all the others after it, say nothing different about you; but they reveal unexpected, surprising activities on your wife's part. For money, obviously. So even if you really didn't know about it before now, don't worry. She did it for money, only for money. . . . You know, once, just once, she even went with my husband."

"I suspected it. I mean, I suspected it in the beginning: I thought your husband got involved with us simply because he wanted to get to my wife. Not that my wife was interested. And then my suspicions vanished: once he'd made clear what he wanted from us, I mean from me, I had no reason to think that he planned to seduce my wife."

"Still a little liaison with your wife was part of my husband's scheme. I think he planned to use it in case you betrayed him, by accident or by carelessness. Then he would have said, 'I had an affair with his wife, he found out and killed mine in revenge,' or 'he'd really come for me, to kill me, my wife resisted, or humiliated him, or somehow provoked him to violence, so he killed her.' But don't start worrying that my husband and your wife are planning to bring the police on your tracks: he doesn't get that good. And anyway, in the end I'm sure your wife would never have agreed to a solution like that. I think I know what sort of woman she is."

"What kind of woman is that?"

"She's like me. Like so many women. . . we adore things; in the sphere of love, we've replaced God with things. Shop windows are our firmament, built-in wardrobes and American kitchens hold the universe for us. Kitchens you don't have to cook in, inhabited by the God of TV commercials. . . . My father, who was middle class, spent his whole life in rented houses without ever feeling the need to possess one of his own. Now there's not a revolutionary who doesn't want to own the house he lives in, who doesn't drown himself in debts, in twenty-five year mortgages, to own a house. The idea of eternity, the idea of hell are contracted in twenty-five year bank mortgages. The banks administer metaphysics. But forget it. . . . Anyway, your wife is like me. . ., we're all the same these days, that's the problem. But aside from that, your wife is either indifferent or naive. I'm sure that she was the one who jumped at my husband's proposal. . . . By the way, what are the terms?"

"He's already deposited a large sum in our name in a bank in Hamburg."

"How much?"

"Two hundred thousand marks."

"So tonight you could have flown to Hamburg instead of coming here and. . ."

"I could have. But if everything went smoothly, in two years I would have four hundred thousand marks on top of that."

"I'll give you five hundred thousand, and in six months. Do you trust me?"

"I don't know."

"You'll have to trust me. And keep in mind that my plan involves minimal risk, while it's a certainty, one could even say a mathematical certainty, that the one you're about to execute would put you behind bars. The detective agency was instructed to send copies of the reports and photographs to the police, in case anything happened to me. . . . And even assuming that I don't carry through or that I actually intend to betray you, the only risk you run is of not getting more money and being indicted for a crime of passion, of honor. After two or three years in prison, there's always amnesty. In fact, if you're smart you'll take my advice: should you get caught, emphasize your wife's betrayal and the horrendous disillusionment my husband inflicted on you. Always emphasize that."

"But thinking it over, it could be you who's setting me up."

"I would think you an idiot if you didn't leave here suspecting that. . . . " She looked at her watch, stood up and asked him, smiling, "Would you think it indiscreet if I asked you how you were planning to kill me?"

"With a pistol."

"Fine. . . . Go now, time is running out, you'll be late for your appointment. And good luck."

She walked him to the door, smiling sweetly, maternally. Before closing the door, as he neared the gate, she called him back. "Take my advice: shoot more than once, he's very sturdy," she whispered as if to urge particular care for a delicate child. And then: "There's a silencer, I imagine."

"On the pistol? Yes, there is."

"Fine, well, good luck again." She closed the door and leaned her shoulders against it. With a smile of seeming enchantment, she tasted every syllable as she said: "The silencer: premeditated homicide." She walked over to the window and watched him go out through the gate.

She sat down in an armchair, then got up. She walked around the room and ran her hands along the furniture and objects with her hands, as if to make music. She looked at the clock. Then she went to the telephone, dialed the number, and asked in an agitated voice: "Is my husband still in the office?. . . He's already left? I'm worried, very worried. . . . Yes, I know it's not the first time he's been late, but something happened tonight that disturbed me. . . . A young man came looking for him, he seemed very upset, threatening even. . . . He was here waiting for him, and he's just left. But how long ago did my husband leave?. . . Yes, thank you, good night, yes, goodbye." She hung up, dialed another number, spoke, her voice even more agitated and pained now. "Police station? Is Commissioner Scoto there? Could you put him on, right away, please?. . . Oh, Commissioner, I'm lucky I caught you at the office at this hour. . . . This is Signora Arduini. . . . Listen, I'm very worried, very worried. . ., my husband. . ., this is embarrassing for me, and humiliating. . . but I have to tell you. . . . My husband is having a relationship with a married woman; she's very young, very beautiful. I know because I hired a detective agency to watch him, I'm not ashamed to admit it. . . . No, I don't want to accuse him of adultery; on the contrary, I'm very concerned that something is going to happen to him. . ., because you see, this evening her husband – he's a young professor – came to see me; he was extremely upset, beside himself. Not thinking, I asked him to come in, and he sat here for a couple of hours waiting for my husband. He seemed violent. I tried to get him to talk, but he answered evasively, in monosyllables. He just left. . . . Yes, a couple of minutes ago. . . . I telephoned my husband to warn him, but he'd already left the office. He should've been here by now. Can you do something? Yes, fine," she said, nearly in tears, "I'll wait another half hour and call you back. . . . Thank you."

C A R L O   S G O R L O N

The Grey Stain

CARLO SGORLON (1930–) Sgorlon's novels, often set in his native Friuli, are
known for their power to distort reality, sometimes to grotesque, sometimes to
oneiric effect, as in the story presented here. The novel, *L'armata dei fiumi per-
duti,* won the Premio Strega. "The Grey Stain" is taken from a collection of
stories written for newspapers and magazines over a twenty-five year period, all
of them set in distant times and places, sometimes historical, sometimes
imagined. "The Grey Stain" is from *Il quarto re mago,* 1986.

My name is Sa' di Ciubak. I am writing this unbelievable story on
my last piece of parchment and some white sheep bones while I live
out my last days in this empty house in a deserted village.

For many years now I have been a merchant. I passed the long
months traveling along the riverbanks of Persia and Mesopotamia by
wagon, horse and camel, and occasionally by barges. But whenever I
could stay home in my own city, I passed time as happily as I could.
My till was always overflowing, and I didn't see any reason why my
money should accumulate in the coffer rather than pass into other
hands in exchange for pleasure. I had no prejudice against wine; yes,
the Prophet forbade it, that's true, but on the other hand, poets and
wise men praised it. I myself had never read the Abu Ali Sima's
poems, or those of the great Omar Khayyám, but on countless occasions I'd heard my friends recite them in the secluded rooms of inns
and hostels where we passed magical nights. The Koran's suras
speak of the streams of honey and wine, sugar and milk which await
us in the hereafter. But the poems which my friends recited said that

it was unwise to barter ready cash for such dubious guarantees, and I was in complete agreement with them.

No matter how much I drank I was never satisfied; whenever I returned to the room where we took our secret pleasures, my throat would go dry and my lips parched, as if I had been trekking through the interminable sandstorms of the desert for three days. My friends would look at me in astonishment each time we raised our glasses, and between toasts they would whisper that they had never seen anyone who could drink like the merchant Sa' di Ciubak.

One day, without warning, I saw a small grey stain appear on a girl's face; she had skin as white as a sheet of linen. I wet the corner of her shawl and rubbed it over the stain, but it didn't disappear. I must have been utterly drunk not to have immediately realized that there was nothing on the woman's face. It was in my own eyes; in fact, wherever I looked, the little stain quickly reappeared. I didn't see it when my gaze was wandering, eager and greedy to drink in everything around me, but only when it rested on something a while.

"What is this all about?" I asked myself when I finally came out of the mists of wine. I tried to smile about it. I figured that the stain had come with the wine and that it should go away with it too, and I threw myself on the jugs with a more ferocious thirst than ever before. But the stain did not disappear. On the contrary, each time that I came out of my drunkenness, I realized with terror that it had grown.

In the end, it came to obsess me. First, I abandoned my trade, and finally my house too. I fled like a fugitive, without even bothering to shut the door. I began going from one dive to another to drink. My friends worried when they saw me. "Sa' di Ciubak is not the same man," they whispered, thinking I did not hear them, as I gazed into their faces which were always blurred by a dark grey stain.

My fear grew greater by the day. I finally fled my city too, and set out for the others I had passed through so often in my travels along the riverbanks or in the mountains. Whenever I saw a familiar face, I would quickly change direction so as not to be stopped and questioned about my condition.

Meanwhile the stain kept growing bigger and bigger. Within instants, whatever I looked at would turn that odious color even while the blinding desert sun went on glittering all around it. It didn't seem to be in my eyes but right in front of them like a mysterious object that was getting closer and closer. "What are you looking at, what the devil are you looking at?" girls would ask me when they saw me gaping at them like a cat in a deserted alleyway in the Casbah.

I never answered. I even stopped drinking and going after girls. I began to spend my days on straw mats in dark rooms because only then did the stain blur in the surrounding blackness. My heart in tumult, I thought that the stain must've been nearly as large as the Black Rock of Mecca which I had seen so many times when I conducted business in that city. It still might've been a hundred feet away, but it was getting closer. And when it was only a hand's length from my face, I would be wholly blind.

Such an idea was so unbearable that I began to consult doctors. They listened in astonishment and racked their minds for some explanation. One said that I must've gotten sunstroke, another that I'd gazed at the solar disk too long, a third that something had gone awry in my mind. Some said nothing or talked nonsense. They made me drink infusions, they rubbed my eyelids with unguents, but still my eyesight didn't improve. Finally, in my desperation, I sought out imans and wisemen in the mosques where they spend their eyesight reading books and gazing at the stars, and the strangest answers came from their lips. In the end, I even consulted the ascetics and magicians who live in the rock caves at the edge of the desert or in horse-skin tents.

I was almost always alone now, dragging myself from one outpost to another, from one cave to another, eating the meat of the jackal, digging up the roots of bushes to quench my thirst, and gazing with growing terror at the swelling stain.

One day out of boredom, I began to follow a vulture that was kicking its way across the scalding stone heaps and stretches of sand. At first I ran after it, then I dragged myself heavily, like an old stumbling man. Finally, I found myself surrounded by houses, mosques, and minarets—a city in the middle of the desert. I took it for a mirage, figuring that I was already delirious from thirst. But the city did not disappear. Instead, the stain disappeared. But now it was as though I were seeing everything through a dense curtain of fog or storm clouds. The whole city was a dark grey, as if it were built of iron and basalt. Nothing, neither the mosques nor the metal objects hung outside the craftsmen's workshops, glittered in such faded light.

As weakened as I was by thirst and fatigue, I quickly realized in great astonishment that this was my own city. Yet it had turned so dark that it was nearly unrecognizable. The men walked silently along the wall, wrapped in their grey wool cloaks; those who recognized me gave me a distracted look but most didn't even bother to greet me. Suddenly I felt an inconsolable and vague desperation overtaking me. I attempted to tell some of my old friends what had happened, but none of them saw anything different about the city, and when I insisted they looked at me as if I were a pitiful madman. Finally, I could endure it no longer, and I left again to live alone in those semi-deserted villages.

All of this really happened to me and I've recorded it. Yet, if there is any meaning in these events, I have not been able to see it. Now that death is approaching, I will wrap the parchment and sheep bones in a goatskin and bury them in the sand, or under the desert rocks. It is the 645th year of Egira. Perhaps one day, a hundred or a thousand years from now, someone will uncover my record and read the dark scroll of my story as if it were a book. Perhaps, who knows? But for me this is the strangest thing that has ever happened in the eternal cycle of the days and nights of this world.

The Seagull

MARIO SOLDATI (1906–) A film director, screen and fiction writer who has enjoyed great popularity, Soldati is known for his stories of intrigue and his accurate psychological portraits. His descriptions of complex and bizarre personalities and situations occasionally border on the grotesque, as in "The Seagull," in which the witness of a metamorphosis is condemned, by the very fact of his experience, to doubt and solitude. Many of Soldati's novels and story collections have been commercial and critical successes. *Le due città* won the Premio Strega in 1964. "The Seagull" is from *I racconti*, 1957.

I'm not going crazy. I'm not asleep. Not dreaming. I'm just as alive as all of you reading this. Believe me. Come and see for yourselves. Come now, and I'll wait till you get here. But hurry. The incredible power I've had since two past midnight could vanish, could go in an instant, as quickly as it came. The clock at the corner of Via Toledo already says three eighteen (wait, let me try again) but I can still do it. Dawn frightens me; when the sun comes up behind the Vomero Hill, I'm afraid I'll become a man again, walking with my feet on the ground like all of you, and plunging back to earth when I jump, even if I hurl myself up, even if my jump would win the Olympics. But come anyway. The miracle might go on for several nights.

Now, I'm writing you with a pencil and pad (I'm in a gas station, next to the neon sign that's still lit; God knows why, I guess for advertising) and I'm going to drop this letter in that red mailbox over there in the corner of the piazza (I'm here in Piazza Dante, in Naples). The envelope is ready, addressed and all. So it should reach you tomorrow morning. Listen, if you take the train now, you'll be in Naples by tomorrow night. I'll plan to meet you near the gas station, at a quarter of two. I hope you don't come for nothing. But who knows, maybe you'll find the piazza full of people yelling, the balconies and windows lit, crammed with spectators, and vendors with carts of almonds and cotton candy, all of Naples celebrating, waiting for the miracle to happen again. But right now there's not a soul in sight. An hour and twenty minutes ago I became the subject of a phenomenon that contradicts all the laws of nature. I am also the only witness.

It happened an hour and twenty minutes ago, as I jumped onto a bench in the garden. I wasn't sleepy and couldn't decide whether to go back to the hotel, so I was wandering around alone. I jumped onto the bench to get a good look at the buds on the chestnut tree, and there I was in midair, two feet above the bench with my head in the branches (my right cheek is still sticky from the blossoms). Suddenly, my hands flapped in the air as if by instinct; I wanted to get my balance in that strange, long leap. Palms facing down, my hands thrashed furiously up and down, like a chicken fluttering to get off the ground, and there I was bewildered, rising higher, grazing the flowering tips of the branches, suspended above the tree. And immediately I looked around, perhaps ashamed, but wanting someone to see me. But the long, wide piazza lit by two rows of streetlamps was completely deserted.

All around, darkness, the tall houses. The shutters on all the windows and balconies dark and closed; all but one. In a building at the corner of Via Toledo, a brilliant light glowed on the third floor. Now, as I'm writing, it's out. Without moving toward it I flapped my hands horizontally at my sides to stay put, and then I noticed that in spite of the night chill, the windows on the balcony were wide open; and looking into the room I saw a desk heaped with papers and piles of open books, all glowing in the lamplight, and a white-haired man huddled over the papers and books, either reading or writing.

It will probably shock you that when I discovered my ability to fly my first instinct was not to see how high or fast I could fly, or how many stunts I could perform. But don't forget, I don't fly like a ma-

chine that engineers have devised and perfected with tedious cal-
culations and experiments, I fly because of a miracle, which is so
simple, so natural, it can't be explained. So you see, I didn't care
about proving how high, how fast. . . . And anyway, a few minutes
later I rose some thirty feet above all the houses until I reached the
top of Vomero Hill: I saw the starry sky and took in the entire countryside in one glance, from the massive black form of Vesuvius all
the way down to the lights of Posillipo; and the vast, dark complex of
terraces and roofs, lined and dotted by the faint lights of streets, al-
leys and courtyards, stretched below me. And then I came down because it was too cold. But my first instinct was to fly over to that
window, to the room where that one brilliant light was burning. I
crossed Piazza Dante heading straight for the window. I held my
body stiff, leaned forward and flapped; long, wide sweeps.

In no time I reach the balcony and grasped the elegant wrought
iron railing like a swimmer grabs on to the side of a boat. I looked into
the room.

The old man's back was turned to me. His shoulders were
rounded, heavy. He was writing. Now and then he put his pen down,
skimmed through one of the many books before him, and started
writing again. He was so absorbed in his work that he didn't hear me.
I couldn't see his face and had no idea who he was. But that white
head of hair under the blinding light and that looming, bent figure so
immersed in study that it was unaware of the cold coming in through
the window, aroused great respect in me.

I was downright impatient to show somebody that I was flying. But
I didn't dare disturb the old man. What difference could it make to
him, to philosophy (he was undoubtedly a philosopher), that a man
might fly?

I blushed thinking how shabby, how tiny my soul must be if an act
which is just a bit strange for a man, but perfectly normal for a poor
seagull, could fill me with such joy.

(And yet I do wish that somebody would see me. What if I suddenly couldn't fly? Nobody would believe I ever did.)

So I turned toward the piazza: nobody. Not a night watchman, not
a beggar picking up cigarette butts, or a prostitute, or a baker who's

finished baking and is going home to bed, or a butcher on his way to the slaughterhouse. Not a soul. Only the stone of the long, wide piazza and halos around the two rows of streetlamps.

At a certain point I thought of screaming, waking up the whole neighborhood. But it seemed ridiculous, maybe even dangerous. Many people still believe in the devil. And some of them have guns. If somebody who believed in the devil and also happened to have a gun went to his window and saw me spinning in thin air a few yards away, he might shoot me down. Seagulls are mortal too.

Several strokes in the air, and I drifted aside. But before leaving the window I called these very words out loudly:

"Philosopher! Father! A poor seagull reveres you and wishes you goodnight."

The old man spun around towards the window. I didn't expect that a man with that white mass of hair and those heavy shoulders could be so alert and agile. As soon as he turned he saw me. But he didn't seem at all surprised that I was suspended like that, in thin air. He stared: two small, intense eyes, sparkling, piercing, smiling at me behind two small, round lenses. Very calmly, he said to me in dialect:

"Why, thank you."

Then I regained my courage. I approached the window again with short, timid strokes of my hands and feet as if I were ashamed to let him see that I could fly. Then I grasped the wrought iron railing on the balcony and asked him anxiously:

"Tell me, father, am I wrong to fly?"

His smile was kind, amused. Without getting out of the chair, he threw his right hand up as if to toss a coin, and said to me:

"Fly sir, if that makes you happy," and turned back to his work.

I let go of the railing, swooped down a few yards, then up and down sensuously, zigzagging, sinking, rising, passing one balcony and then another, trying to cover the entire facade of the building like a bee flies along a flowering trellis. Then, as I've already told you, I rose above all the houses. But it was cold so I came back here, next to the neon sign in the gas station to write the letter. So far the philosopher is the only one who's seen me fly. He wasn't shocked; I'm sure he'll testify for me:

"One April night in Naples, the oddest thing happened to me
. . . " He's an honest man, an important man. Too bad nobody will
believe him.

That is why I'm asking you to come, friends. . . wait, let me see if I
can still do it!

Two strokes.

Yes, that's it. One kick and I'd shatter this neon sign.

Come. Take the train right away. The plane comes to Naples too.
Come now. And let's hope the miracle lasts.

ANTONIO TABUCCHI

The Arhant

ANTONIO TABUCCHI (1943–) In a note at the beginning of his novella *Notturno indiano*, from which the piece here is excerpted, Tabucchi calls his story "not only an insomnia, but a journey." Journey, as a motif, a psychological and narrative process, figures large in Tabucchi's work; the journey leads character and reader toward the cognition and reconciliation of the two sides of reality – that which appears to be and that which is. But reconciliation can only be partial because reality is, inherently, ambiguous. In his essay, "*Doppio senso*" (Double Meaning), Tabucchi wrote: "If life is oblique and surreptitious and essentially ambiguous, I don't find it inconsistent that its invention, literature, true as it may be, is equally oblique and open to the multiplicity of being." One of the most original writers of the younger generation, Tabucchi writes in a spare, refined prose style. Several of his books have been translated into English, *Indian Nocturne* among them. "The Arhant" is from *Notturno indiano*, 1984.

The bus crossed a deserted plain and some sleepy isolated villages. After a stretch of hilly road whose sharp curves the driver took with a carelessness I thought excessive, we sped down huge, empty straightaways in the silent Indian night. I had the impression that it was a landscape of palm groves and rice fields, but it was too dark to see clearly, and only where the road took a sudden turn did the headlights shine across the countryside. I calculated that if the bus followed the official timetable, Mangalore couldn't be much farther now. At Mangalore, two alternatives awaited: either a seven-hour wait for the connecting bus to Goa, or waiting a full day in a hotel for the bus.

I was very indecisive. During the trip, I had slept only a little, and badly at that, and I felt exhausted; but a whole day in Mangalore wasn't a particularly attractive prospect. My guide book said, "Mangalore, situated on the sea of Oman has nearly nothing of its past preserved. It is a modern industrial city with a rational urban layout and a nondescript appearance. One of the few cities in India which really has nothing to see."

I was still trying to decide when the bus stopped. This couldn't have been Mangalore, for we were in open country. The driver turned off the engine and some passengers got off. At first I thought we were stopping briefly for the passengers' convenience, but after fifteen minutes the stop seemed oddly prolonged. Not only that, but the driver had sunken back peacefully in his seat and seemed to be sleeping. I waited another quarter of an hour. The passengers who'd stayed on were sleeping quietly. In front of me, the old man with a turban had taken a long strip of fabric from a basket and was patiently rolling it up, carefully smoothing out the creases with each turn. I whispered a question in his ear, but he turned and gave me a vacuous smile, leaving me to guess that he hadn't understood. I looked out the bus window and saw some sort of dimly lit roadside stand in a sandy space off the road. It looked like a garage made of wooden planks. A woman stood in the doorway, and I noticed someone going inside.

I decided to ask the driver for an explanation. I felt bad about waking him since he'd driven for so many hours, but I felt that it might be better to get some information. He was a fat man and slept with his mouth open; I touched his shoulder and he looked at me, confused.

"Why did we stop here?" I asked. "This isn't Mangalore."

He drew himself up and smoothed his hair. "No sir, it is not."

"Why did we stop, then?"

"This is a bus stop," he said, "we're waiting for a connection."

The stop wasn't listed on the timetable on my ticket, but by now I was used to India's surprises. So I'd asked purely for curiosity's sake and did not appear the least surprised to learn that we were waiting for a bus to Mudabiri and Karkala. I attempted a logical reply. "And the passengers for Mudabiri and Karkala can't wait alone, we have to wait with them?"

"There are people on that bus who will transfer to this bus for Mangalore," the driver answered calmly. "That's why we are waiting."

He stretched out on the seat, making it clear that he would like to go back to sleep. In a resigned tone, I spoke again. "How long is the stop?"

"Eighty-five minutes," he responded. I didn't know whether such exactitude reflected British schooling or was intended as some kind of sophisticated irony. And then he added: "In any case, if you're tired of sitting on the bus, you can get off—there's a waiting room right over there."

I decided it would be better to stretch my legs a bit to kill time. The night was sweet and damp, and there was a strong fragrance of herbs in the air. I walked around the bus, smoked a cigarette by the steps at the rear exit, and then headed for the "waiting room." It was a low, long shed; an oil lamp hung at the door. A divinity of painted plaster which I didn't recognize was fastened to the door jamb. Inside, about ten people were sitting on benches along the walls. Two women stood near the door, engrossed in conversation. The few passengers who had gotten off the bus were scattered on a circular bench in the middle around a supporting pole to which papers of various colors were affixed and a yellowed poster which looked like a schedule or some government announcement. A boy of about ten with short pants and sandals was sitting on a bench in the rear. A monkey was perched on his shoulder, its face hidden in his hair, and its little hands laced around his neck in a posture of affection and dread. In addition to the oil lamp by the door, two candles were burning atop a packing crate: the light was very dim and the corners of the shed were dark. I paused for a couple of minutes to look at the people who didn't even seem to notice me. Seeing the boy alone there with his monkey struck me as strange, even though one frequently sees children alone with animals in India; it reminded me of a little boy I was very fond of and how he hugged his doll before falling asleep. Perhaps it was that association that compelled me toward him; I sat down next to him.

He looked at me with his beautiful eyes and smiled, and I smiled back; it was only then that I realized in horror that the little being he was carrying on his shoulder was not a monkey at all but a human being. A monster. Some natural atrocity or some terrible illness had stiffened his body, distorting its shape and proportions. His limbs were contorted and altered beyond any order or measure save for those of grotesque atrocity. Even his face, which was now peering out from his master's hair, had not escaped the devastation of deformity. His rough skin, the wrinkles as deep as wounds, combined with his features gave him the monkeylike appearance that had prompted my error. The only human aspect of that face was the eyes: two tiny, sharp, intelligent eyes that flashed in every direction as though they were possessed by the knowledge of some great impending danger, by fear.

The boy greeted me in a friendly manner. I wished him a good evening and found myself unable to get up and walk away.

"Where are you going?" I asked him.

"We're going to Mudabiri," he said, smiling, "to the temple of Chandranath."

He spoke a good English without stumbling. "You speak English well," I said. "Who taught you?"

"I learned at school," the boy said proudly, "I went for three years." Then, turning his head slightly, he made an apologetic gesture. "He doesn't know English, he couldn't go to school."

"Of course," I said, "I understand."

The boy caressed the hands wrapped around his chest. "He's my brother," he said affectionately, "he's twenty years old." Then his expression became proud again and he said, "but he knows the Scriptures, he knows them by heart, he's very intelligent."

I tried to maintain a nonchalant attitude, to look as though I were slightly distracted and lost in my own thoughts, to hide the fact that I lacked the courage to look at the person in question. "What are you going to do in Mudabiri?"

"There are festivals," he said, "and Jains from all over Kerala, many pilgrims, will be coming there in the next few days."

"Are you pilgrims too?"

"No," he said, "we travel around to the temples. My brother is an *Arhant*."

"I'm sorry but I don't know what that means."

"An *Arhant* is a Jain prophet," the boy explained patiently. "He reads the pilgrims' *karma*, and we make a lot of money."

"So he's a seer."

"Yes," the boy said candidly, "he can see the past and the future." Then he made a businesslike connection and asked me, "Would you like to know your *karma?* It only costs five rupies."

"Fine," I said, "ask your brother."

The boy addressed his brother gently, who replied in a whisper, all the while looking at me with his flashing eyes.

"My brother wants to know if he can touch your forehead," the boy informed me. Waiting, the monster nodded in agreement.

"Sure he can, if he has to."

The seer stretched out his little contorted hand and rested his index finger on my forehead. He kept it there for several moments, his gaze fixed intently on me. Then he withdrew his hand and whispered something into his brother's ear. A little impassioned discussion followed. Talking excitedly, the seer seemed vexed and irritated. When they were through talking, the boy turned toward me with an afflicted expression.

"So," I said, "will you tell me?"

"I'm sorry," he said, "but my brother says he can't do it – you're somebody else."

"Oh, right," I said, "who am I?"

The boy turned to speak again to his brother who replied briefly. "That doesn't matter," the boy told me, "it's only *maya*."

"And what is *maya?*"

"The appearances of the world," the boy answered, "but it's only illusion; what matters is the *atma*." Then he consulted with his brother and confirmed this with conviction: "What counts is the *atma*."

"And the *atma* is?"

The boy smiled at my ignorance. "The soul," he said, "the individual soul."

A woman came in and sat down on the bench facing us. She was carrying a basket with a sleeping baby. I looked at her, and raising her hands to her face, she made a quick gesture of respect.

"I thought that we only had *karma* within us," I said, "the sum of our actions, and of what we've been and will be."

The boy smiled again and spoke to his brother. The monster looked at me with his little sharp eyes and indicated the number two with his fingers. "Oh no," explained the boy, "there's the *atma* too, it's with the *karma* but it's a separate thing."

"But if I'm somebody else, then I'd like to know where my *atma* is, where I can find it right now."

The boy translated for his brother and another intense conversation followed. "It's very difficult to say," he informed me after a while, "he cannot tell you."

"Why don't you ask him if ten rupies would help," I said.

The boy asked him and the monster stared me in the face with his little eyes. Then he uttered some words directly at me very quickly. "He says it isn't a matter of rupies," the boy translated. "You're not here, and he can't tell you where you are." He gave me a big smile and continued, "But if you want to give us ten rupies we'll accept it all the same."

"Sure, I'll give it to you," I said, "but at least ask him who I am right now."

The boy smiled again benevolently and then said, "But that's just your *maya* – what's the point of knowing?"

"Of course, you're right," I said, "there's no point." Then I had an idea and said, "Ask him to try to guess."

The boy looked at me in astonishment. "Guess what?"

"Guess where my *atma* is," I said. "Didn't you say he was a seer?"

The boy repeated my question and the brother made a brief reply. "He says he can try," he translated, "but he can't guarantee anything."

"That doesn't matter, let him try anyway."

The monster stared at me with great concentration for a long time. Then he gestured with his hand and I was expecting him to speak, but he didn't say anything. His fingers moved lightly in the air to indicate waves, and then he cupped his hands as if to gather imaginary water. "He says that you're on a boat," the boy whispered to me. The monster made a sign with his palms out and then froze.

"On a boat?" I said. "Ask him where, fast, what boat it is."

The boy put his ear to the lips of his whispering brother. "He sees many lights. But nothing else – there's no use insisting."

The seer had reassumed his initial position, his face hidden in his brother's hair. I took out ten rupies and handed them to him. Then I went out into the night and lit a cigarette. I paused to look at the sky and the dark margin of vegetation on the edge of the road. The bus for Mudabiri couldn't be far now.

MARIO TOBINO

A Personal Missive

MARIO TOBINO (1910–) A psychiatrist and director of the Psychiatric Hospital in Lucca, Tobino began as a poet. Not surprisingly, introspection, lyricism, and an attention to rhythm characterize his fictional work as well. His experience during the war became the subject of this story and of *Deserto della Libia*, considered to be among the most powerful books about the war. However Tobino is probably best known for his moving portrayals of the lives of the institutionalized patients he has worked with, as in *Libere donne di Magliano*.

"A Personal Missive" is from *La bella degli specchi*, 1976.

The most elegant doorman in all the Italian universities was undoubtedly Birindelli. His frock coat, cinched at the waist with its soft and shiny skirts that flowed down to his knees, was unmistakably him. He was pale, thin, and scrupulously shaven. He took in everything in a flash and then averted his eyes as if he'd seen nothing. He was cordial, every student's friend and at their disposal, while remaining detached and stately, for he knew his position – the doorman at the University of L., the oldest in Italy! He was a little over forty. Among the students, especially the freshmen, he was a legend: "Birindelli! I talked to Birindelli today! I brought my scrapbook for him to sign. I know him quite well. Have you seen his daughter? What a beauty." To have Birindelli return your greeting in a certain way was to be someone.

Birindelli moved through the Sapienza like the lord of a castle. His office, just beyond the historic portals, was a large room with a dusky ceiling. There were numerous mailboxes along the wall for the students. Birindelli watched over all of them. He was most talkative around young people.

Though seldom in his office, he was always wandering through the university, through the Sapienza, the main seat of all the departments. He often stationed himself in the administration building where students register and pay tuition, but he would also show up in the literature department where all the humanities students gathered, and in the department of engineering; and he seemed to have a particular liking for the school of law.

Birindelli held to schedules as if they were ceremonies. At eleven he would post himself under the historic portal and lean against the right-hand side. With his long, lustrous black outfit, the university stems sparkling on the lapels of his frock coat, and that vague, generalized scorn on his face, he was not unlike Velazquez's painting of the prince after the hunt.

L. is a city of porticos, a picturesque place, with its maze of columns all leading toward the center and the Tower. He stood with his legs slightly crossed, in the shadows of the portico, and watched over the coming-and-going with an air of distraction.

And between five and six in the evening, he would repeat this ritual. There was no student who passed him without trying out some greeting, whose eyes did not, at the very least, graze him swiftly, if he felt too unfamiliar to expect a reply. Birindelli showed a superior condescension toward everybody; toward the professors, he was merely courteous, formal – no servility there!

It was said of him too, with frank admiration, that he owned his own car and that during vacations he loaded up his whole family and drove to Rimini, to Cattolica, like a real gentleman. The students were proud to have a doorman of that ilk.

Only a few had noticed this particular charm, a detail worthy of mention: with what swift elegance the skirts of his frock coat moved, how eager he became whenever he pointed out the plaques.

Along the central corridor of the Sapienza, there were two plaques, two strips of marble commemorating the young men who had perished in the name of freedom, who had died during the Risorgimento. Birindelli often loitered near those marble plaques, and, as soon as he caught sight of a freshman, would go over in a rush of sincerity, to make his acquaintance, all zealousness.

"And if things are different today," and he would raise his arms pathetically towards the marble, "what did they die for? Courage, we must take courage!" Fascism was in full force. Birindelli made other bitter exclamations.

There were some students who fell for it, others no. These others, the instinctively cautious ones, were slow to answer, evasive; and thus, they saved themselves. The naive ones, on the other hand, those with no head for politics, were snared; they answered without thinking, confessed their antifascist sentiments, and sometimes even their hatred for the regime. Whenever that was the case, Birindelli drew closer, became fraternal, engaged them in his intimate warmth, and while exploring certain details of the conversation, got around to asking their names and advised prudence. In his monthly report to his superiors at the O.V.R.A, he would provide precise information. Those Adriatic vacations he took with his family were hard earned.

Inevitably, the years pass, and the war comes; everyone is more watchful now, everybody's sentiments more intense. Those who side with the police become more and more like them as though an accelerating motion, a physical law were at work. After the eighth of September, Birindelli finds himself dealing with the Germans, as well as the fascists.

Right in the Sapienza, in the little house at the back of the garden, live two young people, the caretaker's children; both belong to the Action Party. The Civil War is raging, and the Action Party is a minor group, but it will fight to the death for freedom. Its members are similar, even in their outward appearance, to those of Young Italy; some grow beards, their eyes are intelligent, they talk of Mazzini, of Benedetto Croce, of a modern, civil Italy. These two are literature students; their father, a modest caretaker, has labored so they could study at the university. The Sapienza is their house, they were born there, and naturally, they know all its secrets. They also know all about Birindelli, why he makes certain moves; they know what his garments are woven of, and what sad devil lurks in the skirts of his frock coat.

Birindelli quickly perceived that these kids were plotting something underhanded; he saw them as sentimental, confused souls who had been spurred on by their father, for the simple caretaker envied him and had illusions of climbing the social ladder. He watched more carefully and finally noticed that there was traffic going in and out of the caretaker's hut; meetings were held there; the visitors came in through the small gate at the back of the park, in the Botanical Institute. And they even looked like conspirators; some left with packages under their arms.

Birindelli tipped off the Germans, who broke into the house the following night and found a large quantity of printed propaganda, a duplicating machine, and even a radio transmitter.

The two youngsters were taken to the barracks and tortured to reveal the names of their comrades. But they did not utter a word, they just stared with sad, intelligent eyes. Then they were taken to the usual spot, behind the wall used for target practice, and shot in the head.

Birindelli didn't seem terribly perturbed; the caretaker of the literature department, the father, still greeted him. Birindelli must have had some rigid block, something hard and obtuse inside him, or at least some arrogance that blinded him. He couldn't even acknowledge that he was under suspicion, that word of his spying had gotten out. For him the established authority was his only light, his only altar, so it must've been so for everyone else too. He couldn't imagine that a man might yearn for revenge, that men could nurture the flame of passion, of hope for a new world.

Doorman Birindelli kept to his schedule like a man turning a wheel; at eleven in the morning and after lunch, he would lean against the right side of the door with a feigned indolence, returning greetings with a benevolent smile.

Meanwhile, the town talked of nothing but the two young people, their character, the tortures they had suffered, their faith, the serenity of death, and of how their father had sacrificed so they could study. And especially amongst their companions in the underground, in the *Quinta Gap*[1], the group they belonged to, grievous remarks and resolutions were made.

---

1. Fifth Patriotic Action Group

One night, two workers showed up at a *gappista* meeting and followed the proceedings with great concentration. Afterwards, when they were alone, they talked it over and came to a decision. The next day they went to the commander of the *Quinta Gap*.

"The only thing we're not sure about is the letter. Take a look, we might have made a mistake. You can add anything you want."

"No, it's fine as it is."

The workers found out that Birindelli loitered at the right side of the main portal of the university between eleven and twelve o'clock; they'd already planned every move.

From their homes on Via Nosarelli, it was easy to get to the top of Via della Sapienza on bicycle. One of them had the pistol in the pocket of his overalls; the other was holding the letter in his hand carefully, so as not to crease it. Both were rather young. They pulled up in front of the columns of the Sapienza, on their bicycles.

They picked him out at once, with that lustrous black coat down to his knees, that look of apparent distraction on his face and superior air. He was exactly as they had imagined.

Each worker had assumed a different task: one was to be the humble messenger, the other the assassin. They walked under the portico, leaning their bicycles against the wall just before the main portal.

The first worker approached him. Birindelli, having noticed his overalls, paid him no attention. The worker drew nearer, the letter in hand: he stopped in front of Birindelli, waiting.

Finally Birindelli turned to him, and proferring the letter, he asked him respectfully:

"Pardon me, are you the doorman, Signor Birindelli?"

"Yes."

"This letter is for you."

"Give it to me."

Birindelli took the letter with a slightly careless gesture, and slipping his index finger in a corner, ripped it open.

The worker who had handed it to him was already walking back toward his bicycle.

Now his friend stepped forward. Birindelli was examining the letter and began to read. The second worker waited for two or three more seconds to elapse, then reached for the pistol, assuming that Birindelli had had time to read the personal missive. He pulled the trigger. Then he too ran to his bicycle and the two men made off together, swiftly.

Birindelli slumped, his shoulders sliding down against the door. He was still clutching the letter that read: *This is how traitors of the patria die.*

Name and Tears

ELIO VITTORINI (1908–1966) Vittorini is a major figure of twentieth-
century Italian letters, both as a writer and, in his work as editor, translator, and
critic, as a promoter of literary culture. It is thought that his writing made an essential transition in the evolution of twentieth-century literature, from the
hermetic tendencies of the pre-war period to the political engagement of post-
war neorealism and the later avant garde. His work is marked by musicality, and
by a reliance on the mythopoeic, which sometimes create a haunting, dreamlike
atmosphere, as in "Name and Tears." This famous short piece was preface and
title of the first edition of Vittorini's *Conversazione in Sicilia*, written under the
constraints of fascist censorship and, ironically, considered his most successful
work. "Name and Tears" and "The Cart" are from *Nome e lagrime*, 1971.

I was writing in the gravel path of the garden, and already it was
dark; dark for some time, the lights on in all the windows.

The caretaker walked by.

"What are you writing?" he asked me.

"A word," I answered.

He bent down to look, but he didn't see.

"What word is it?" he asked again.

"Well," I said, "it's a name."

He shook his keys.

"Not a 'long live'? Not a 'down with'?"

"Oh no," I exclaimed.

And then I laughed.

"It's somebody's name," I said.

Then the caretaker walked off and I went back to writing. I wrote until I hit earth under the gravel, I dug and wrote, and the night grew blacker.

The caretaker came back.

"Still writing?" he said.

"Yes," I said. "I wrote some more."

"What did you write?" he asked.

"Nothing more. Nothing besides that word."

"What!" the caretaker yelled. "Nothing besides that word!"

And he shook his keys again and lit his lamp to look.

"I see," he said. "There's nothing but that name."

He lifted his lantern and looked into my face.

"I wrote it deeper," I explained.

"Ah, like that?" he said. "If you want to keep on, I'll give you a hoe."

"Give it to me," I answered.

The caretaker gave me the hoe and walked off again, and I dug with it and wrote the name deep, deep down into the earth. Truthfully, I would have written right down to the carbon and iron, right down to the most secret metals, which are ancient names. But the caretaker came back again and said, "You'll have to leave now. We're closing here."

I climbed out of the grave of the name.

"All right," I answered.

I put down the hoe and dried my forehead, and I looked at the city all around me, beyond the dark trees.

"All right," I said, "all right."

The caretaker sighed.

"The person didn't come, huh?"

"The person didn't come," I said.

But then I quickly asked him: "Who didn't come?"

The caretaker lifted his lantern to look me in the face like he had before.

"The one you were waiting for."

"Right," I said.

But again, quickly, I asked him: "What person?"

"What the devil!" the caretaker said. "The person whose name it is."

And he shook the lantern, he shook his keys, and added, "If you want to wait a little bit longer, feel free."

"That's not what matters now," I said. "But thank you."

But I didn't leave, I stayed, and the caretaker stayed with me, as if to keep me company.

"Beautiful night!" he said.

"Beautiful," I said.

Then he started off with his lantern, toward the trees.

"But," he said, "are you sure the person isn't there?"

I knew she couldn't come, yet I was startled.

"Where?" I whispered.

"Over there," said the caretaker, "sitting on the bench."

At those words, leaves rustled; a woman stood up out of the darkness and began walking on the gravel path. I shut my eyes at the sound of her footsteps.

"So she did come?" said the caretaker.

Without answering, I headed off after the woman.

"Closing time," the caretaker shouted, "closing time."

Following after the woman, I walked out of the garden then into the city streets.

I followed what had been the sound of her footsteps on gravel. I could even say: led by the memory of those footsteps. And I walked for a long time, followed her for a long time, first amidst crowds and then on deserted sidewalks until at last, for the first time, I raised my eyes and saw her, a stroller, in the light of the last store.

The truth is, I saw her hair. Nothing else. And afraid of losing her, I began to run.

In that part of the city there are fields, then tall houses, dark parade grounds, then bright fair grounds, with the red eye of the gas generator in the distance. Over and over again, I asked, "Did she come this way?"

Everybody said they didn't know.

But a playful little girl on swift roller skates approached me, and she was laughing.

"Aaah!" she laughed. "I bet you're looking for my sister."

"Your sister?" I exclaimed. "What's her name?"

"I'm not telling," said the little girl.

And she laughed again; she circled me on her skates, she did a dance of death around me.

"Aaah!" she laughed.

"Then tell me where she is," I said to her.

She wheeled around me in her death dance for another minute, and then skated off down the endless boulevard, and she was laughing.

"She's in a doorway," she shouted from afar, still laughing.

Abject couples stood in the doorways, but I walked to one that was deserted, bare.

The door opened when I pushed it. I took the stairs and then I heard crying.

"Is that her crying?" I asked the doorkeeper.

The old woman was sleeping upright in the middle of the stairs, holding her rags; she woke up and looked at me.

"I don't know," she answered. "Do you want to take the elevator?"

I didn't, I wanted to go straight up to that crying, and I kept climbing, past the black, open windows, up the stairs. Finally I reached the place where the crying was — behind a white door. I went in, and it was nearby; I turned on the light.

But I didn't see anyone in the room. And I didn't hear anything then. And yet, there on the divan, was the handkerchief of her tears.

The Cart

I t climbs the road full of dust, then encounters the wind and runs along the sky. From that point of view, the peaks of the mountains appear below.

The colored cart of the man returning from Saturday's work advances, advances and creaks. And he is not alone. Already he has picked up a companion who was going home on foot; and now he picks up another. "Oi, Michelino," he calls, "Michelino."

The cart stops, and the mule turns to observe from between the blinders the man who will be his new burden.

"Hello Giona. Hello Baba," Michelino says slowly.

He is small, he is black-skinned, with a week's growth of black beard on his cheeks, and he carries his spade and shoes on his shoulders.

"Fine, aren't you coming on?" says Baba. Michelino is absent-minded, he doesn't smile, but he approaches and puts a foot on the hub, his spade and shoes still on his shoulders. Finally he is up, and he squats behind his companions, in the great green stain overflowing in the cart.

"Didn't you hear the cart?" asks Giona.

"Sure," Michelino says. And the mule begins pulling again. The mule pulls; and the cart creaks. Evening is approaching.

"So many ceci beans," Michelino cries.

He is talking about the green stain he is sitting in, and he runs his hand through it, breaks open a kernel and eats it. The ceci beans, carried up from the valley, make a great green stain in the cart, the only green in the whole high countryside.

"They're good," Michelino says.

"Sure they're good," says Giona, who picked them.

"Can I taste them too?" asks Baba.

He turns and rips off the top of a frond with three or four ceci pods, tastes them. "Very soft!" he exclaims.

"Sure they're soft," says Giona.

And turning back to Michelino, he adds: "Give me a couple." He is the oldest of the three, the blackest of all with his week's growth of beard, he's tired and wants some comfort, some happiness: as the mule knows, that's why he called his companions into the cart.

"Go on, eat, eat," he says. And he watches his friends eating and hopes for a little happiness.

"So fresh," says Baba.

"Sure they're fresh," Giona says.

And Baba winks at him. "Where'd you find them?" he asks.

"Where?" Giona asks in surprise. Then he says, "Not in your fields, I'm sure."

Baba laughs. "On no! That's for sure!"

And Giona is content; he can laugh. "Not in your fields. Not in your fields."

Only Michelino is still gloomy; he breaks one kernel after another and eats and eats until he says gloomily: "It seems a little early for them."

"For the ceci?" asks Baba.

"Not for the fava, but for the ceci, yes," he answers.

And Baba says to Giona: "He thinks it's early."

"Early?" Giona says in surprise.

"Isn't it early?" Michelino says.

Giona and Baba look at one another. Is it early? Isn't it early? They ask one another with their eyes because their companion worries about such things. But they don't want to lose the happiness they believe they have won.

"No, it's not early!" Giona shouts.

"No!" shouts Baba.

"No?" says Michelino.

The cart sways, advances, and the evening descends, the sun gone now, set between the low peaks of the mountain. "It's already April," says Baba.

And Michelino cries, "April?"

KATHRINE JASON has published poetry in the *New Yorker* and other magazines. She is the recipient of a Fulbright scholarship and a grant for translation from the National Endowment for the Arts. Her previous translation, *Words in Commotion and Other Stories* by Tommaso Landolfi, was published by Viking Penguin in 1986. She lives in New York City with her husband and daughter and teaches at Hunter College.

Scott Walker, ed. / *The Graywolf Annual 7: Stories from the American Mosaic*

Scott Walker, ed. / *The Graywolf Annual 8: The New Family*

Will Weaver / *A Gravestone Made of Wheat*